PRAISE FOR CATHY GLASS

'Poignant and revealing ... real-life stories such as these have helped to move and inspire a generation'   *Sunday Mirror*

'A true tale of hope'   *OK!* Magazine

'Heartbreaking'   *Mirror*

'A life-affirming read ... that proves sometimes a little hope is all you need'   *Heat* Magazine

'A hugely touching and emotional true tale'   *Star* Magazine

'Foster carers rarely get the praise they deserve, but Cathy Glass's book should change all that'   *First* Magazine

'Cannot fail to move those who read it'   Adoption-net

'Once again, Cathy Glass has blown me away with a poignant story'   The Writing Garnet, book blogger

'Brilliant book. I'd expect nothing less from Cathy ... I cried, of course'   Goodreads review

'... gripping page-turner from start to finish ... emotive and heart-wrenching ...'   Kate Hall, book blogger

A Life Lost

ALSO BY CATHY GLASS

CATHY GLASS

A Life Lost

**Jackson is haunted by a
secret from his past**

A TRUE STORY

HARPER
element

Certain details in this story, including names, places and dates,
have been changed to protect the family's privacy.

HarperElement
An imprint of HarperCollins*Publishers*
1 London Bridge Street
London SE1 9GF

www.harpercollins.co.uk

HarperCollins*Publishers*
1st Floor, Watermarque Building, Ringsend Road
Dublin 4, Ireland

First published by HarperElement 2021

7 9 10 8 6

A catalogue record of this book is
available from the British Library

ISBN 978-0-00-843661-2

Printed and bound in the UK using
100% Renewable Electricity at CPI Group (UK) Ltd

ACKNOWLEDGEMENTS

A big thank you to my family; my editors, Kelly and Holly; my literary agent, Andrew; my UK publisher HarperCollins; and my overseas publishers, who are now too numerous to list by name. Last, but definitely not least, a big thank you to my readers for your unfailing support and kind words. They are much appreciated.

'For life and death are one,
even as the river and the sea are one.'
Kahlil Gibran

CHAPTER ONE

A DIFFICULT START

I knew it was going to be difficult, so I waited until my family had left the house that morning before I began to clear out Lucy's room. Armed with cardboard boxes, bags, wrapping paper, sticky tape and a good dose of courage, I went upstairs and into her bedroom. Or rather, I should say, what had been her bedroom. Lucy, aged twenty-five, the elder of my two daughters, had moved out and was now living with her partner, Darren, and their baby, Emma. Of course, that's the natural cycle of life. Children grow up, leave home and start families of their own. Fine in theory, but I wasn't finding it so easy to accept in practice, even though I saw Lucy often.

She had come to me as a foster child many years before and stayed permanently to become my adopted daughter. We'd been through a lot over the years and now, at very short notice, I was having to clear out the last of her belongings to make room for Jackson, a ten-year-old boy I'd been asked to foster. Lucy had already taken what she needed, so her shelves, drawers and wardrobe contained only those items she didn't require at present or had grown out of. She'd said a few times she'd come over and sort out her belongings, but she was busy with her baby and I'd told her there was no rush. There hadn't been a rush until Joy, my supervising social worker (SSW), had told me the day before that they needed to move Jackson from his home very quickly and had asked me to look after him.

My first reaction had been to say no, but as a foster carer that's very difficult when you're aware a family is in crisis and a child needs a home quickly. So I'd asked Lucy, my son Adrian, my other daughter Paula and Tilly, the young lady I was already fostering, what they thought about having Jackson stay with us. Lucy had said she was fine about him having her old room, as her home was with Darren now. Adrian, aged twenty-seven, had concerns I might be taking on too much, which I'd secretly thought too. While Paula, aged twenty-three, wasn't overjoyed we'd be fostering another child with behavioural issues, as we'd had plenty of experience of that before and knew it wasn't easy. (Jackson's behaviour was the main reason his mother was putting him into care.) Tilly said yes and offered to help look after him. That was very kind of her, although I doubted she knew what it was like to live with a child who was continually kicking off and challenging you.

So, with no one in my family really objecting, and aware that there was always a shortage of foster carers, I said I would take Jackson. Lucy's was the only free room, so I now needed to get a move on and clear it, for, if all went according to plan, he would be with us later today.

It was strange, the little nostalgic reminders that brought a tear to my eye. It wasn't the rest of Lucy's clothes that made me well up as I cleared them from her wardrobe, although I could smell her perfume on them.

Or the soft toys and ornaments she'd lovingly collected as a child that I removed from her bookshelves and carefully packed. Or the boy-band memorabilia from when she'd had a crush on the lead singer. No, it was a couple of old hair braids that sent a tear down my cheek as I remembered plaiting her hair for school and then teaching her to plait it herself.

And the birthday and Christmas cards we'd given to her over the years. All of them, wrapped in tissue paper in a drawer. I also found a partially composed note from her, handwritten one time before she'd decided to apologize in person. It was from her teenage years and I remembered the incident that had led to it. One of a number when she'd been testing the boundaries and had wanted to stay out very late. The letter began:

Dear Mum, I'm sorry I shouted at you. I know you make the rules to keep me safe, but ...

Then she had come to me to say sorry. I remembered those cross words and the hugs and kisses that followed as we made up. 'Never go to sleep on an argument' was my mother's philosophy, and my family and I very rarely did. Now, my darling daughter was a mother herself, and in years to come would probably face similar situations with her own daughter, Emma. My heart swelled with pride, love and admiration for everything Lucy and my other children had achieved.

Having paused for trips down memory lane, it took me over two hours to clear out the rest of Lucy's room, then I thoroughly vacuumed and dusted it, and put fresh linen on the bed. I stacked the boxes and bags on the landing to store in the loft later, where they could stay until Lucy was ready to sort them out. Now the room was clear it had lost its personal touch and I returned downstairs rather melancholy and deep in thought.

But if this had been upsetting, it was about to get a whole lot worse. Shortly, I would be meeting Jackson, whose father and older brother had recently died – the reason given for his anger. Or was there more to it? So often in fostering a child arrives with one story and then gradually you discover another. Time would tell, but for now I needed to get through what was going to be a very upsetting meeting with his mother.

CHAPTER TWO

TRAGIC

Whatever can you say to a woman whose husband has died and whose teenage son has committed suicide? I didn't know if the two tragedies were connected; Joy, my SSW, who'd given me the details, wasn't sure. I was now driving to the council offices where the meeting was being held with thoughts of the family going through my head.

I knew from the placement information forms that Jackson's mother, Kayla, was thirty-nine and had been widowed two years ago. A year after she'd lost her husband from cancer, her eldest son, Connor, aged seventeen, had hanged himself. Yet somehow, she'd managed to carry on and I admired her courage. I supposed she felt she had to for the sake of Jackson and her two daughters, Jenna, aged seven, and Grace, five. My heart went out to them. What they had all been through was unbelievably sad; truly the stuff of nightmares and devastating for the whole family. I understood that concerns about Jackson's behaviour had been raised by his school the previous term, then during the summer holidays Kayla had reached breaking point and had gone to her doctor, who had contacted the social services.

Kayla had admitted she was unable to cope with Jackson's behaviour any longer and had agreed to him going into care. How long he would be with me I didn't know.

I parked the car in a side road close to the council offices and, summoning my courage, got out. Tragedies like this one reminded me how lucky I was. My children were all healthy. I'd lost my father a few years before, but he'd been in his eighties when he'd died. Thankfully my mother was still doing well. It seemed to me Jackson's family had been given an unfair share of life's misery.

Going into the council offices, I registered at reception and, with my ID pass looped around my neck, went upstairs to the room where the meeting was to be held. I'd brought a small photograph album with me to show Kayla so she had some idea of where her son would be living. Because she had placed Jackson in care voluntarily under what's known as a Section 20 (of the Children Act), and there were no safeguarding issues, she would probably be given my contact details. If a child is brought into care as a result of abuse and is the subject of a court order then generally the parents aren't told where they are, although some find out.

I knocked on the door of the meeting room and went in. Seated at the table were two women and a young lad who I took to be Jackson. I was slightly surprised to see him there, as Joy had said this meeting was just for Kayla to meet me.

'Cathy, I'm Frankie, the family's social worker,' said one of the women, greeting me. 'This is Kayla and her son Jackson.'

'Pleased to meet you,' I said, joining them at the table. 'I am so sorry for your loss.'

'Thank you,' Kayla said in a small voice, while Jackson glared at me.

Although he was sitting down, I could see he was tall for his age but willowy and slightly built. He had dark hair and beige skin, the same as his mother. But whereas her eyes showed deep sadness, Jackson's shouted anger and confrontation. Having thrown me a disparaging look, he concentrated on the mobile phone he held in his lap. It might surprise you to know that nearly half of all children aged five to ten have a mobile phone. I hoped his mother had put parental controls on it.

'We thought it best if Jackson joined the meeting,' Frankie said to me. 'Kayla's daughters are being looked after by a neighbour.'

I nodded. The schools didn't return from the summer vacation until the following week, so Kayla would have had to make childcare arrangements to attend this meeting. I hadn't met Frankie before but she had a calm, confident manner.

'How are you, Jackson?' I asked, trying to engage him.

He shrugged and continued to tap the keypad on his phone. His mother looked at me, slightly embarrassed, and I threw her a reassuring smile.

'Kayla asked to meet you,' Frankie said to me. 'She thought it might help. Perhaps you could tell us a bit about yourself, your home and family.'

'Yes, of course. I've brought some photographs with me.'

I placed the album on the table in front of Kayla and Jackson. As Kayla began to turn the pages, I said a few words about each photo. The first was a group photo of us standing at our front door as if welcoming in our new arrival. I told them the names and ages of my children, including Tilly, aged fourteen, who I was fostering, and said that Lucy now lived with her partner and their baby not far away. The rest of the photos were of the house – downstairs, upstairs and then the back garden. The very last was another group photo, taken in our back garden with a selfie stick and including our cat, Sammy. 'Do you like cats?' Frankie asked Jackson as I finished.

He shrugged dismissively and stared at his phone.

I hadn't had time to include a photo of Jackson's bedroom because until now it had been Lucy's room, so I showed them the photo I'd taken on my phone before I'd left the house. Jackson kept his gaze down. Kayla thanked me and handed back the album. I then talked a bit about my family, our routine and what we liked to do in our spare time, which was expected at these introductory meetings.

'How long has Tilly been with you?' Kayla asked.

'Eight months.'

'Is she staying for good?'

'I don't know,' I replied truthfully.

'Why is she living with you?' Kayla asked.

'I'm afraid I can't really go into details,' I said awkwardly, glancing at Frankie. 'It's confidential. She can't live at home, so she is staying with us for the time being. She's settled in very well.' (I tell Tilly's story in *A Terrible Secret*.)

'Thank you, Cathy,' Frankie said, then to Jackson: 'I expect you have lots of questions. Is there anything you would like to ask Cathy now?'

He shook his head and tapped his phone.

'Jackson, can you please put down that phone!' his mother exclaimed, desperation in her voice. 'People are talking to you. It's rude to ignore them.'

'So?' he snarled aggressively. 'You can't tell me what to do.'

'You would never have spoken to me like that if your father had been here,' Kayla said, tears springing to her eyes.

'And we both know why he's not here!' Jackson retaliated.

There was a second's pause before he suddenly jumped up, sending his chair clattering across the room, and stormed out, kicking the door shut behind him.

'I'll go after him,' Frankie said, and left the room.

Kayla took a tissue from her bag and pressed it to her eyes. 'I'm so sorry,' she said. 'I don't know what to do with him any more. He's so angry. He blames me for his father's death.'

'But why is he blaming you?' I asked. 'I thought your husband died of cancer.'

'He did, but Jackson says I should have made him go to the doctor sooner. He'd been complaining of stomach pains after he'd eaten, but I thought it was just indigestion. We're not a family that's always running to the doctor. By the time they found the cancer it was too late. It had spread all over his body. He was dead three months after diagnosis – two years ago now.'

'I am so sorry,' I said, and felt my own eyes fill. 'What a dreadful loss. But it wasn't your fault.'

'He was a good man. I loved him so much. Jackson wasn't able to talk about his father or what he was feeling, and would storm off if he was mentioned. Then a year later Connor, my eldest son, took his own life, and Jackson fell apart. He blames me for his death too.'

Words failed me. Sometimes a person's loss is so great that it's impossible to find the words to express meaningful sympathy. 'I am sorry,' I said again quietly.

We were silent for a few moments and then I asked: 'Has Jackson had any bereavement counselling? I know it can sometimes help.'

'No. Our doctor suggested it, but he won't go. He's closed in on himself. The only way he expresses his loss is through anger. It builds up and then he explodes. My daughters are different. They talk about their dad and brother and say how much they miss them. They come with me to the cemetery, but Jackson won't.'

'I expect Frankie will suggest counselling. It's usually with CAMHS – Child and Adolescent Mental Health Services.'

'Yes, she's mentioned it.'

'I'll do my best to get Jackson there.'

'He needs something,' Kayla said, dabbing her eyes. 'I'm petrified he might do something silly and follow Connor.'

'Has he told you he's contemplated suicide?' I asked, very concerned.

'No, but I've lost one son that way – I know it's possible – and Jackson was close to his brother, despite him being seven years older.'

'You've told Frankie all of this?'

'Yes.'

The door opened and Frankie returned. 'Jackson is being looked after by a colleague,' she said, and sat at the table. 'I suggest we give him time to calm down, and then, when we've finished, he can go straight home with Cathy.'

Clearly arrangements had changed.

'I haven't brought any of his things with me,' Kayla said. 'I thought I'd have time to go home first.' Then to me she said: 'Jackson was supposed to be with my daughters, but he kicked off so badly I had to bring him with me.'

'As Jackson is finding this all very difficult, I think it's better he goes with Cathy now,' Frankie said. 'I can take you home so you can gather together what he needs for the next few days, then I'll drop it off at Cathy's later. Is that OK?'

Kayla nodded.

'I've got spare clothes that will fit him,' I said, 'but obviously it's better if Jackson can have his own. What's happening about contact?'

'I'd like to see him for a while every day,' Kayla said.

I doubted this would be practical. 'School returns next week,' I pointed out, and I looked at Frankie.

'Jackson will need time to settle in at Cathy's,' she said gently to Kayla. 'And he'll have school work to do. I suggest, to begin with, you see him for an hour after school on Monday, Wednesday and Friday and two hours at the weekend. Then we can review arrangements in a month or so.'

'All right,' Kayla said quietly. I made a note of the days.

'Where is Jackson seeing his family?' I asked.

'At his home,' Frankie said. 'You will be able to take and collect him?'

'Yes.' The foster carer usually takes the child to and from contact as well as doing the school run. Carers who don't drive use public transport or cabs. In exceptional circumstances the social services provide transport.

'Will he be going to see his family straight after school?' I asked. This was what usually happened.

'Does that suit you?' Frankie asked Kayla.

'Yes.'

'I'm guessing we'll arrive around four o'clock,' I said. Jackson's home address and that of his school were on the placement information forms, so I knew the travelling time involved. 'I'll return to collect him at five?' I clarified.

'Yes, please,' Frankie said.

'And contact at the weekend?' I asked. 'Which day?'

'Saturday, please,' Kayla said. 'He can come for lunch, but he can stay as long as he likes.' I thought Kayla was now feeling guilty for placing her son in care.

'I think we need to firm up a time for the weekend visit,' Frankie sensibly said, 'so Cathy knows when to collect him. Shall we say twelve till two?'

Kayla agreed. 'But he can phone me any time,' she said. 'I've put credit on his phone.'

'Perhaps you could phone on those days you're not seeing each other?' Frankie suggested. Although in practice, once a child has a mobile phone, this type of contact is virtually impossible to control. It's not such a worry in cases like this where there are no safeguarding concerns (as far as we knew), but I knew of instances where a child was removed from home as a result of parental abuse and the parents continued to threaten the child over the phone, until the foster carer found out and reported it to the social worker and took away the phone.

'Is there a parental control app on his phone?' I now asked.

'Yes,' Kayla replied. 'Connor set it up not long before he died. Connor always looked out for his young brother. He felt Jackson was too young to have a phone, as he'd had to wait until he was twelve.' She smiled reflectively and I saw her eyes well up again.

With nothing further to discuss, Frankie suggested we go to collect Jackson; Kayla would then say goodbye and he would come home with me. I wasn't expecting it to go smoothly and I was right.

CHAPTER THREE

JACKSON

Frankie led the way into a small room where a colleague of hers was sitting, talking to Jackson. 'Thanks, Aaron,' she said.

Aaron nodded, said goodbye and good luck to Jackson, then left.

Frankie sat in the chair Aaron had vacated. The room was just big enough to take a small desk, two office chairs and a filing cabinet. Kayla and I stood to one side. The room was on the third floor and looked out over the car park below.

'Jackson, I know this is difficult for you,' Frankie began gently. 'How are you feeling now? A little less upset?'

Jackson shrugged despondently. He wasn't holding his phone, so I guessed it was in his pocket.

'I've talked to you about why you're staying at Cathy's for a while,' Frankie continued. 'Do you have any questions?' Jackson shook his head. 'OK. We think it's best if you go straight to Cathy's now and then I'll bring some of your belongings later. Is there anything you would particularly like me to bring today?'

Jackson kept his head down and didn't reply.

'I'll make sure I put in your phone charger,' his mother said.

Jackson said nothing.

'You'll be able to collect some more of your belongings another day,' Frankie said. 'And obviously you'll want to see your mother and sisters regularly. So we thought tomorrow and then Monday, Wednesday and Friday after school. You and your mother can also phone on the days you don't see each other. How does that sound?'

'Not fussed,' Jackson said with another shrug, head down.

But of course he was 'fussed'. He was hiding behind a couldn't-care-less attitude to protect himself from further hurt. He'd be feeling rejected – most children coming into care do, even though the reasons for the move have been explained to them.

'I want to see you,' Kayla said touchingly.

'What if I refuse to go with her?' Jackson asked, raising his head and glaring at me. 'You can't make me go. None of you can.'

'We think it's best for you at present,' Frankie replied sensitively. 'It will be a bit strange to begin with, but it will allow you some space. You will be able to attend the same school, so you'll see your friends.'

'You could have some friends back at the weekend,' I suggested, thinking this might help.

There was a moment's pause, then Jackson jumped up and, barging between his mother and me, left the room.

We all went after him. Aaron was in the main office and, seeing Jackson run off angrily, gave chase. He went ahead, trying to catch up with him, as Frankie, Kayla and I followed. We went through some double doors and down a flight of stairs. Aaron and Jackson weren't in view. I was even more anxious now. If Jackson felt he could behave like this with all of us present and in front of an open-plan office full of social workers, what chance did I have of controlling his behaviour when it was just him and me? I shuddered at the thought. Sometimes a child's behaviour is so challenging that they can't live in a foster home and have to go to a therapeutic children's home to receive the help they need.

We went down a second flight of stairs and arrived in reception. Aaron and the security guard had Jackson standing between them. We went over.

'Thank you,' Frankie said to the guard and Aaron.

But at that moment the main doors automatically opened as someone came in and Jackson seized the opportunity and shot out. Kayla let out a small cry. Aaron went after him, followed by Frankie, Kayla and me. There was a busy main road not far away, but thankfully Aaron managed to stop Jackson before he got there. Lightly holding his arm, he began to talk to him, trying to calm him down.

'Aaron is one of our outreach workers,' Frankie told me and Kayla.

We waited a little way off as Aaron continued to talk to Jackson and slowly he seemed to calm down. Aaron took his hand from Jackson's arm and continued talking to him in a low, even tone. Kayla's phone bleeped with a text.

'I need to go,' she said anxiously as she read the message. 'I promised my neighbour I'd be back by four-thirty to collect my daughters. I'll catch the bus.'

'I'll wait until Jackson is on his way to Cathy's,' Frankie said. 'Then I'll come to see you later.'

Kayla went over to say goodbye to Jackson, but he turned his back. The poor woman – I felt so sorry for her. I instinctively wanted to tell Jackson not to be so rude to his mother, but he'd only just calmed down and I knew it would do more harm than good. Kayla seemed used to his rudeness and went on her way to catch the bus.

'Where is your car?' Frankie asked me.

'Parked in a side road about a five-minute walk away.'

'Could you bring it here? It might be easier to get Jackson in.'

I could see why Frankie thought that would work better than walking him to where my car was parked. There is a drop-off/collection bay at the front of the council building that takes one car at a time.

But as I went to fetch my car, I again wondered how I was going to manage Jackson when it was just him and me. I was already stressed; my heart was pounding. It's always a bit nerve-racking meeting a child and their parents for the first time, but this was far worse than usual. Not because of Kayla – she was lovely. It was Jackson. I'd looked after children before with challenging behaviour, but his habit of bolting when he was angry or upset was very unsafe for him and difficult to control.

Arriving at my car, I engaged the child-locks on the rear doors so they could only be opened from the outside, just in case Jackson had any plans to make a dash for it if I stopped at traffic lights. I drove to the council offices, wondering if I was taking on more than I could manage, but then I chided myself. Jackson was only ten. He was angry and upset because his father and brother had died.

I needed to concentrate on helping him through the grieving process so that hopefully he would eventually come to terms with his sad loss.

As I pulled into the collection bay at the front of the council offices, Frankie and Aaron came forward with Jackson between them. Setting my face to an encouraging smile, I got out.

'OK, love?' I said to Jackson, opening the rear door. 'It's about a twenty-minute journey to my house.'

He hesitated, glanced around, but then got in. I breathed a sigh of relief, as I'm sure Frankie and Aaron did.

'Look after yourself,' Aaron said.

'I'll see you later,' Frankie told Jackson. But he was already concentrating on his phone.

I closed the rear door and got into the driving seat as Frankie and Aaron returned to the council offices.

'Can you put on your seatbelt, please?' I said to Jackson, fastening my own. He ignored me so I turned in my seat to face him and said more firmly, 'Jackson, you need to put on your seatbelt, love.'

He ignored me for a while longer and then, annoyed, did as I'd asked, ramming the metal tongue into the buckle.

'Well done,' I said. Before pulling away I quickly texted Paula and Tilly, who were at home, to say we were on our way.

As I drove, I periodically glanced in my rear-view mirror at Jackson, checking he was all right. I talked to him, trying to put him at ease, and asked him about his school and friends. He didn't reply, look up or make eye contact in the mirror, but kept his head down, concentrating on his phone. It was only when I pulled onto the drive at my house that he finally spoke.

'I'm not staying here,' he said. 'I'll run away.' He tugged hard on his door handle. 'You've locked me in!'

'I keep it locked for when I transport younger children,' I said, bending the truth slightly. 'Stay there and I'll open it for you.'

I got out and went round. At the same time our front door opened and Tilly and Paula appeared.

'Hello,' I said with a brightness I didn't feel, and opened Jackson's door. 'Come and meet Paula and Tilly.'

As Jackson got out, I saw his gaze flicker up and down the street. Our small driveway was open plan, so there was nothing to stop him running off.

'Come on, this way,' I said feigning confidence.

'Hi, Jackson,' Tilly called enthusiastically from the front door.

He ignored her but did come with me into the house. I quickly closed the front door.

'This is Tilly, who is also staying with us, and my daughter Paula,' I said.

'Hi, how are you, Jackson?' Tilly asked. Then she looked hurt when he ignored her. Paula, on the other hand, having grown up with fostering, appreciated that our new arrivals often needed time to settle in and adjust.

'Would you like a drink and a snack?' I asked him. 'Or to see your bedroom first?'

He shrugged.

'I can show you your room,' Tilly offered.

'No. I'll see it myself,' he replied grumpily, and began upstairs.

'It's on the right,' I said, going after him.

As we went into his room, I heard Tilly say to Paula, 'He's so rude.'

I guessed Paula would explain and I would have a chat with Tilly too, later.

'The room is a bit bare, but it will look better once you have some of your belongings in it,' I said to Jackson. 'Frankie is going to collect them and bring them here later.'

He went over to the window, glanced out, then sat on the bed and concentrated on his phone.

'Are you playing a game?' I asked him, trying to establish some communication. I'd caught glimpses of the screen and thought that might be so, although I doubted Jackson was getting much pleasure from the game. It seemed more like mindless tapping as a displacement for what he was really thinking and feeling.

He didn't reply so, going over, I said, 'I know it's difficult, love. You've suffered a great loss and now you're having to live in a strange house with people you don't know. It will get easier, I promise, and I am here to help you.'

'I don't need your help,' he said resentfully.

'I think we all need help sometimes. Do you have any questions you would like to ask me now?'

He shook his head, although I knew he must have plenty.

'Would you like to see the rest of the house?' I asked. I usually show the child around early on as it helps them settle and feel at home. Jackson shook his head again. 'Maybe later then. What would you like to do now?'

He ignored me.

'I was thinking of making a lasagne for dinner. Do you like that?'

'Not fussed.'

'OK, but I don't want you sitting up here by yourself.'

'Can if I want,' he replied.

Despite his bravado, I felt sorry for him. He looked so lost and alone, sitting there on the edge of the bed, shoulders slumped forward, pretending he didn't care. I'd seen children before trying to put on a brave face when they were scared and hurting inside. His mother had said he wouldn't talk to her about his feelings, but not opening up was only prolonging the agony for him. I was about to suggest he come down and sit in the living room when his phone rang.

'It's Mum,' he said, his face brightening a little. But instead of answering, he rejected the call.

'Why did you do that?'

'I don't want to talk to her.'

'Couldn't you just say hello and let her know you're all right?' I suggested.

He didn't reply.

'I'll give her a ring then,' I said. 'She'll be worried about you.'

'No, she won't,' he retaliated.

'Jackson, I know you're feeling rejected. But your mother loves you and will be missing you a lot. You all need some time and space to get through this, but she has feelings too. She's grieving like you and your sisters are, but she's having to hold your family together as well.'

'We're not a family any more!' Jackson snapped, and I could hear the pain in his voice.

'You are a family, love, just a different one. I know this isn't exactly the same – my husband didn't die, but he left us many years ago when Adrian and Paula were little. We all had to adjust to life without him, difficult though it was, so we could see a way forward. In time and with counselling, you will be able to see a future too.' I had no idea if I was saying the right thing, as I'd never experienced the devastating bereavement Jackson had, so I was relying on common sense.

Jackson didn't say anything, but he must have heard what I'd said. Hopefully he would think about it and know I was there for him, just as his mother was.

A knock sounded on his bedroom door – I'd left it ajar – and Tilly appeared. 'Hi, I'm in care too,' she said to Jackson. She was bright and sparkly and wanting to help, but the timing was wrong.

'So?' Jackson said under his breath.

'I'm just saying. I thought it would help.'

I threw her a reassuring smile. Jackson's phone rang again and this time he accepted the call. 'What do you want, Mum?' he asked, his voice flat. But at least he'd answered.

'Come on,' I said quietly to Tilly. 'We'll leave Jackson to talk to his mother.'

We went out and I drew the door to but didn't completely close it. I went with Tilly into her room. 'He's very moody,' Tilly said.

'Don't take it personally. He's had a lot to cope with.' I'd already told her and the rest of my family what they needed to know about Jackson's loss.

'Can Abby come round this evening?' Tilly asked. Abby was her best friend and they saw a lot of each other.

'Yes, if her parents can collect her. I can't leave Jackson with Paula at present.' My daughter Paula was one of my nominated sitters – police checked and approved by the social services – but I'd never leave a new arrival with her. They needed to have settled in first.

'They should be able to,' Tilly said. 'Can Abby stay for dinner?'

'Yes, it's going to be lasagne.'

'Great.'

Although this would mean another new person for Jackson to meet, I'd found in the past that it helped the child to relax if everyone continued with their plans as usual.

'I'll phone her now,' Tilly said. Then she paused and looked at me seriously. 'Jackson's very young to have a mobile phone, when you think what happened to me.'

'I know, love, but I understand there is a parental control app on it. I'll check it when I have the chance and make sure it's up to date and doing its job.'

Tilly had learnt the hard way that while having a mobile phone had many advantages, it was also open to abuse. The poor girl had been to hell and back and as a result of what had happened still wasn't talking to her mother.

Leaving Tilly to call Abby, and Jackson on the phone to his mother – listening rather than talking – I went downstairs. Paula was in the front room using the printer. We all had our own laptops but shared the printer. Having graduated in the summer, like many young people she was finding it difficult to get a permanent job and was temping in the meantime. We chatted for a few moments and then I said I was going to start dinner and asked her to let me know if she heard Jackson moving around. From his room to the front door was a straight run down the stairs, and I wouldn't have put it past him to try to leave. Foster carers can't lock children in the house, even if it is for their own good, so I put the safety chain on the front door, which would at least slow him down a bit.

I was right to be cautious, for five minutes later I heard footsteps on the stairs and then Paula ask, 'Are you OK, Jackson?'

I went quickly into the hall in time to see him at the front door.

CHAPTER FOUR

GET INTO TROUBLE

Paula was in the hall too.

'The living room is this way,' I told Jackson, pretending I thought he'd lost his bearings. 'Would you like to watch some television or help me make dinner?'

He remained by the front door. Tilly appeared on the landing. 'I'll watch television with you until Abby arrives,' she said, and came down.

'This way,' I said positively to Jackson. And with the three of us there, I think refusing became less of an option.

He came with us into the living room where I turned on the television and handed him the remote control. Disgruntled, he sat on the sofa. Tilly sat beside him and Paula returned to the front room to finish printing her document.

'Would you like a drink?' I asked him.

'Water,' he said, staring at the television.

'Please,' Tilly added. I threw her a look that said not to worry about lack of politeness. I realized she was trying to support me but, given all the issues Jackson was having to deal with, 'please' and 'thank you' were the least of my concerns. Stopping him from running away was more important.

I went to fetch his drink, making sure I left the door to the living room open. One of our safer-caring rules was that a looked-after child shouldn't be in a room with someone with the door closed. Leaving the door open meant that I and others could hear what was going on, reducing the chances of an allegation being made. Also, the child could leave the room easily if they wished. It was impossible to know what a shut door could mean to an abused child. All foster carers have a safer-caring policy and follow similar guidelines to keep all family members feeling safe.

Returning to the living room, I gave Jackson the glass of water and he drank it straight down. 'You were thirsty. Would you like another one?'

He shook his head.

'I'll be in the kitchen making dinner if you want me,' I said. 'We'll eat just as soon as Adrian and Abby are here.'

'Abby's on her way,' Tilly said. 'And her dad will collect her later.'

'Good.' I left the room, again making sure the door was open.

I didn't know what time Frankie would arrive with Jackson's clothes, so we'd have dinner as planned. The first few days after a new child arrives are always a bit unsettling, so we would continue our routine as best we could. I had some concerns, though, about how Jackson would react to Adrian. Most boys we looked after quickly bonded with my son and appreciated time spent with him. However, Jackson had lost his father and older brother, and although Adrian was ten years older than Connor had been when he'd died, I wondered how Jackson would react. Would he accept Adrian and bond with him as the only other male in our household or would he react against him?

A short while later I heard a key go in the front door and then the door bang against the safety chain. I went into the hall and let Adrian in.

'Are you trying to keep me out?' he joked, kissing my cheek.

'No, to keep Jackson in,' I said quietly. I'd already texted Adrian to say Jackson was here.

'Is it as bad as that?' he asked, taking off his shoes.

'He's in the living room with Tilly. Abby is joining us for dinner. And Jackson's social worker will be coming at some point to drop off his clothes.'

'Another nice, quiet evening then,' he quipped, and I smiled.

Adrian went into the living room to say hello before going to change out of his work suit. I'd just replaced the safety chain again when the doorbell rang. 'That'll be Abby!' Tilly cried and came rushing down the hall.

I opened the door and welcomed Abby. Tilly ushered her into the living room to meet Jackson. I think it was a novelty having Jackson stay, for until now she'd been the only looked-after child in the house.

I went into the living room and checked they were all OK and then returned to the kitchen to see how dinner was doing. The landline rang. It was Joy Philips, my SSW, checking that Jackson was there and all was well. I updated her. All foster carers have a supervising social worker whose role is to support, monitor, advise and guide the carer and their family in respect of fostering. She thanked me and said she'd phone on Monday to see how the weekend had gone and then visit us the following week.

Dinner was ready and I was about to call everyone to the table when the doorbell rang. With a sigh, I returned the lasagne to the oven and answered the door. It was Frankie holding a large zip-up bag.

'How is Jackson?' she asked, coming into the hall.

'Quiet. He's in the living room.'

'Did his mother phone?'

'Yes, he spoke to her.'

'She's very upset. She's wondering if she's done the right thing in putting him into care. I've told her she will need to give him a chance to settle in. She's only packed what he needs for tonight and a change of clothes for tomorrow. Hopefully she'll feel a bit better soon. She remembered his phone charger, though.'

Leaving the bag in the hall, I went with Frankie into the living room where I introduced her to Tilly and Abby. She knew Tilly was staying with me but hadn't met her before. Aware that Frankie might want to talk to us alone, Tilly told Abby they'd go to her room. Adrian and Paula were in their rooms too.

'I won't stay for long,' Frankie said to Jackson, who was pretending to concentrate on the television. 'There are some of your clothes in a bag in the hall. You can bring some more back when you see your mother tomorrow. She remembered to put in your phone charger.'

'I'm not seeing her,' Jackson said.

'Yes, tomorrow, twelve till two,' Frankie said.

'I'm taking and collecting you,' I added.

'No, I'm not going. I don't want to see her ever gain. I hate her. I want my dad!'

Throwing down the remote, Jackson stormed out of the room, and for a moment I thought he was going to the front door, but he ran upstairs instead. We heard his bedroom door slam shut.

Frankie looked at me, concerned and world-weary. Jackson wouldn't be the only case she'd dealt with that day and it was now after 6 p.m. on a Friday.

'You go, I'll see to him,' I said.

'Thank you,' she said gratefully. 'I've got reports to write this evening. Try to persuade him to see his mother and sisters tomorrow. If you have any problems over the weekend, you'll need to contact the duty social worker. You've got their number?'

'Yes.'

'I'll phone you on Monday and arrange to see you next week. Thanks again.'

I saw Frankie out and then asked Adrian, who'd just come down, to dish up dinner while I talked to Jackson.

Many children are upset when they first come into care, even if they've been removed from a violent and abusive home. They are rarely relieved and often remain fiercely loyal to their parents and crave the only home they've known. Jackson had more reason than most to be upset. Not only had he left his family, but he'd suffered a double bereavement – a challenge for an adult, but for a child it was shattering and would change the course of his life forever. As I knocked on his bedroom door, I felt the huge weight of his sorrow.

He was sitting on the floor with his back against the bed. I went over, leaving the door slightly open. 'Can I join you?' I asked him quietly.

He shrugged, so I took that as a yes and sat beside him. We were silent for some moments – he was gazing at his hands while I was trying to think what to say for the best. He hadn't been able to talk to his mother about his loss and had refused counselling, so I doubted I would fare much better. But I had to try.

'What hurts most?' I asked him presently.

He looked a bit taken aback and then shrugged.

'You've had a huge amount to cope with. Not many children your age have had to deal with what you've been through. We all cope with loss in different ways. Some people cry a lot, others go very quiet and some get angry. Sometimes we do all of those things, which can be very confusing.'

He remained quiet.

'If you could change one thing in your life, what would it be?' I tried.

A moment's pause and then: 'My dad.'

'You mean your dad not dying?' I asked.

He nodded. Which was interesting. I would have thought the greatest pain would have come from his brother's suicide at seventeen, compared to his father, who, while young, had died from natural causes.

'Your dad was very ill,' I said. 'The doctors did all they could to make him better, but sadly they couldn't help him. I looked after another boy some years ago who'd lost his mother and father. He was very brave too, like you are. When you think of your dad, do you remember him when he was well or ill, or a bit of both?'

'Mainly when he was ill,' Jackson replied.

'That must be very upsetting for you. It can be diffi-cult to remember back to all the good times, but I think counselling will help you. Frankie is going to arrange for you to talk to someone who is good at helping children with their feelings.'

He shrugged.

I didn't know if I was handling this right, but at least he was engaging with me on some level.

'You obviously miss your dad loads, and what about Connor? You must miss him too.'

'Yes.'

'Does it make you angry that he left you in the way he did?' I knew that often the loved ones of those who have committed suicide feel angry with them in some way, seeing it as a selfish act over which they had some control. I'd had previous experience of this with Joss, whose story I tell in *Girl Alone*.

But to my surprise Jackson said, 'I'm not angry with Connor. It was Dad's fault.'

'In what way, love?' I asked gently.

Jackson was quiet and stared straight ahead.

'You think Connor committed suicide because your father died?' I asked. 'That he couldn't get over the loss?' I assumed this was what he meant.

Jackson looked confused.

'If Dad hadn't become ill, none of this would have happened and we wouldn't have needed help.' He shook his head in frustration, unable to verbalize what he was thinking. This was where a bereavement counsellor would have known what to say to draw him out. But I hadn't had that training; most foster carers haven't.

'Did Connor talk to you about his feelings?' I asked.

Jackson nodded.

'That must have been a worry for you. Did you tell your mum?'

'No. Connor said I mustn't. He said she had enough to cope with as Dad was ill, and it would only upset her more. He said he'd get into trouble if I told, because he was old enough to know it was wrong.'

'Wrong, love? What was wrong?'

'I can't tell you,' Jackson said quietly, and abruptly stood, signalling that the conversation was over.

I too stood. 'I'm pleased we've had this chat,' I said. 'Hopefully we can talk again. Now let's get some dinner – you must be hungry. I know I am.'

Jackson came with me downstairs and into our kitchen-diner. I took the meals that Adrian had plated up for us from the oven and we joined the others at the table.

It was noisy. Tilly and Abby had finished eating and were now laughing as they shared a WhatsApp video joke on their phones. Adrian and Paula were talking more seriously about job applications and Sammy, our cat, was sitting by the table hoping for some leftovers.

I sat opposite Jackson, occasionally glancing at him as he ate. I was puzzled by what he'd said about not telling their mother because Connor would get into trouble as he was old enough to know it was wrong. The only reason I could think of for this was that Connor had told Jackson he was contemplating suicide. It would explain why he'd also said it would upset his mother if she knew. Would a seventeen-year-old see it in those terms? I thought so. I also knew that sometimes those thinking of taking their life gave clues of their intention to other family members or friends. If I was right and Connor had confided in Jackson, it was a huge burden for him to carry. I would need to tell Frankie what Jackson had said when I next saw her and also make a note of it in my log when I wrote that up later. All foster carers in the UK are required to keep a record of the child or children they are looking after – either in a diary or digitally. This includes appointments, the child's health and wellbeing, education, significant events and any disclosures the child may make about their past. As well as charting the child's progress, it can act as an aide-mémoire. When the child leaves, this record is placed on their file at the social services.

Adrian finished his conversation with Paula about job applications and then tried talking to Jackson, but he just shrugged in response, much as he'd been doing with us. Adrian knew it would take time for him to settle in and feel at ease, if indeed Jackson stayed. For, in truth, because Kayla had placed him in care voluntarily, there was nothing to stop her taking him home. Frankie had said she was having doubts. The social services would only intervene if they felt the child was at risk, which as far as I knew Jackson wasn't. However, if Kayla did remove him from care now, I thought it was likely he would return quite quickly. I doubted she was in any better position now to manage his behaviour than she had been before.

After dinner Adrian went out to see Kirsty, his long-time girlfriend. Paula went to her room to phone a friend and Tilly took Abby to her room to listen to music. I asked Jackson to help me unpack his bag, mainly to keep him occupied. Also, once he had some of his things in his room, it wouldn't seem so strange.

'Do you have a room of your own at home?' I asked

him as I unpacked. If a child is used to sharing, sleeping alone can be very unsettling to begin with.

'I do now,' he said. 'I used to share with Connor.' His face clouded over and I could have kicked myself for not thinking.

'Sorry,' I said.

He shrugged and then said he wanted to phone his sisters. I waited as he used his mobile to make the call, but his mother said they were already in bed.

'You'll see them tomorrow,' I said, aware of how disappointed he was.

Another dismissive shrug. I tried to talk to him about his sisters, but he wouldn't engage. I then persuaded him to come downstairs with me, where I asked him if he'd like to play a game of cards or similar, but he said he didn't. He wanted the television on and flicked through the channels until he found a cartoon. I sat with him and at eight o'clock I said it was time for bed. Immediately he switched off the television and went upstairs. In some ways his quiet compliance was more worrying than an angry outburst, for at least it would have given vent to some of his emotions.

He didn't want a shower so I said he could have one in the morning, then I left him in the bathroom to wash and change. Once he'd finished, I pointed out where my bedroom was. 'If you need me in the night, call and I'll come to you,' I said. 'It's bound to be a bit strange to begin with, but don't wander around at night by your-self.'

He didn't want to say goodnight to anyone, so I saw him to his room and he got into bed. On the first night I always ask the child how they like to sleep: the curtains open or closed; the light on or off; the bedroom door open or shut. It's little details like this that help a child settle in an unfamiliar room, but Jackson replied to all my questions that he wasn't fussed. I also said that mobile phones needed to be switched off or left downstairs at night. With a sigh, he switched it off. I said goodnight and asked him if he'd like a hug or goodnight kiss but he didn't, so I came out, closing the door. I would check on him later.

At ten o'clock Abby's father came to collect her. I'd met him and Abby's mother before collecting or dropping off one of the girls. It's important that looked-after children see their friends regularly, just as it is for our own children. Once Jackson was settled, I hoped he too would be inviting his friends to our house to play or sleep over.

I checked on him before I went to bed and he seemed to be asleep, but a few minutes later, as I was reading, I heard him moving around his room. Putting on my dressing gown, I went round the landing, knocked on his door and went in. He was sitting on the edge of his bed.

'Come on, love. It's late. You need to sleep,' I said.

With a huff, he got back into bed. I said goodnight and returned to my room. Fifteen minutes later I heard him again. It was going to be a very long night.

CHAPTER FIVE

A NEW DAY

I lost count of the number of times I had to resettle Jackson that first night. It seemed that every twenty minutes or so I was putting on my dressing gown and going to his room, having heard him moving around. His room was directly next to mine, so I was able to hear him before he woke anyone else. One time I went in he said he needed to use the bathroom, which was fair enough, but the other times I found him out of bed, wandering around, saying he wasn't tired. I said I was and took him back to bed, keeping our exchange to a minimum as I would when resettling a baby or young child. However, when I heard him at 3 a.m. I found him playing a game on his mobile phone.

'I'll look after that,' I told him. 'You can have it back in the morning.'

'I'll switch it off,' he said.

'Yes, switch it off and I'll look after it until tomorrow.' I held out my hand for the phone in a manner that said I was expecting my request to be obeyed. There was a short stand-off before he slapped the phone into my hand.

'Thank you. Well done for making the right choice. Now into bed and stay there, please. You won't fall asleep if you keep getting up.'

He huffed, annoyed, but got into his bed. I returned to my room and lay in bed wide awake, tense and listening out. It was quiet for a few minutes and I was tempted to believe he was asleep, but then he began coughing loudly. Not a real cough but forced and designed to annoy. I didn't think he could keep it up for long, so I stayed in bed and waited. The coughing stopped and instead he began humming a tuneless noise that would wake the whole house. Grabbing my dressing gown, I went round the landing again and met Paula coming out of her room. 'It's OK, love, I'll deal with it,' I said. 'You go back to bed.'

Giving a brief knock on Jackson's door, I went in. He was in bed, still making the ridiculous humming noise at the top of his voice. He didn't stop when he saw me. It might have been funny had I not been so tired and worried he would wake everyone else. 'Stop that now,' I said firmly. 'Or you won't be watching any television tomorrow.'

'You can't do that,' he said, challenging me.

'Try me,' I said, my face serious. I could have done without this now, I thought, but if I didn't set in place the boundaries I expected tonight, it would be even more difficult tomorrow. 'I mean it, Jackson. If you keep making silly noises, I'll stop your television for the whole of tomorrow. If you've got a problem, we can talk about it, but I'm not having you wake everyone. Is there something you want to share with me now?' I waited. He pulled a face but didn't say anything. 'Then go to sleep and I'll see you in the morning.'

Assuming an air of expecting my instructions to be followed, I left and returned to my room. He gave a few angry thumps on our adjoining wall and then it went quiet. I waited ten minutes and then checked on him and he was fast asleep.

The following morning I slept in until nearly eight o'clock. I had Jackson's phone and the first thing I did on waking was to check the parental control app that Connor had installed. It was working and up to date. I also checked what he was actually using his phone for. This wasn't an invasion of his privacy. He was ten years old and I had a duty to keep him safe. I'd looked after children before who'd left themselves vulnerable or got into trouble from misusing their phone. But apart from calls to and from his mother and a text to a friend, he seemed to be using it mostly for playing games. The games were age-appropriate and while some of them required access to the Internet, the controls in place meant that he shouldn't be able to access adult or inappropriate material.

Jackson slept until nine o'clock, by which time I was washed, dressed and in the kitchen having some breakfast. As soon as I heard him moving around, I went upstairs to his room. I always like to start each day afresh, regardless of what has happened the day before.

'Good morning,' I said brightly as I went in. 'I'm pleased you managed to get off to sleep. Here is your phone.'

He had the decency to look a bit guilty as he took the phone. 'Would you like a cooked breakfast? I usually do one at the weekend.'

He nodded.

'How does egg, bacon and tomatoes sound?'

'OK.'

'Good. I'll cook it while you're having a shower.' I took the change of clothes his mother had sent from his drawer. 'Come with me and I'll show you how the shower in the bathroom works, then I'll leave you to it.' With a young child or those with special needs I would help them with their personal hygiene, but Jackson was capable of looking after himself, as children his age usually are. I led the way into the bathroom where I showed him how to use the shower and checked he had everything he needed.

'When you've finished, come down and your breakfast will be ready.'

It was only a short shower, but at least he'd done as I'd asked. He'd even washed and towel-dried his hair, so I praised him. I placed his breakfast on the table in front of him together with the glass of apple juice he wanted, then left him to eat while I went upstairs to clear up the bathroom. I knew from experience the state in which a bathroom could be left. It was as I expected. Water had been splashed on most of the walls and glass surfaces; the shower gel had been left with its top off, leaking over the sponge and flannel he'd used; his wet towel was in a heap on the floor, on top of the pyjamas he'd just taken off. This was pretty normal behaviour for a young person and it didn't matter, although once Jackson had finished his breakfast I would explain some of our more important house rules. I liked to do this soon after the child arrived, so we all knew where we stood.

I joined Jackson at the table as he drained the last of his juice.

'All right?' I asked him with a smile. 'Did you enjoy that?' His plate was empty, so I assumed he had.

'When am I seeing my mum?' he asked a little grump-ily.

'Twelve o'clock. We'll leave at eleven-thirty so you're there in plenty of time.' Children in care often worry about being late to see their parents, although it was a good sign that Jackson was even asking. Yesterday he hadn't wanted to see his mother at all.

'You'll be able to bring back some more of your belong-ings,' I said. 'And choose some of your favourite games.'

'I'm not coming back,' he said. Which I guessed would be another hurdle to overcome.

'What would you like to do now?' I asked him. 'We have over an hour before we need to leave. There are plenty of games and puzzles in that cupboard there.' I pointed. 'It would make a change from playing on your phone. Also, I need to mention a few house rules that we all follow to keep us feeling safe.'

He looked at me warily.

'It's nothing to worry about.' I smiled. 'So, our bedrooms are our own private spaces and we don't go into each other's. We knock on the door if we want the person, just as I knocked on your door last night before I went in. We always try to be kind, caring and polite to each other. If we are angry, we talk about our feelings rather than shout and get annoyed, and we never hit anyone. One of the adults in the house will answer the front door if someone calls, and we usually take off our shoes when we come into the house. OK?'

He shrugged.

'Lastly, mobile phones. We don't have them at the table while we're eating, and at night they're either switched off or left down here. I think it might be best if you leave yours downstairs so you are not tempted to use it in the night.'

'I keep it with me at home,' he said. 'My mum doesn't mind.'

'That's her decision. Things are a bit different here. What would you like to do now?'

'Phone my sisters,' he said.

'All right, although you'll be seeing them shortly.' While phone contact was supposed to be on the days Jackson wasn't seeing his family, he'd only just come into care and was clearly missing his sisters – he'd tried to phone them yesterday evening, but they'd been in bed. He was in care under a Section 20, so I didn't see a problem with him phoning them on this occasion as long as his mother didn't mind. 'Make sure it's all right with your mum,' I said.

I began clearing away the breakfast dishes as Jackson made a video call home on his phone. His mother answered.

'Can I talk to Grace and Jenna?' he asked.

'Why? Aren't you coming to see us later?' Kayla asked, immediately anxious.

'Yes, but I couldn't talk to them last night.'

'Oh, I see. I'll put them on.'

I heard her call their names and then their little happy voices came on the phone, a stark contrast to Jackson's sombre, flat tone. 'Where are you?' one of them asked. I didn't know if it was the younger one, Grace, aged five, or Jenna, who was seven. 'What are you doing?' 'What does the house look like?' 'Who else lives there?' They vied to have their questions answered with the natural exuberance and intrigue of young children.

Jackson gave short, sometimes single-word answers. When they asked if I was there and what I looked like, Jackson could have turned his phone so the lens was pointing towards me in the kitchen, but he didn't.

'Is she there?' they persisted.

'Yes – hi, girls!' I called.

'Can we see her?' they asked.

'No. I'm going now,' he said testily, and ended the call.

'They're only interested,' I said. 'We could ask your mother and sisters here for a visit one day so they can see where you're staying.'

'Can I watch television?' he asked, ignoring my suggestion.

'Yes, if you wish.'

We went into the living room and switched on the television. The rest of the household began to rise.

The weekends are more leisurely and gradually, one by one, Adrian, Paula and Tilly came downstairs, said hi to Jackson and made themselves breakfast. We discussed our plans for the weekend. I usually saw my mother at the weekend, but I wasn't going this time as I wanted to wait until Jackson's behaviour was more settled and predictable. Mum was in her late eighties and, having lost my father a few years before, she lived alone. I didn't want her upset. I saw her every week and phoned her most evenings. When I told Adrian and Paula I wasn't going they said they'd go tomorrow. Lucy, my eldest daughter, lived with her partner and their baby, and they visited Mum separately, although sometimes we all went together. Adrian also asked Tilly if she wanted to go, but to our astonishment she said, 'I can't, I'm going to see my gran tomorrow.'

In normal circumstances this wouldn't have been surprising, but Tilly had consistently refused to see her grandmother, Nancy, and her mother, Heather, since her stepfather's abuse had been discovered. He was now in prison, but Tilly was still angry with her mother for not doing more to protect her. Her grandmother, on the other hand, wanting to leave the past behind, thought it was time for Tilly to forgive her mother so they could all move on with their lives. Originally there'd been plans for her to live with her gran and mother, but all that had changed when the truth had come out. Tilly was an integrated member of my family now and could stay for as long as was necessary, but I felt she should see her gran, who hadn't been well, and try to forgive her mother. I was therefore very pleased that Tilly had said she was going, as I knew Nancy would be.

'I've spoken to my mother on the phone,' Tilly added.

'Well done,' I said, doubly pleased. Although I tempered my enthusiasm, as I knew how tenuous the peace would be. 'How are they both?'

'OK. I'm going to have lunch there tomorrow.'

'Good. Have you told your social worker you're going?'

'Not yet.'

'I'll email her.'

There was no reason why Tilly couldn't visit her gran and mother again, although Isa, Tilly's social worker, needed to be informed.

'I'm seeing Abby today,' Tilly said.

'Fine, but have you done all the school work you were supposed to? You return to school next week,' I reminded her.

She looked at me sheepishly. 'I'll do some now before I go out.'

'Yes, good idea.'

With all the worry of what had been going on in her house before coming into care, Tilly had got very behind with her school work and was supposed to be catching up during the summer holidays. When she returned to school, she'd be in her exam year and her predicated grades were poor. Her teachers were concerned, as I was. However, Tilly had made progress in other aspects of her life. She had arrived angry, upset and confused, but had settled well. She was now in therapy and I was proud of the progress she'd made, just as I am proud of all my children. I don't ask them to strive to achieve the impossible, just to do their best and be happy and contented. But I was realistic and if Tilly didn't achieve the passes she needed, she could always take the exams again.

'Can we go now?' Jackson asked me a little before 11 a.m.

'We don't have to leave until eleven-thirty,' I reminded him. 'If you've had enough of watching television, let's find a game we can play.'

'I don't want to play a game,' he replied moodily, and returned to the television in the living room.

Ten minutes passed and he came to me and said quite firmly, 'We have to go now.' He could tell the time but seemed used to having his wishes acted on.

'It's not time yet.'

'Why can't we go now?' he asked, disgruntled.

'Because your social worker said we should get there for twelve o'clock, and that is the time your mother is expecting us.'

'She won't mind,' he said, and disappeared up to his room.

He reappeared five minutes later, put on his jacket and trainers, and stood pointedly by the front door, where the safety chain was in place. I kept an eye on him as I continued with what I was doing. I was pleased he wanted to see his mother, but I wasn't going to be dictated to by a ten-year-old boy. He sat by the door, playing on his phone, and at eleven-thirty I said it was time to leave. I called goodbye to Adrian, Paula and Tilly as we left. I was carrying the bag Jackson's mother had sent.

'Why have you got that?' he asked as we got into the car.

'It's your mother's and it may be useful for packing more of your belongings. I need to ask her for your school uniform,' I added, thinking aloud.

'I don't go to school,' he said.

I glanced at him in the rear-view mirror as I started the engine and pulled away. 'Yes, you do. I have details of your school on the paperwork I've been given.'

'I only go sometimes,' he said. 'When I want to.'

'That doesn't sound right.'

'It's true!' he exploded. 'Ask my mum if you don't believe me!'

'I will,' I said, and changed the subject.

CHAPTER SIX

A MIXED WEEKEND

As soon as Kayla opened her front door, Jackson shot in. I heard squeals of delight come from his sisters who were so very pleased to see him. Kayla invited me into the hall.

'How's he been?' she asked anxiously.

'Not too bad. He had a restless night, but that's only to be expected. He ate a good breakfast and has been looking forward to seeing you all. I've brought his bag back to refill. Could you include his school uniform for next week, please?'

She looked at me uncomfortably and I guessed what was coming next.

'I've had second thoughts about all of this,' she said. 'The girls missed him last night, so did I, and I feel guilty for sending him away. I know I haven't been coping, but perhaps Jackson has learnt his lesson and will be better behaved in future.'

'I understand,' I said. 'And obviously it's your and Frankie's decision, but I think you need to give him a bit longer and see how it goes. If you remove him now, the social services won't keep the placement open. There are too many other children in need of homes, so if it doesn't work out and he has to come into care again, it will almost certainly be with another carer. Possibly out of the area.'

'I've been thinking that if I had some support here and he goes to school each day, I might be able to manage him better.'

'I suggest you discuss it with Frankie on Monday,' I said. 'And what is the situation regarding his school? Jackson told me in the car that he only goes when he wants to. What's that all about?'

She sighed. 'After Connor's death, Jackson's behaviour got so bad at school they kept sending him home, although they knew I was struggling. I was called to a meeting with the deputy head and his teacher and they suggested he needed more time to adjust to his loss and I shouldn't send him if he was having a bad day. To be honest I think it was easier for them if he wasn't there playing up, so he began only going in when it suited him.'

'Did it help his behaviour?' I asked, not wholly surprised by the school's action. I'd fostered children before who'd been repeatedly sent home or excluded for bad behaviour – it's the easiest option.

'No, it got worse,' Kayla said. 'He wouldn't get up in the morning and when he did he was rude and uncooperative. He needs school.'

'I'll talk to Frankie about it on Monday. All children have to receive an education by law and if he really can't be accommodated in a mainstream school, then an alternative needs to be found. I am sure his social worker will agree.'

'Yes, when I told her she said he should be in school. But I can't force him.'

I felt sorry for Kayla having to deal with this on top of everything else, and it didn't sound as though the school had been much help. Although I knew many of the schools in the area from twenty-five years of fostering, I wasn't familiar with Jackson's. Once I'd spoken to Frankie, I would be doing all I could to make sure Jackson attended school, for the sake of both his education and his social development.

Jackson's sisters suddenly appeared at the end of the hall and rushed excitedly towards us. I guessed from their ages who was who. 'Hi, Jenna. Hi, Grace,' I said.

'Are you Jackson's foster carer?' Jenna asked.

'Yes. I'm Cathy.'

'Why's he staying with you?' Grace asked. 'Is he naughty?'

'Not any more,' Kayla said, which I thought was kind but rather naive.

The girls looked at me quizzically as if expecting a foster carer to look different, but, having seen Jackson in, it was time for me to leave.

'I'll see you later, at two o'clock,' I said, and, saying a general goodbye, I left.

I returned home, where there was just enough time to have some lunch before I had to leave again to collect Jackson. I'd been half expecting a phone call or text from Kayla telling me not to go back as Jackson would be staying at home. But to my astonishment, as I drew up outside his house I saw him sitting on the front doorstep with the door behind him closed. I quickly got out.

'What's the matter?' I asked, going up the path. 'What are you doing there?'

He shrugged, stood and went to my car.

I pressed the doorbell. It was opened immediately by Kayla, close to tears.

'Where's he gone?' she asked anxiously.

'He's in my car. What's happened?'

She shook her head in exasperation. 'It was stupid of me to think I could cope. Jackson was all right for the first half an hour and then he started getting angry with me and the girls. They got upset so I told him off and he stormed out. He's been sitting on the front doorstep ever since. I've been checking on him and telling him to come in, but he refused. He can be so stubborn when he has a mind to.'

'You should have phoned me and I could have collected him early,' I said.

'I didn't think. Here is his bag.' She had it ready in the hall. 'I've put in his school uniform, but it's too small. He hasn't worn it for a while.'

'Don't worry, I'll replace it.'

'Mum!' Jenna cried from the back room. 'Grace has taken a piece of my puzzle.'

'I have to go,' Kayla said. 'Can I phone you this evening once the girls are in bed?'

'Yes, of course. If you could make it after eight-thirty, Jackson will be in bed too.'

'Mum!' Jenna cried again.

'I'm coming!' she called back, her face full of anguish, and said goodbye.

I returned to my car. The poor woman had so much to cope with, bringing up her young family alone as well as coming to terms with her own grief. I put Jackson's bag into the boot of the car and got in. Jackson looked at me carefully as though he thought I would tell him off. But he wasn't really to blame. He needed help. The whole family did.

'Are you all right?' I asked him, turning in my seat to face him.

He shrugged despondently.

'Do you want to talk about what happened?'

'No.' He looked out of his side window.

'I think once your mum gets some help and you start attending counselling and school regularly, everyone will be much happier.'

He seemed relieved that he wasn't in trouble and gave a small nod. It wasn't his fault the family situation had deteriorated in the way it had. Two bereavements in two years must have been agonizing, and it had resulted in an intense and complex mixture of painful feelings and unresolved issues that would hopefully heal with time and therapy.

'Can I still see my mum?' Jackson asked as I drove.

'Yes, of course, love. On Monday, and you can phone tomorrow. Jenna and Grace were pleased to see you.'

'They are nicer than me,' he said pitifully, and I could have wept.

'You're all nice,' I said. 'It's just that you seem to be carrying a lot of the pain from what happened and blaming yourself.'

'It *was* my fault,' he said. 'I wish Connor hadn't told me.'

I looked at him in the rear-view mirror. 'Told you what?' I asked. I'd looked after children before who'd disclosed from the rear of the car while I was driving – it seemed easier than telling me face to face – but Jackson looked away.

'You mean that Connor told you he was thinking of taking his own life?' I asked, which was what I'd assumed before when Jackson had said something similar. He shook his head.

'What was it then, love?' I asked gently.

'I can't tell you. I promised I wouldn't.'

'Have you told your mother or anyone else?'

'No. I can't break a promise now he's dead.'

'I understand, but sometimes promises we make seem right at the time and then the situation changes and it's better to tell someone and share our pain. It seems to me that whatever Connor told you could be like that. He said you shouldn't tell as it would upset your mother, but now it's upsetting you. I don't think he would have wanted you upset, would he?'

'No,' Jackson said quietly. 'But I still can't tell you.'

I stopped off on the way home and bought Jackson a new school uniform and school shoes.

'I don't think they'll have me back,' he said, referring to his school.

'If not, we'll find you another school,' I told him positively. Although I knew it might not be that easy. If a child has been excluded from one school, others are reluctant to take them.

Once home, I hung his uniform in his wardrobe and unpacked the bag his mother had sent. Then, after dinner, I persuaded him to have a game of draughts with me. For a short time – while he was involved in playing the game – the weight of his sadness seemed to lift and he was just another child playing to win, then it descended again. I tried to talk to him about his problems, but he wouldn't be drawn. A shutter came down, which I guessed had probably happened with his mother too.

That night at bedtime, I waited on the landing while he washed and then changed into his pyjamas in the bathroom. It was Saturday night, so Adrian and Paula were out and Tilly was in her bedroom watching a film on her laptop. As I went with Jackson into his room I remembered to ask him for his phone. He hadn't been using it during the evening because he'd been playing a game with me.

'It's downstairs,' he said. 'I left it in my place at the table like you said.' You could have knocked me down with a feather! I struggled to hide my surprise. 'Well done. Good boy.' I smiled.

Not only did this arrangement mean that the child wasn't tempted to use their phone at night, but it had the added advantage of being an incentive for them to get up in the morning, which can be a problem, especially on a school day.

'I think you'll sleep better tonight,' I told Jackson as I waited for him to get into bed. 'If you're upset or need anything, call me, but I don't want any silly noises. It's not fair on everyone else.'

I asked him if he'd like a goodnight kiss or hug, but he shook his head, so, saying goodnight, I came out and closed his door. I waited on the landing for a few minutes to see if he would get out of bed, but all remained quiet. I looked in on Tilly to make sure she was OK and then went downstairs. I sat in the living room and wrote up my log notes while the day's events were still fresh in my mind. At 8.45 Kayla called my mobile.

'How is he?' she asked, concerned.

'He's in bed, hopefully asleep.'

'The girls are too. I told them Jackson didn't mean to be nasty, but he can't help himself sometimes. Cathy, you've been fostering a long time and must have looked after a lot of children; do you think there is something wrong with him?'

'Like what?' I asked.

'I don't know. Autism?'

'No.' Sometimes, if a parent is struggling with a child's behaviour, they can wonder if it's autism. 'I don't think he's autistic, but I do think he's grieving for his father and brother.'

'So are we all,' Kayla said.

'I know, but Jackson seems to feel guilty about something Connor told him. Has he ever said anything to you?'

'No. He won't talk about his father or Connor. I know it's not healthy, but what can I do? A neighbour of mine, Jerry, offered to talk to him. Jerry was good while my husband was very ill, but Jackson won't have anything to do with him and he's quite rude.'

'Can you think of anything that Connor might have confided in Jackson?'

'No. Connor was seven years older than Jackson – why would he confide in his little brother? What's Jackson been saying?'

'Only that Connor told him a secret that he mustn't tell because he'd get into trouble and it would upset you.'

'I've no idea what that could be. Perhaps he's making it up.'

'Maybe, although I don't think so. Hopefully he'll be able to talk to a counsellor once Frankie has put that in place.'

'Jackson never used to be like this,' Kayla said with a heartfelt sigh. 'I just wish he'd start behaving himself so we can all be together again.'

'Yes, that's what we're all working towards,' I said. Although quietly I thought that wasn't going to happen for a long time – not until Jackson shared the burden he was carrying.

Jackson only woke once during the night to use the bathroom and then went straight back to sleep. I think he was exhausted from the previous broken night – so was I. The following morning I told him he'd done well and left him to get dressed. It was Sunday, the start of September, and the sun was shining in a clear blue sky, making everyone feel brighter.

We all had breakfast together and then once I'd seen Adrian and Paula off at the door to visit my mother, and Tilly to see her gran, I took Jackson to the local park with a football. We kicked it back and forth for a while and then he went off to dribble it around the park by himself, although he was never out of my sight. Another boy joined him for a while and they played together until the boy's father said it was time for him to go.

On the way home I told Jackson that my other daughter, Lucy, and her partner Darren were going to stop by later with their baby Emma, so he would meet them. I had suggested to Lucy that they come for dinner, but she'd said she had no idea what time they would be able to leave the house. Emma was only four weeks old, and they were up a lot at night and tried to doze when she slept during the day. Also, leaving the house required a lot of organization with nappies, bottles of formula and so on, as many new parents know. Lucy and Darren had met at the nursery school they both worked at, although Lucy was now on maternity leave. I liked Darren, and his parents were nice too.

I felt the day was going well. Once home, Jackson wanted to phone his mother. I asked him to make the call in the living room, where I was, so I was on hand if necessary. I knew how emotional these phone calls home could be. Phone contact was on my list of matters to discuss with Frankie when we next spoke. I thought that Jackson was too young to simply go off and phone his mother whenever he pleased.

As it turned out, it was just as well I was present when he phoned her – although not for the reason I'd anticipated. Kayla didn't answer his call and it went through to voicemail.

'Mum's not there!' he said, immediately becoming angry.

'I expect she's busy,' I said. 'You can try again later.' I would suggest to Frankie that we had a set time to phone to avoid this type of disappointment.

Jackson didn't follow my advice to wait but immediately called his mother again, with the same result, and then again, getting more and more agitated each time she didn't answer.

'She could be out,' I suggested. 'Or the battery on her phone might have died.' There were any number of reasons why Kayla might not be able to answer, but Jackson, being vulnerable and in a dark place, chose to believe the most negative and hurtful.

'She doesn't want to talk to me,' he said sorrowfully. 'She'd rather be with Grace and Jenna.' But his next assumption was the most telling. 'Perhaps she's dead too. Perhaps they all are!' And he burst into tears.

I went over and tried to give him a hug, but he stepped back, so I gently took his hand and sought eye contact. 'Jackson, love, they're not dead. I expect your mother is busy and isn't aware you've called. Of course she wants to talk to you. She loves you. As soon as she checks her phone and sees your missed call, she'll phone.' This wasn't a reassurance I'd give all children I'd fostered, but I thought it was true of Kayla.

'No, they could be dead,' he persisted.

'They're not,' I replied firmly. But I could see why he might think that. We are shaped by our experiences and his experience was that loved ones could suddenly die.

Eventually he allowed me to dry his tears and give him a little hug. And of course the next time he phoned his mother she answered and was pleased to hear from him.

'I saw your missed call when I came in from hanging the washing on the line,' she said. 'I was just about to phone you when you called.'

His face lightened and they had a good conversation, but Jackson's initial reaction was an indication of just how fragile he was. It was very worrying, and I knew he should receive bereavement counselling as soon as possible.

CHAPTER SEVEN

CHALLENGING BEHAVIOUR

When Lucy and family visited that Sunday after-noon, we tried to include Jackson as we did every child we looked after, but he wasn't interested. He spent some time with us in the living room playing on his phone, either ignoring us or shrugging when anyone spoke to him. Then he said he wanted to go into the garden, so I unlocked our shed and took out everything he wanted to play with, then locked it again as there were tools in there that could have been dangerous to a child. I asked Jackson to play on the grass, which covers most of the bottom half of our garden. It's the children's area and includes an outdoor ball pond, sandpit, small trampoline, goal posts, climbing frame and swing. It was where my children had played when they were little, and where I encouraged our looked-after children to play. I made sure he had everything he wanted and returned indoors where I re-joined Lucy and family in the living room.

I sat in the chair by the patio windows, where I could see Jackson. When he thought I wasn't watching he began purposely throwing the balls from the ball pond over the fence into our neighbour's garden. I knocked on the window and motioned for him to stop. He shrugged and pretended to play, but as soon as he thought I wasn't looking he began doing it again. I went out.

'Keep the balls in the garden, please,' I said to him.

I waited until he was playing again and then went indoors. A few minutes later he was throwing them over the other fence. My neighbours would return them, so I decided not to go out, but when he began throwing sand from the sandpit over the fence I had to go out again.

'Don't do that, please,' I said firmly. 'You've got all these toys out to play with. Why don't you ride the bike or scooter?' He shrugged. 'If you've had enough of being out here then come in and join us.'

Scowling, he threw another handful of sand.

'You've lost half an hour of your television,' I said.

'Don't care,' he said. He stormed past me and went indoors, slamming the back door.

I followed him in just in time to hear him stamp upstairs and then his bedroom door slam shut.

'Are you all right, Mum?' Lucy called.

'Yes,' I said, going into the living room. 'We'll give Jackson time to calm down.'

We tried to carry on as before, but it was very difficult. Jackson was stomping around his bedroom and opening and shutting his door, so I had to keep going up to settle him.

I could guess why he was being so disruptive while Lucy was here; I'd seen it before with other children I'd fostered. If you're not living with your own family then witnessing a happy family gathering just makes your own loss a whole lot worse, regardless of how welcoming the host family is. Lucy and Darren had gone out of their way to include Jackson, as I had, but he wasn't having any of it. Christmas is often the worst for this. If you are picturing a deprived child overjoyed and grateful for what will probably be their first proper Christmas – with presents, games and sumptuous food – forget it. Occasionally that's true, but more often the child is disruptive and angry at Christmas because they're not with their own parents and they never had a decent Christmas in the past.

Despite Jackson's negative behaviour, I enjoyed spending time with Lucy, Darren and my granddaughter Emma. They said they were sorry to have missed Adrian, Paula and Tilly but would see them another time. As soon as they'd gone, Jackson came down from his room and wanted the television on. I reminded him he'd lost half an hour, and he stormed up to his room again. It was quiet and then I heard an almighty bang. I ran upstairs, my heart pounding. Giving a brief knock on the door, I went in. The chair that was usually under the desk had been thrown against the wall. Jackson glared at me and then looked around for something else to throw.

'I wouldn't,' I said, although there wasn't much else to throw anyway. He only had his clothes and phone with him.

At that moment the front door opened as Adrian and Paula returned from seeing my mother. 'Hi, Mum, we're back!' Adrian called. It seemed to defuse Jackson.

'Come down and find something to do for half an hour,' I said to him. 'Then you can watch some television.'

'I want to stay here.'

'OK, but don't throw anything else or you will lose more television time. I'll be downstairs if you need me.'

I left his door open and went to talk to Adrian and Paula. I'm acutely aware of how easy it is for the foster carer's own family to take second place because of the needs of the looked-after child, so I always make time for them, even though they are adults now. Adrian and Paula told me of their day and said Nana was well and she sent some fairy cakes she'd made. I phoned her to thank her and also to let her know that Adrian and Paula were home safely.

Jackson must have been counting off the minutes for when half an hour had passed he came downstairs to watch television. He liked watching television, so depriving him of it was a good sanction when needed. Hopefully next time he'd think twice before he did something he shouldn't. He also enjoyed two of Mum's cakes.

When Tilly arrived home I made time for her, and asked how her visit home had gone. 'Gran's good,' she said. 'And Mum told me she was truly sorry for everything that happened.'

'I'm sure she is,' I said.

Heather, Tilly's mother, had apologized to Tilly before, but unlike then, I now felt Tilly was more open to accepting her apology. I hoped so, for in many ways Heather had been a victim as much as her daughter.

Jackson had another reasonable night, only waking once when I resettled him. Monday was the last day of the summer holidays before school began again on Tuesday. It turned out to be a day of phone calls. Joy phoned first to ask me what sort of weekend we'd had, and I updated her on both Jackson and Tilly. Children in care have their own social worker, but the foster carer's SSW oversees all children the carer is looking after. She said she was due a visit and made an appointment to see us at 4.30 on Thursday.

Next to phone was Isa, Tilly's social worker, who was calling in response to my email advising her that Tilly was going to see her grandmother and mother on Sunday. She'd also spoken to Tilly that morning, who had then gone out with Abby – making the most of her 'last day of freedom', as she put it. Tilly had told Isa she was going to her gran's next Sunday but wouldn't be going after school as well as her gran wanted her to. Isa thought, as I did, that this was sensible. Their peace was still fragile and Tilly needed time to heal. Isa asked me about Tilly's school work and said the school would need to update her PEP (Personal Education Plan) in the new term. All children in care have a PEP – a document that sets out goals and achievements to help the child or young person reach their full academic and life potential. Tilly was seeing a counsellor at CAMHS once a week, which would continue in the new term. It was the same service I hoped Jackson would access. It's part of our wonderful National Health Service, so free to the user, and gives children access to therapy when their families might not otherwise be able to afford it. Isa arranged to visit us on Friday after school at around 4.30. The week was filling up.

Then Frankie called and I updated her on the ups and downs of Jackson's weekend. We agreed that he needed to be in school again as a priority, but Kayla had told her the school wouldn't take Jackson back without a reintegration meeting. She said she'd phone them now and try to set one up for tomorrow. Although the school wasn't open for the students until tomorrow, the staff were in. That afternoon, as I was about to leave the house to take Jackson to see his mother, my phone rang. It was Frankie to say we had a reintegration meeting with the deputy head at 8 a.m. tomorrow.

When I told Jackson he pulled a face but did say his mother would be pleased.

I saw Jackson to his front door and said hello to Kayla and the girls but didn't go in. They only had an hour together, so they needed to make the most of it. It wasn't worth me going home so I went to a local store and bought some groceries we needed. When I returned to collect Jackson he was clearly in a bad mood. I looked questioningly at Kayla, but she just shook her head in exasperation. Whatever had gone wrong in such a short time? I wondered as we went down the path to my car. They were supposed to be seeing each other four times a week, but this didn't bode well.

'What's the matter?' I asked Jackson once we were in my car. I turned in my seat so I could see him.

'You told Mum on the phone that Connor had a secret,' he said, his face tightening in accusation.

'Yes, because she is your mother and she's worried about you, as I am. There is clearly something wrong beyond the fact that you have lost two people close to you.'

'No, there isn't! It's none of your business,' he snapped.

'I hope that in time you will make it my or your mother's business so we can help you,' I said.

'I don't need help,' Jackson protested. 'I promised Connor I wouldn't tell Mum and I won't.'

'I know, but you didn't promise him not to tell me,' I pointed out, hoping this would help him open up.

'But you'll tell Mum,' he returned.

'Probably, and certainly your social worker. As your foster carer I can't keep secrets. They would have to know. Sometimes it's easier to write things down, Jackson. Have you ever thought of keeping a diary?'

'No, and I don't want to.' He scowled.

'OK, let me know if you change your mind and we can buy you a nice diary to write in. It's helped other children I've looked after.'

I started the car and drove away. Jackson remained glum, staring out of his side window during the journey home. I tried talking to him, but he ignored me, so we completed our journey in silence.

Thankfully Paula was home with some good news.

'I've been offered temporary work for the rest of the week and I've got an interview for a permanent post next week.'

'Well done. Fantastic!' I said.

She was as pleased as I was. She'd filled in dozens of online application forms and this was only her second interview. She'd done well to get temporary work and another interview for a permanent post, but with fierce competition we were realistic about her chances of being offered the position. Last time she'd come second.

We all had dinner together and although Jackson ate plenty, he was very quiet. We tried drawing him into the conversation, but he didn't respond. His shutters were down. I hoped that eventually he could be as chatty and relaxed as we were, talking, laughing and sharing our day as we ate. But I knew he was a long, long way from that yet.

That night I began a bath and bedtime routine for Jackson that would see us through the school weeks and was earlier than at weekends or in the school holidays. Tilly was also planning on having an early night, ready for school the following morning. At the start of the long summer holidays the days seem to stretch endlessly ahead, then suddenly they're over and you're faced with a new term and the school routine resumes. Adrian and Paula had to be up early too, for work.

Jackson was restless that night and I had to resettle him a number of times. He wasn't always out of bed, and his phone was downstairs, but he kept asking questions about school so I guessed he was worrying about it. 'Who will be at the meeting?' I told him the deputy head, Frankie and us, as far as I knew. Will he be in the same class as he was last time? I said I didn't know. And so forth. I told him I understood he was apprehensive about going to school again, but he'd be fine once he was there and in the routine. Of course, I didn't know for certain he would be allowed back into the same school, but I thought now he was a looked-after child, and with his social worker present, we were in with a good chance. Generally, allowances are made for challenging behaviour when children are in care. Some schools are more supportive than others.

The following morning Jackson took a long time to get out of bed and then dress in his new school uniform. I said he looked very smart and he scowled. I asked him what he wanted for breakfast and he said nothing, and that he wasn't going to school. He eventually had some breakfast but kept telling me he wasn't going to school. However, with the rest of the household also preparing to leave, his protests got lost in all the hustle and bustle. He got swept along with everyone else and found himself in my car on his way to school. I could imagine it was very different in his house, where Kayla had to get his two younger sisters ready to take to school as well. At some point his obstinate refusal would have got the better of her and she would have given in and let him stay at home as the school had suggested.

As I drove, I kept glancing at Jackson in the rear-view mirror; he was usually scowling or deep in thought. I reassured him there was nothing to worry about, and he replied with a grumble about not being allowed to bring his mobile phone. I'd told him to leave it on the table until I'd checked with the school what their policy was on mobile phones. Some schools published their policy on their website, but Jackson's hadn't.

We arrived outside his school ten minutes before the reintegration meeting was due to take place. I parked in the road a little way from the main entrance and we got out. Jackson looked the part in his new school uniform with his school bag, which his mother had sent, on his back, although his expression gave a different message: annoyed, irritated and resentful.

'Try to look a bit more positive,' I said as we walked along the pavement to the main gate.

'I don't want to be here,' he said grumpily. 'I'd rather go to another school.'

'Why? Is there any specific reason?' I asked, wondering if he was being bullied. I pressed the security buzzer.

'No. I just would,' he said.

The gate opened and I saw Jackson hesitate and glance around as if he might be thinking of running away.

'We'll see how it goes,' I reassured him. 'In you go.' I stood aside to let him go in first. The playground was empty at this time. 'It's bound to be a bit strange to begin with,' I said as we continued to the main door. 'Do you have any questions you want me to ask?'

He shook his head.

I pressed the security buzzer beside the door and we were let in to reception, where I gave our names to the school secretary and the reason for our visit. 'Sign here,' she said, opening the visitors' book, 'then take a seat over there.'

Jackson was already sitting on one of the four chairs that were in a line on the far side of reception, and I joined him. The reception area was typical of that of many schools, with their achievements displayed on the wall together with a list of staff and their photographs.

'Who was your teacher last year?' I asked him.

'Miss Whitecloth,' he said. 'We called her Rags.' And finally his face lightened to a small smile.

'That's better,' I said, also smiling. 'Whitecloth is an unusual name. I wonder who you will have this year.'

'Don't know,' he said. The school year ran from September to July, so Jackson would now be in the class above – his final year at primary school. Had he been in school when the last term had ended, he would have met his new teacher with the rest of his class.

The security buzzer sounded and Frankie came in. She said good morning, registered at reception and then joined us. 'You look very smart,' she told Jackson. 'How are you?'

He shrugged.

'A bit apprehensive, understandably,' I said.

Frankie and I made some light conversation as eight o'clock, our appointment time, came and went. I saw Frankie glance at the wall clock, then she checked some messages on her phone. Jackson was becoming increasingly anxious and kept tapping his foot and shifting position in his chair. At 8.10 Frankie said, 'I wonder why the delay?' At 8.15 she stood and went to the secretary. 'We had an appointment with Ms Gainsborough at eight o'clock,' she said pointedly.

'Yes, she's very busy as deputy headmistress,' the secretary replied. But she didn't reassure us that she was on her way or phone her to check.

'We're all busy,' Frankie said quietly to me as she returned to her seat.

'It's not fair, keeping Jackson waiting all this time,' I said. With every passing minute I could see he was becoming more and more agitated, like a simmering pot. I thought before long he'd make a run for it.

At 8.25 Frankie went to reception again. 'I'm afraid I can't wait indefinitely,' she said.

'I'll phone Ms Gainsborough,' the secretary replied brusquely, clearly expecting us to just sit and wait.

Jackson, however, who hadn't wanted to come to school in the first place, had now run out of patience. As the secretary made the call, he jumped to his feet and, rushing to the door, tried to open it by yanking on the handle, which made the whole door rattle. He hadn't spotted the release button. Frankie and I went to him and he gave the door a good kick. At that moment a smartly dressed woman in her thirties appeared from the corridor behind us and I knew instantly it was Ms Gainsborough, the deputy headmistress, now witnessing Jackson's outburst.

CHAPTER EIGHT

ON TENTERHOOKS

'Whatever is going on here?' the deputy head asked sternly.

Jackson stopped kicking the door and stared at her. Frankie and I were looking at her too.

'We don't tolerate that sort of behaviour in school, do we, Jackson?'

'No, Miss.'

I immediately came to his defence, as I would any child I was looking after. 'Jackson was very anxious about coming back to school,' I said. 'I'm afraid the wait hasn't helped. I'm Cathy Glass, his foster carer.'

'I'm Ms Gainsborough, deputy head,' she said. 'Even so, there are ways to behave and Jackson knows that kicking is not allowed. Don't you?'

'Yes, Miss.'

'Frankie Streete, Jackson's social worker,' she said, introducing herself.

'Take a few deep breaths and calm down,' I told Jackson.

'I apologize for the delay, but it was unavoidable,' Ms Gainsborough said. 'Let's go to my office.'

I threw Jackson a reassuring smile, but he looked

angry as we followed the deputy head through a set of double doors and along a corridor, past empty class-rooms. School didn't start until nine o'clock so the children would be outside gathering in the playground. We turned left and stopped by a door marked 'Headmistress'. As the deputy, Ms Gainsborough was acting headmistress and I had the feeling she wasn't completely confident in her role, hence her rather severe approach.

'Jackson, you can sit there while we talk in the office,' she said, referring to two chairs to the right of the door.

'Can't he come in with us?' I asked.

'It's school policy after exclusion to speak to the parent or carer first,' she said. Then to Jackson: 'Have you got your reading book in your bag?' I knew he had as I'd looked in his bag.

'Yes, Miss,' Jackson said.

'Read your book then and I'll call you in to join us in a few minutes.'

'Good boy,' I said. I waited until he'd sat down before I followed Ms Gainsborough and Frankie into the office.

It was a spacious room with a large wooden desk, bookshelves and an area to the right with four easy chairs arranged around a mat and coffee table. 'Sit down,' she said, and I felt like a child.

She took a folder from her desk and joined us.

'So, Jackson is in care now,' she said. 'Let's hope his attitude improves, because if not, I can't really see him staying with us for long.' I assumed Frankie had given her some general background information when she'd phoned to arrange this appointment.

'I'll do all I can to help him,' I said. 'Jackson has been through a very difficult time recently.'

'I appreciate that,' Ms Gainsborough said. Then, opening her folder, she spent some time talking about the incidents that had led to him being sent home on fixed-term exclusions. Frankie made notes. 'Other pupils would have been permanently excluded by now, but we have made allowances,' she concluded.

'Thank you,' I said.

Ms Gainsborough then asked if Jackson was seeing his mother and if there were plans for him to return home. Frankie gave details of contact and said that Kayla had placed Jackson in care voluntarily as she felt she'd be able to cope better with just her daughters there. And the care plan was that ultimately Jackson would return home.

'His sisters also attend this school,' Ms Gainsborough said, which I knew from the placement information form. 'They are in the infants, which is in the adjoining building. They don't appear to be having the same difficulties Jackson is.'

'Jackson seems to have assumed responsibility for the tragedy in his family,' I said.

Frankie agreed and said, 'I'm making an urgent referral to CAMHS.'

I then asked Ms Gainsborough if Jackson had been assessed as having any special educational needs. Although none had been mentioned so far, I knew this could have an impact on a child's behaviour at school.

'No,' she said. 'But he's missed a lot of school so has fallen behind. We sent work home when he was excluded, but it was rarely completed. Then there were all the days he took off because he wasn't up to coming to school.'

Frankie nodded. 'We'll need another meeting to draw up a PEP,' Frankie said, and Ms Gainsborough made a note. She then looked at me, 'How is Jackson with you?'

'It's early days yet but he's getting into a routine.'

'And his behaviour?'

'It's manageable.'

'It might be for you, but here Jackson will be in a class of thirty. I was going to suggest he returns part-time to begin with – mornings only. We could review his progress at half-term.' Which was seven weeks away.

There was silence for a moment and then Frankie said what I was thinking. 'We need to try to reintegrate him into full-time school as soon as possible. He's missed a lot of school and we expect our looked-after children to receive a proper education.'

'Also, if he was part-time,' I said, 'I think it would single him out from other students. He needs the education but also to form friendship bonds. He doesn't seem to have many friends. Do you have a Pastoral Support Programme [PSP] here? I've seen it work well with other children I've fostered. Then Jackson would have a mentor, someone he could go to if he was struggling.'

'Our teachers usually provide pastoral support,' Ms Gainsborough said. 'But I can speak to Mrs Bryant, our Special Educational Needs Coordinator [SENCO].'

'Thank you,' Frankie said as she wrote. 'So we'll start him full-time with support.' Which Ms Gainsborough accepted.

'The infant school that Grace and Jenna attend comes out ten minutes earlier than this one,' she said to me. 'We do this to stagger the number of cars in the road. But you might still see Kayla collecting Grace and Jenna. Is that going to be a problem? When Jackson lived with his mother they all went home together.'

'We'll have to see how it goes,' I said, for it had the potential to be upsetting for all three children on the days when there wasn't contact.'

'Do they share a playground?' Frankie asked.

'No, they're separate.'

'Cathy will be taking Jackson to see his sisters and mother after school on Mondays, Wednesdays and Fridays,' Frankie said. 'And Saturdays for two hours.'

Ms Gainsborough made a note and then ran through some practical information relating to the school, including school times, permission slips for outings and school uniform, most of which I'd read on their website. I then asked her about their mobile-phone policy.

'Jackson has had problems with his mobile phone in the past,' Ms Gainsborough said. 'Our policy is to discourage children from bringing them to school. But if a parent wants their child to have their phone with them then they are asked to sign a permission slip. We don't take any responsibility for the phone being lost or damaged on school premises. If they are brought into school then they have to be kept switched off all day. They are not allowed on school excursions. As Jackson struggled to keep his switched off, I would suggest his phone stays with you. I'm assuming you will be bringing him to school and collecting him?'

'Yes,' I said.

'So there are no safety issues that might require him to have a phone with him?'

'No,' I replied. 'He can leave his phone at home as he has done today.'

'Good, well done,' she said, and I felt I had been awarded a gold star. 'We'll call Jackson in now and then he can join his class. Would you like to fetch him?' she asked me.

I stood, went to the door and opened it, expecting to see Jackson sitting on the chair where we'd left him. He wasn't. I stepped out and drew the door to behind me. His bag was on the floor beside the chair, but there was no sign of Jackson. My heart sank. Where on earth was he? Surely he hadn't left the building? I walked hurriedly to the end of the corridor and couldn't see him, then turned and went to the other end. I was about to return to the room and tell them he'd gone when Jackson appeared along the corridor. 'Where have you been?' I asked, annoyed. 'You were supposed to sit and wait for us.'

'I needed the toilet,' he said. But his smirk told me otherwise. This was Jackson deciding not do as he'd been told.

'Come on, hurry up. You're going to be allowed back into school, but Ms Gainsborough wants to talk to you first.'

He groaned and I threw him a warning look. I picked up his school bag and held the door open for him to go in. I was on tenterhooks as he sat down and Ms Gainsborough talked to him about his behaviour. I thought that at any moment he might storm off, shouting abuse. She reminded him of the school's expectations – that every member of the school community should behave in a considerate and respectful way towards others and achieve their personal best. I was relieved when she'd finished.

'I'll take Jackson to meet his class teacher now,' she said, standing. 'Mr Burrows has just joined our school this year and is an excellent teacher.'

'I've got a man teacher?' Jackson asked.

'Yes.'

I couldn't tell from his expression if he was pleased or not.

'I'll stop by Cathy's later and see how your first day has gone,' Frankie told him. We said goodbye and the two of us left the school together, then went our separate ways.

My thoughts kept returning to Jackson during the day, wondering how he was getting on. I thought about Tilly too, who also had her first day back at school today, and Paula, who was starting a new temping position. Adrian was settled in his job, so I didn't worry about him so much. At midday I texted Paula and Tilly to see how they were doing. Tilly was in secondary school and they were allowed to switch on their phones at lunchtime. She replied: *You were right! I should have done more work in the holidays*, with an unamused emoji face.

Paula texted back: *OK. The people are nice.* She was on reception at a firm of solicitors.

I then texted Adrian and Lucy to see how they were. Adrian replied: *I'm fine, Mum. How are you?* While Lucy asked: *Are you free to talk?*

Yes, I replied. Worried that something was wrong, I phoned her straight away. 'Are you all right, love?' I asked.

'I can't settle Emma,' Lucy said anxiously. 'I don't know what's the matter with her. We were up most of the night. She doesn't have a temperature, but she won't let me put her down.'

'Is she feeding?'

'Yes. I don't know what I'm doing wrong.' I heard her voice break.

'You're not doing anything wrong, love. Babies can become unsettled sometimes for no obvious reason. If she's feeding and doesn't have a temperature, I doubt she's ill. Do you want me to come over?'

'Yes, please, Mum.'

'I'll leave now,' I said. 'But I'll have to collect Jackson from school later.'

'Thank you.'

Picking up my bag and jacket, I quickly left the house. I could remember how it felt as a new mother not being able to settle my first baby. They seem so small and vulnerable that you feel you should be able to cope, but their crying – loud and persistent – can make you feel utterly helpless and incompetent. We are led to believe that parenthood is natural and instinctive, but it rarely is first time around. Added to this, Lucy had confided in me that she was worried she wouldn't be a good mother and would take after her birth mother, Bonnie, who hadn't been able to bring her up. I'd reassured her there was no comparison. Bonnie had had a lot of issues, including drug and alcohol misuse, which is why Lucy had gone into care in the first place. Lucy and I were far more mother and daughter in real terms than she and Bonnie had ever been. She saw Bonnie a couple of times a year and was realistic in what she could expect from her. Lucy was the opposite of her birth mother. Responsible, compassionate and reliable, she was a qualified nursery nurse so knew how to care for infants. But tired from the constant demands of her new baby, her self-esteem had plummeted and allowed misgivings to return.

Although the flat where Lucy and Darren lived was only a mile away, I used my car as I had to collect Jackson when I left her. I arrived ten minutes later, but by then Lucy had succeeded in settling Emma and she was asleep in her cot in the living room.

'I told her Nana was on the way to sort her out,' Lucy joked. 'She let out a large burp and went straight off to sleep.'

I smiled. 'It was probably trapped wind all along,' I said as I gazed adoringly at little Emma.

Lucy made us a cup of tea and we sat in the living room and talked, keeping our voices low so we wouldn't disturb Emma. I saw Lucy's eyes begin to close. 'Why don't you have a sleep?' I suggested. 'I'll keep an eye on Emma.'

'I will, if you don't mind,' she said, and went to her bedroom for a lie-down.

While Lucy and Emma slept, I did the washing-up and tidied the kitchen. When Emma woke she was happy to lie in my arms for a while, but then it became clear she needed feeding. I knew Lucy was breastfeeding and using formula as a top-up. I gently woke her and put Emma in her arms. After she'd fed and changed her, we returned to the living room. Lucy seemed refreshed after her nap and better able to cope. Darren, who'd been on the early shift at the nursery, would be home in a couple of hours. Presently I had to leave to collect Jackson, so I kissed them goodbye. Most new mums need a helping hand from time to time, and I still remember how wonderfully supportive my parents were.

As I parked outside Jackson's school I saw Kayla waking along the pavement, having collected her daughters. They didn't see me and were heading away from me, I assumed walking home; their house wasn't far from the school. I went into the junior school playground where I waited for school to end, and soon Jackson come out. I spotted him straight away, standing beside the only male teacher. They both came over and for a moment I thought his teacher wanted to see me because there'd already been a problem, but he just wanted to introduce himself.

'I'm Mr Burrows, Jackson's class teacher,' he said with a smile.

'Nice to meet you, I'm Cathy Glass. Has Jackson had a good day?'

'Yes, a very pleasing start.'

'Excellent,' I said. 'Let me know if there is anything I can do to help him.' Jackson was looking a lot happier.

'Homework will start tomorrow and Jackson has a copy of the homework timetable,' Mr Burrows said. 'I've spoken to our SENCO, Mrs Bryant, and she will be providing Jackson with pastoral support. She saw him for a few minutes at lunchtime today to introduce herself. She will be seeing him twice a week and Jackson knows where to find her if he needs her at other times.'

'That's great, thank you,' I said, pleased that support had been put in place so quickly.

However, as Jackson and I walked to my car he grumbled about having to see Mrs Bryant. 'I'm not going,' he said. 'It's in my lunchbreak and the other kids don't have to go.'

'It's to help you manage at school,' I told him.

'Don't care. Not going.' His face set.

'You need to give Mrs Bryant a chance and see how it goes,' I said. 'And Frankie is stopping by soon,' I reminded him.

'I'm not seeing her either!' he said, looking like thunder. I had the feeling we were in for a rough evening.

CHAPTER NINE

HARD WORK

Despite trying to draw Jackson into conversation by asking him about his day at school, he sat in moody silence while I drove home. Once indoors, he went straight to the table in our kitchen-diner, retrieved his phone and went upstairs to his bedroom. That morning I'd taken the opportunity to check his phone again, as I would be doing regularly, but there hadn't been anything untoward on it.

Tilly arrived home as I began preparing dinner and came into the kitchen for a chat. She was a bit down, because all her subject teachers had emphasized to the whole class the importance of working hard this year, as exams began in less than eight months. I suggested to her – as I had before – that she set aside a few hours each night to study so it wasn't left until the last minute. She agreed, but then said, 'I'll start straight after dinner.'

'Dinner isn't until six o'clock so why not do an hour before, and then two hours after?'

'Three hours a night!' she exclaimed.

'I think that's what is needed or more.'

She grumbled about not having time to see her friends, poured herself a glass of juice and took that and a bag of crisps to her bedroom, supposedly to study. Almost immediately I heard her talking on her phone. Not the exact words, but the rise and fall of her voice. I guessed she was talking to her best friend Abby, despite having seen her at school. I gave her ten minutes and then went up and knocked on her door. She knew why.

'Sorry! I'm going to do some work now,' she replied.

'Good.'

I checked on Jackson. He was sprawled on his bed, playing a game on his phone. I'm sure parenting was much simpler before mobile phones! 'Why don't you come downstairs?' I suggested, not wanting him to spend too much time alone.

'Don't want to,' he replied sulkily. 'I tried to phone Mum but she's seeing to Jenna and Grace.'

'It's a busy time of the evening if you have young children,' I said. 'Did she say she'd phone you back or are you going to call her?'

'She'll phone,' he said.

I tried again to persuade him to come downstairs but didn't get anywhere, so I returned to the kitchen. Eventually Tilly's phone call ended and Jackson quietly came down and sat in the living room. At 5.15 the doorbell rang and it was Frankie. I showed her through to the living room.

'Did you have a good day?' she asked Jackson, sitting next to him on the sofa.

'It was all right,' he said, concentrating on his phone.

'I won't keep you long, I just wanted to see how you are.'

Jackson didn't reply so I told Frankie that Mr Burrows had said he'd had a good day and he'd also seen Mrs Bryant at lunchtime.'

'Great,' Frankie said. 'Well done.' And taking out her notepad, she made a note.

I asked Frankie about phone contact. 'I wondered if we could set a time for Jackson to call his mother? Sometimes she's not available and Jackson is disappointed.'

'No, I'm not,' he said moodily, glancing up from his phone.

'I'll ask her,' Frankie said, making another note. 'I've made a referral to CAMHS. Hopefully it will come through in weeks rather than months, although there is a waiting list. I knew the number of referrals had risen sharply in recent years as more and more young people struggled with mental-health issues.

'Have you got all Jackson's belongings now?' Frankie asked me.

'No. Just another bag of clothes.'

'I'll ask Kayla to pack more so you can bring them back tomorrow.' She looked at Jackson. 'While you're there, you can check for anything you want to bring with you. OK?'

He shrugged.

'Cathy will give you pocket money and also put credit on your mobile phone. Is there anything you want to ask me?'

'No.'

Frankie looked at me apprehensively, clearly worried that Jackson wasn't engaging with her, but I couldn't offer much as he wasn't talking to me either beyond the basics.

'If there is anything you need, you can ask Cathy,' Frankie said. 'I'll leave you to have your dinner now. Something in the oven smells good.'

'It's cottage pie,' I said.

'Mmm, my favourite. Do you like cottage pie?' she asked Jackson.

'It's all right,' he said.

I saw Frankie to the door.

'Kayla is very worried about him,' she said.

'Yes. So am I, but I'm doing all I can to support him.'

'I know. Thank you.'

It was only a short visit to check on Jackson in placement.

Once Adrian and Paula were home, I served dinner. Tilly was in a better mood having done half an hour's homework. She tried to make conversation with Jackson – asking him if he liked his school and what his favourite subjects were, but he just shrugged and concentrated on eating.

'I met Mr Burrows, Jackson's form teacher today,' I said, trying, as Tilly had done, to draw him in. 'He seems very pleasant.'

'He's not,' Jackson retorted.

'He seemed nice to me,' I said.

'We're not allowed to talk in lessons. He said it's in preparation for next year when we go to secondary school. You can't talk in lessons there.'

'That's right,' I said, pleased that Jackson had finally contributed something.

'Connor used to tell me,' Jackson added.

I looked at him. Mentioning his older brother was a big step forward and, wanting to build on this, I asked. 'Was he in the sixth form?'

Jackson nodded.

'What was he studying?'

He didn't reply. The shutter had come down again. I knew virtually nothing about Connor and I hoped in time Jackson would feel able to talk about him and his father and share some of the wealth of memories he must have. It's part of the healing process to be able to talk about our loved ones who have passed. Although painful to begin with, it's therapeutic and helps keep the person's memory alive.

The rest of the evening flew by as weekday evenings do, and it wasn't long before it was the following morning and we were all getting up and leaving the house: Adrian and Paula to work, Tilly to school on the bus and Jackson with me in the car. His protests about not going to school again being lost in the general hubbub of a busy household preparing to leave.

Ms Gainsborough had told me that the infant school Jackson's sisters attended came out ten minutes before the junior school, but she had omitted to mention that both schools started at the same time. I realized this as I pulled in to the road and saw the parents and children going into both schools, so it was likely we were going to see Kayla and the girls.

Jackson spotted them first, coming along the pavement towards us. 'There's Mum, Grace and Jenna!' he shouted, and ran to greet them.

They were as pleased to see him as he was them, especially little Grace, who threw her arms around him. His mood lifted for a while. I said hello to all of them and reassured the girls that they'd be seeing Jackson again after school as they had contact.

'Jackson may as well walk home with us,' Kayla suggested. 'It seems daft you coming all the way here just to bring him to my house when I live close by.'

I agreed it made sense, but I thought I should check with Frankie first. I told Kayla I'd confirm it with their social worker and then call her. We all said goodbye and went into our respective playgrounds to wait for the start of school. Jackson's previous good humour disappeared, his scowl returned and he moved away so he was standing some distance from me. Other children his age were in small groups, many without a parent or carer, but I wouldn't be leaving Jackson in the playground until he could be trusted not to run away.

The bell sounded for the start of school and the students began going in. I went to him and said, 'If I'm not here this afternoon to meet you, your mother will be. Then I'll collect you at five o'clock after contact. Have a good day.'

He ignored me and joined the queue of children filing into the building. I waited until he'd gone in before I left the playground.

It was midday when I finally managed to reach Frankie to ask her if Jackson could go home with his mother on the days he had contact. She said it should be fine, but to inform the school. Primary schools like to know how their children are getting to and from school and to be kept informed of any change in the arrangements to keep the children safe. This is even more important for looked-after children, when a parent might try to snatch a child from school. Kayla was allowed to take Jackson home with her because there were no safeguarding concerns in respect of her abusing or neglecting her children and Jackson was in care voluntarily.

I telephoned the school secretary and told her that Jackson would be going home with his mother on Mondays, Wednesdays and Fridays, starting today. She said she'd inform Mr Burrows and also Ms Gainsborough who, as well as being acting head, was also the designated teacher for looked-after children. All schools in the UK have one. I then telephoned Kayla and confirmed the arrangements, adding, 'Are you sure this is OK with you? I can easily collect Jackson and take him to your house.'

'No, it's a waste of your time, and it will be nice for Jackson. People have already started talking because I wasn't there yesterday to meet him.'

'OK. I'll see you at five o'clock then, but if you need him collected earlier, call me.'

I knew that families with children in care often struggled with what to tell people, especially other parents, feeling there was a stigma in having a child in care. The children themselves sometimes told their friends they were staying with an aunty or family friend rather than admit that the person standing in the playground was their foster carer. Usually when the truth came out they were pleasantly surprised to find that others were only interested and there was no stigma. But I was aware that adults could be different and sometimes liked a good gossip.

Without having to meet Jackson at the end of school, my day suddenly grew longer and I made the most of it. My fostering memoirs were being published and I'd stopped the admin work I'd been doing in my spare time to make ends meet so I could write. I'd always had an interest in writing and I'd previously had poems and short stories published, but the success of my fostering memoirs was overwhelming. I was soon receiving thousands of messages from people all around the world, and I replied to as many as I could.

I write my books to raise awareness of children in care, with the hope of improving the system. Only time will tell if I have been successful in this respect. The royalties from my books have allowed me to start clearing my mortgage and paying off my children's student loans as well as helping others – children I've fostered in the past, and I donate to various charities. Details of some of these can be found on my website. However, while I enjoy writing, my first priority is my family and the children I foster.

Tilly arrived home at 4.30 p.m. as I was about to leave to collect Jackson from his mother's. I trusted Tilly enough to leave her alone in the house for short periods but not enough to do her homework.

'Remember, an hour's study before dinner,' I reminded her.

'I will, but I need to get a drink and a snack first.'

'Of course. I'll see you at five-thirty!' I called as I left the house.

When I arrived at Jackson's Kayla had another small bag ready, containing his belongings. 'The rest can stay here,' she said, and I nodded.

While it is better for a child in care to have their own belongings with them, I could appreciate why it was so difficult for parents to pack and send them. Packing seemed to compound their feelings of guilt and there's a finality in the act, although all the children's belongings go back with them when they return home. If they can't return home, then they go with them to their permanent home. Sometimes their belongings arrived a few items at a time over weeks and months, but I always bought the child what they needed.

Kayla had answered the door but there was no sign of Jackson. I asked her how he'd been, and she said generally all right, but he was very quiet and seemed to have a lot on his mind. She said he could suddenly snap and become angry for no obvious reason – as he had when he'd been living with her. I said I'd experienced similar. She knew Frankie was making an urgent referral to CAMHS and hoped this would help. I could see how guilty she was feeling for placing her son in care and reassured her it was for the best at present. I also asked her what time would suit her for Jackson to phone on the days he wasn't seeing her, as I hadn't heard from Frankie. She said early evening around seven o'clock was good.

She called Jackson and he appeared in the hall, looking very sullen. He was quiet in the car. I tried talking to him about his sisters and what they'd played but got nowhere. I asked him about his day at school and was met with, 'It was all right.'

When we arrived home Tilly was in her bedroom on her phone but stopped the moment she heard us come in. I encouraged Tilly to study, but ultimately at her age the responsibility was hers. There was only so much I could do.

While I put the finishing touches to dinner, Jackson watched television, and then, once Adrian and Paula were home, I called everyone to the table.

'I was talking to my gran on the phone,' Tilly said.

'How is she?' I asked. I'd got to know Nancy from looking after Tilly.

'She wants me to stay there over the weekend like I used to, but I told her I'm not ready for that.'

'OK. We're seeing your social worker on Friday so you can discuss it with her then.' But as I spoke, I realized I had a clash of appointments. At the time Isa had arranged to come I would be leaving to collect Jackson from contact. 'Actually, I might have to reschedule that,' I added.

After dinner I emailed Isa, Tilly's social worker, and explained the problem so she'd read the email first thing in the morning. I then asked Jackson about his homework.

'Haven't got any,' he replied.

'Mr Burrows said it started tonight,' I pointed out.

Jackson shrugged dismissively, so I switched off the television and explained that he could watch it again once he'd done his homework. He folded his arms crossly and ignored me.

'Sit at the table to do it and I'll help you. It won't take long.' I had little idea what standard Jackson was at, only that he didn't have any special needs but had missed a lot of school.

'I want the television on,' he said, his face setting.

'Yes, I know, and you can watch some more once you've done your homework. It's one of my rules – homework first.' As Jackson's foster carer I had a duty to ensure he reached his full potential at school. Also, on a personal level, I wanted him to do as well as he could, as I did with my own children.

Jackson sulked, muttered under his breath and then stamped up to his bedroom and slammed the door. A few minutes later he stamped down again and, picking up his school bag, took out his homework diary.

'I can't do it. I need a computer,' he announced triumphantly.

'Not a problem,' I said. 'I have a laptop you can use.'

I fetched it from the front room and set it up on the table in the kitchen-diner. 'Come on, do your homework, and then you have the rest of the evening free.'

He huffed and glared at me but must have decided it was easier to do as I'd asked than protest further. Throwing himself into a chair at the table, he began working on the laptop as I cleared up the kitchen, able to see him and on hand to help if necessary. After some minutes I went over to check what he was doing – researching Ancient Greece. I suggested he copied and pasted what he needed into a Word document and then we could print it out. Ten minutes later he said he'd finished and I showed him how to send the Word document wirelessly to the printer in the front room. While he went to collect it, I checked his homework diary and saw he had some maths homework too. We were right back to square one!

Jackson said he wasn't going to do his maths and wanted to watch television instead. I replied that homework was a priority and had to come first. Eventually I tempted him back to the table with a drink and a slice of chocolate cake – Jackson liked his food. I sat in the chair beside him and looked at the maths worksheet as he ate and drank.

'Mmm, decimals,' I said. 'They can be complicated.'

'No, they're not, they're easy.'

'Really? Show me,' I said.

And before he realised it, he was completing the worksheet and getting them right.

'Well done,' I said as he finished. 'That didn't take long.'

I then sat with him in the living room while he watched some television. Getting Jackson to do his homework had been hard work, but I hoped tomorrow it would be a bit easier. Tilly had also done some studying, so all in all I felt the evening had gone well. However, a short while after seeing Jackson into bed I heard him moving around. I went up to resettle him and found he'd been crying.

CHAPTER TEN

ANOTHER DIFFICULT EVENING

'You're upset,' I said, going further into Jackson's bedroom. 'What's the matter, love?'

'Nothing.' He was sitting on the edge of his bed, turned away from me.

'Can I sit beside you?'

'No.'

'I can't leave you like this,' I said, going over. 'I want to help. What is it?'

'You can't help. No one can,' he said. Then, jumping up, he shouted, 'Go away!' And gave my shoulder a hard push.

'No, don't do that,' I said, backing away.

'Can if I want.'

I realized my presence was only antagonizing him and, concerned for my safety, I said, 'I'll wait outside until you're calmer.' I went out, leaving his door slightly open. A moment later he slammed it shut.

Adrian was out for the evening, but Tilly and Paula were in. Having heard Jackson shout and slam the door, they came out of their rooms. 'He can't treat you like that!' Tilly said indignantly.

While Paula, who'd heard worse, said, 'Jackson is angry and needs time to calm down.'

I didn't tell them he'd pushed me. I wasn't hurt and it would only have upset them.

'It's all right. You carry on with what you're doing and I'll wait here until he's calmer,' I said. 'If he comes out and finds us all here, it could make things worse.'

They returned to their bedrooms while I waited on the landing. I'd found in the past with children I'd fostered that often their hurt came out as anger and other challenging behaviour. Having said that, I wasn't going to put myself in danger. I tried twice more to talk to Jackson, but each time I went into his room he shouted at me to get out. On the third time he was in bed asleep. I felt bad that I hadn't been able to help or comfort him and he'd gone to sleep upset, but there wasn't much else I could have done in the circumstances. I didn't know Jackson that well and he was volatile, so I needed to be cautious. When a young child was upset or angry it was easier to scoop them up and hug them until they felt better, but Jackson was ten and nearly as tall as me. I would make a note of what had happened in my log, as I was supposed to.

Of course I didn't sleep well that night. I listened out for Jackson, but he only got up once to use the toilet, then went straight back to bed. The following morning he was subdued and wanted to phone his mother at breakfast. I said she'd be busy with the girls as they'd be getting ready for school, and he'd see them all briefly soon anyway.

'But I want to phone,' he said.

'Text instead and then she can read it when she's free,'

I suggested. 'We agreed you would phone at seven o'clock.'

I thought he was following my advice as he put down his phone and finished his breakfast. But after he'd eaten, he went up to his room and called his mother. I was on the landing and the call must have gone straight through to voicemail, for I heard him say in a very sad voice, 'Mum, it's me. I miss you.'

I felt for him and knew the effect those touching words would have on Kayla, and probably compound her feelings of guilt.

When Jackson came out of his room, I said, 'I thought I told you to text your mother.' I left it at that. I didn't make an issue of it, as there were other, more pressing matters that needed addressing. I reminded him to leave his phone on the table before we went to school, and reluctantly, after a lot of protesting, he did as I said. It was a continuous battle to get Jackson to do as I asked, and it was very wearing.

'I got your voicemail message,' Kayla said to Jackson when we saw her outside the school. 'I tried to phone but you didn't pick up.'

'That's because I have to leave my phone at Cathy's!' Jackson retorted, annoyed. He glared at me. Kayla was looking at me too.

'Ms Gainsborough thought it best,' I said. 'When Jackson took his phone to school last year it caused him problems. He doesn't need it in school and he's phoning you tonight at seven.'

'Yes, I'll be ready,' she replied, and the matter was dropped.

I spoke briefly to Jenna and Grace and then, wishing them a good day, we went our separate ways into school. Again, Jackson distanced himself from me in the playground, but he didn't interact with any other students. He stood, hands in pockets, staring gloomily at the ground. Once he'd gone in, I left the playground but didn't see Kayla as I returned to my car.

At home I checked my emails. Isa had replied saying she would still visit Tilly as arranged on Friday and hopefully see me when I returned from collecting Jackson. I confirmed the arrangement and made a mental note to tell Tilly, Paula and Adrian. I then set about doing some housework, hung the washing on the line and, with a cup of coffee to hand, phoned Lucy. She was in good spirits and was going to meet another new mother she'd become friends with through the antenatal clinic for lunch. We didn't talk for long as she was still trying to get ready while keeping Emma amused.

I was planning on visiting my mother on Sunday and would take Jackson, although I had some concerns about how he would behave. I phoned Mum and told her that he was still settling in so we wouldn't stay for long. She understood. I said I'd bring something to cook there for lunch. For many years Mum had cooked a full roast dinner on Sundays, but now she was older we usually went out or I cooked.

'I'll look forward to meeting Jackson,' Mum said. 'I'm sure he'll be well behaved here.'

Mum was always very positive and saw the best in people. She went out of her way to make the children we looked after welcome and one of the family. My father had too when he'd been alive. I couldn't have wished for better parents.

Having chatted with Mum, I spent a few hours writing before it was time to collect Jackson. Mr Burrows came over to see me again and once more I wondered if Jackson was in trouble. Thankfully he said he'd had another good day. I was delighted and we both praised Jackson. Although his behaviour was challenging at home, he seemed to be better now in school. I'd found this before, or the opposite – that children were sometimes very well behaved at home but a nightmare in school. I think this can be because if you carry a huge burden around with you, as many of our looked-after children do, you can only hold it together for some of the time. Perhaps Jackson felt it was easier to kick off with me rather than risk a permanent exclusion from school. Although, of course, it was only the start of the term and we had a long way to go yet.

On the way home I reminded Jackson that Joy Philips, my supervising social worker, was coming to see us. I said she visited us about once a month to make sure I was looking after him and Tilly properly and to give me any guidance I might need.

'I'm not talking to her,' Jackson said bluntly. 'I'm going to do my homework.'

I smiled. 'Excellent. She will be impressed.'

'Mr Burrows was in care,' Jackson said after a moment.

'How do you know that?' I asked, glancing at him in the rear-view mirror.

'He told me at lunchtime, so the other kids couldn't hear. He said he had to go into foster care and knew what it was like, and if I wanted to talk to him I could.'

'That was nice of him. Did he tell you why he was in care?'

'No, but he said he still visited his foster mum some-times, although she was old now and had stopped fostering.'

'I'm sure she'll be very pleased. Some of the children I've fostered are still in touch. I look forward to hearing from them. In fact, I'll probably Skype one boy I looked after on Sunday. We are due for a chat.'

'I'm not keeping in touch with you when I leave,' Jackson said.

Joy arrived promptly at 4.30. An experienced social worker in her late forties, she was caring, efficient and level-headed. Jackson was in the living room watching television, so she met him first, but only briefly.

'How are you?' she asked him as I switched off the television.

'OK,' he replied sulkily.

'How is school?' Joy asked, sitting beside him.

'OK. I'm going to my room now.'

And off he went.

'How are you all?' she asked me with a smile. 'Coping?'

'Just about.'

'And how is Lucy and the baby?'

'Good, thanks.'

Joy took out her laptop, ready to make notes, and I updated her on Jackson. I described his behaviour, dispo-sition, routine, eating and sleeping, contact and what he liked to do in his spare time.

'How does he get on with Adrian?' Joy asked.

'The same as the rest of us, really,' I said. 'Hopefully things will improve in time, once he loses some of his anger.'

'Has Kayla said any more about taking him out of care?'

'Not to me.'

The front door opened and Tilly let herself in. 'Hi!' she called brightly from the hall. 'It's me!'

'We're in the living room,' I replied.

'One of your success stories,' Joy said quietly to me.

'Thank you, yes.' But it had been very different when Tilly had first arrived, having fled from her parents' house.

Once Tilly had taken off her jacket and shoes, she came into the living room. 'Shall I talk to you now?' she asked Joy, aware she'd want to see her at some point. 'Then I need to phone Abby.'

'And do some studying,' I added with a smile.

'Yes, and that!' Tilly laughed.

'I won't keep you long,' Joy said. 'How are you? You look very well.'

'I'm good,' she said, sitting down. She then answered Joy's questions about her routine, school, hobbies, contact – she was going to see her gran and mother again on Sunday – going out socially, pocket money and so forth. She was used to these visits now.

Once Joy was happy that Tilly had everything she needed, she thanked her for her time and Tilly went to her bedroom, while Joy continued with the other routine matters of her visit. We discussed my future training – all foster carers have to attend a set number of training sessions per year, and experienced carers are expected to facilitate some training too. She read and signed my log notes, and I read and signed the minutes from her last visit. These were also stored digitally now. We arranged a date for her next visit in a month's time and she concluded by looking around the house. Tilly was studying when we knocked on her door.

'Well done,' Joy said, having a quick look in.

When we went to see Jackson he was playing on his phone. Joy tried to talk to him, but he didn't respond so she said goodbye and take care.

'Bye,' Jackson said, his voice flat.

'Keep an eye on him,' Joy said to me once we were downstairs. 'He worries me.' Which did nothing to lessen my sense of foreboding.

We all had dinner together and Tilly did most of the talking. Her year had mock examinations coming up and her teachers were increasing the pressure. The results of the mocks would go towards their predicted grades, which in turn would govern their choices in respect of what they could study in the sixth form. They were also expected to continue with their course work.

'It's impossible!' Tilly declared dramatically.

'Just do a bit each day,' I said. 'As long as you're doing your best, no one can expect more.'

'Miss does!' she replied.

Jackson was his usually pensive self, although he ate well, which was a blessing. I'd looked after children in the past who'd stopped eating because of stress and it's very worrying. Sometimes they required specialist help to get them eating properly again, but usually their appetite returned once they felt more settled.

As we talked over dinner, I said I was going to see my mother on Sunday and Paula immediately said she'd come. Adrian said he would visit Nana with Kirsty another day, as would Lucy and Darren. Tilly was seeing her gran on Sunday.

'Do you have a grandmother?' Tilly asked Jackson.

He nodded.

'Do you see her?'

He shrugged.

I knew from the placement information forms that Kayla's mother was dead and she had limited contact with her father, who lived with her stepmother some distance away. Jackson's paternal grandparents lived closer, but they seemed to have lost contact since his father's death, which was a pity. Good grandparents are invaluable, especially in times of trouble. I'd had experience of this when my husband had left us when my children were little. My parents were fantastic, and my father was a good male role model – although I appreciated that not everyone is as fortunate.

As dinner ended Jackson said he was going to phone his mother. It was six-thirty so I said I thought he should wait half an hour until seven o'clock, and in the meantime, I'd help him with his homework. 'I want to phone her now,' he said confrontationally.

'I know, but seven o'clock is a good time for your mother, and you will be disappointed if she doesn't answer or is too busy to talk.'

'I'm going to phone her now,' he persisted.

Tilly left the table in disgust, saying she would smack

him if she didn't leave, while Paula began clearing away the dishes, probably hoping Jackson would just do as he was told for once. But Adrian, still at the table and one of the most patient people I know, said, 'Why stress, Jackson? Just get your school bag and do your homework until it's time to phone your mother.'

'I don't want to,' he said.

'Sometimes we have to do things we don't want for our own good. This is one of those times.'

For a moment Jackson looked as though he was going to argue with Adrian but then seemed to think better of it. Abruptly pushing back his chair, he went to fetch his school bag.

'Thanks, love,' I said to Adrian.

'It's OK, Mum. But when you've finished with Jackson, I need to talk to you.'

'What about, love?' I asked, immediately concerned. 'Is something wrong?'

'No, but we do need to talk. I'll wait until you've got time.'

CHAPTER ELEVEN

THE BLINK OF AN EYE

Jackson sat at the table reluctantly doing his school work while I busied myself in the kitchen, keeping an eye on him and ready to help if necessary. But my brain was working overtime. What was it Adrian wanted to tell me? He'd given no clue but had seemed very serious. He'd always been on the quiet side; reserved, thoughtful, sometimes internalizing his feelings. But he was also rational, sensible and not given to flights of fantasy. Whatever he wanted to talk to me about, he would have considered it carefully first. He worked hard at his job with a firm of accountants, and his long-time girlfriend Kirsty was a teacher. Was it about his job or her? I wondered. Or something entirely different?

Was he ill? I thought with a stab of horror. Had he been experiencing symptoms and, not wanting to worry me, secretly gone to the doctor? It was possible, although he'd said there was nothing wrong. In that case, why hadn't he just told me there and then what he had to say? Lucy had suddenly announced she was pregnant the year before. Was Kirsty now expecting too? I doubted it. Adrian had told me they were saving up to buy a place of their own first, but of course not all babies are planned.

'I'm finished,' Jackson said, jolting me from my thoughts.

'Good boy.' I went over to check his work, but he hurriedly packed away his books.

'I'm phoning my mum now,' he said, and went into the living room to make the call.

I could only hear one side of the conversation, but his voice was flat. I guessed his mother kept asking him if he was all right and what was wrong, because he said, 'Nothing,' in reply a number of times in the same gruff voice. His other short replies didn't reassure me either. 'Yes.' 'Don't know.' 'No.'

When he spoke to his sisters he was a bit more animated, although they did most of the talking. I went into the living room. 'Tell them about your day at school,' I suggested. But he didn't.

They spoke for a few minutes longer and when he ended the call he picked up the remote control for the television.

'Would you like to play a game instead of watching television?' I asked.

'No.'

I looked at him carefully. 'Jackson, what can I do to make your life easier?'

'Nothing!' he replied grumpily, and switched on the television.

I stayed in the living room, checking and replying to the messages on my phone, while he watched television, but my thoughts were elsewhere. Now I was concerned not only for Jackson, but for Adrian too. I would wait until Jackson was in bed before I heard what Adrian had to say so I could give him my full attention. At 7.45 when the programme Jackson was watching finished, I said it was time for him to get ready for bed. He protested but then went upstairs, and once he'd showered and was in bed, I went up to say goodnight and clear up the bathroom. I knocked on his door and went in. He was sitting on the edge of his bed playing on his phone.

'I'll take that downstairs for you,' I said non-confrontationally.

He ignored me.

'Jackson, I want to put your phone downstairs on the table ready for morning, like you have been doing.'

Without any warning, he suddenly turned and threw the phone at me. It missed me but banged against the wall.

'That's not good,' I said, picking it up. 'You've lost half an hour of your television tomorrow.'

'Don't care!' he shouted, his anger flaring.

'I'll wait outside until you're calmer,' I said, and left the room. Just in time. There was a loud crash as something hit the door. I guessed it was the chair. But it didn't stop there. He began banging it against the door. Paula, Adrian and Tilly shot out of their rooms.

'What the hell's that?' Tilly cried.

'He's not going to trash the place,' Adrian said, and he pushed open the door. 'Enough!' he said loudly. Adrian was taller than Jackson and more solidly built. 'Stop now! What do you think you're doing?'

'Nothing,' I heard Jackson say.

'Put the chair where it's supposed to be and get into bed,' Adrian said.

I went into the room in time to see Jackson return the chair to the desk and get back into bed. 'Good boy,' I said. 'Do you want to talk?' I asked him.

'No! Hate you.'

'We'll leave you to calm down then,' I said, and Adrian and I left the room.

Foster carers are expected to remove themselves from danger and I could see my presence was antagonizing Jackson. I drew the door to and waited. 'Thanks,' I said to Adrian.

Tilly and Paula both looked a bit shaken. 'He'll be all right. You continue with what you were doing,' I reassured them. 'I'll wait here.'

'We'll have that chat when you're ready,' Adrian said to me. 'I'll be downstairs, but don't go in his room again until he's calmed down. If that chair had hit you, it could have killed you.'

'All right, love.'

Concerned, Adrian went downstairs as I waited on the landing until it went quiet in Jackson's room. I gingerly opened the door and looked in. He was asleep. Relieved, I joined Adrian in the living room. He had his laptop open and a mug of coffee beside him. 'Do you want a drink?' he asked

'No, thanks, love. I just want to hear what you have to say.' He was looking even more serious now. He set his laptop aside and I sat beside him on the sofa. 'Well, what is it?'

'Kirsty and I are going to get married,' he announced, turning to me.

'That's wonderful, Adrian!' I kissed his cheek. 'But why are you looking worried?'

He frowned. 'Because I have big concerns about leaving while you're still fostering. Jackson's behaviour tonight has confirmed it.'

'Oh Adrian, you don't have to worry about me.'

'Yes, I do,' he replied firmly. 'I realize not all children we foster are as badly behaved as Jackson, but …'

'No, some are worse,' I put in.

'Mum, I'm serious. What would have happened if I hadn't been here tonight?'

'Jackson would probably have done more damage, but eventually he would have calmed down,' I replied.

'And if he hadn't?'

'We would have kept out of his way until he did. If it escalated, I would have called the police. Adrian, I appreciate your concern, but I've been fostering a long time – even before you were born. There have always been children with challenging, even disturbing behaviour. Jackson has problems, but he's not the most disturbed child I've looked after, and we got through that. You were away at university for three years,' I pointed out. 'I managed then.'

'I know. But I'm not sure I appreciated then how difficult fostering could be. You just got on with it.'

'And I still do,' I said. 'Look, love, I know you mean well and Jackson is a handful, but he will turn a corner before too long.'

'You always say that, Mum.'

'And it's true. Well, mostly,' I added, remembering a couple of instances when that hadn't been the case, but it's crucial when fostering to stay positive.

'Supposing you just looked after babies and very

young children?' Adrian suggested. 'They couldn't hurt you like an older child could.'

'I'll think about it,' I said. 'But you need to stop worrying about me and get on with your life just as Lucy has. When is the wedding?'

'June next year.' His expression finally brightened.

'Wonderful. I'm so pleased for you both.' It wasn't before time. They'd known each other since college.

'And the other piece of news is that we have found a flat to buy,' Adrian added.

'Really? Where?'

'Watling Road – you know, off Blueberry Park?'

'Yes, not so far away then.'

'No. The flat is one of three converted from a large Victorian house,' Adrian said enthusiastically. 'Ours is the whole of the second floor. There is no conveyancing chain so it should go through quickly.' I nodded. 'It needs some work doing to it, but hopefully we'll complete the purchase ahead of the wedding so we can do it up before we move in.' It was typical of Adrian that he'd thought all this through.

'Fantastic,' I said. 'Sounds great.'

'As soon as we've exchanged contracts – so we know for certain the flat is ours – we'll show you and Kirsty's parents around. There are some photographs on the estate agent's website. Would you like to see them?'

'Yes, please.' I kissed his cheek again.

Smiling, he picked up his laptop and opened the bookmarked page. The first view of the flat was of the exterior of the building, which I recognized from driving past. It was in a road of similar large Victorian houses, many of which had been converted into flats. He began the slide show of the interior of the flat, which showed a spacious kitchen-diner, living room, a bathroom and three bedrooms – two doubles and a single. I could see why they wanted to do some work on it, though, as parts of it were dated.

'The bathroom and kitchen need modernizing,' Adrian said, bringing the pictures on screen again. 'But the other rooms just need a coat of paint, and we'll get rid of that awful orange carpet.'

I laughed. 'Yes, I think I would. But, Adrian, the flat is terrific. You and Kirsty have done so well to save up for the deposit. And I couldn't wish for a better daughter-in-law.'

'Thanks, Mum.'

'Now, about the wedding,' I said. 'I'll help towards the cost and I'm assuming you'll want to invite your father?'

'Yes, I feel I should.'

'Of course. It's one of those occasions when divorced parents have to come together for the sake of their children,' I said. When Adrian and Paula had been little I'd had to work with my ex-husband, John, to organize contact. Now they were adults they made their own arrangements and usually met him in a café. They saw each other about every three months, but I hadn't seen him for some years.

'Has Kirsty met John?' I asked.

'Not yet.'

'I suppose you'd better invite John's girlfriend too,' I said magnanimously.

'They aren't together any more,' Adrian replied.

'OK,' I said easily, but I didn't comment. Since leaving us, John had remarried, divorced and then had a number of girlfriends. While I'd been very upset when he'd first left, it was history now and I'd come to believe I was probably better off without him, although I'd never tried to turn the children against him.

'I'll tell Paula I'm getting married,' Adrian said, 'and then phone Nana and Lucy.'

'Yes, they'll be delighted. And Adrian, please don't worry about me. You've done a good job of being the man about the house and now it's time for the next stage in your life. I'm proud of you. I'll miss you when you've gone, but you mustn't worry about me.'

'And you'll think about my suggestion of just fostering newborns or little ones?'

'I will, love.'

When I write my log notes each evening I always include the positive as well as the negative. Tilly's was easy as she was settled now, but Jackson's got me thinking. I included the feedback from Mr Burrows and that Jackson was eating well. But I also had to detail Jackson's angry outbursts and what had led to it. Tonight, I included that Adrian had intervened. As far as my family and I were concerned, the matter had been dealt with, but I might need to justify my actions in days, weeks or months to come, which is one of the reasons for logging events. Without them you only have your memory to rely on and details of incidents can fade with time. Foster carers are sometimes called upon to give evidence in court, when their logs may be requested.

While I sat in the living room Adrian was upstairs sharing his good news with Paula, who was obviously very pleased for him. He also told Tilly; her view of marriage was tainted by her mother's experience, but still she wished him 'Good luck'. He then phoned my mother, who was delighted and immediately asked what he would like for an engagement present. When he came down I asked him if he'd had any thoughts about an engagement party, and he said Kirsty's parents would be in touch with me as they were arranging something. Not wanting to risk disturbing Lucy by phoning her if she was seeing to Emma, Adrian texted her instead. She replied by text congratulating him, and then texted me – *About bloody time!* with emojis of wedding celebrations and a thumbs-up.

While I was pleased for Adrian, as I was for Lucy, who now had her own home and family, I also felt a pang of sadness. All those wonderful years I'd spent bringing up my children, as well as fostering, when time seemed to stand still. Birthday parties, Christmas, friends to play, days out to the coast and theme parks, holidays. Then suddenly, in the blink of an eye, it was all over and they were adults moving out. I felt I'd made the most of their childhood, but could I have done things differently? Undeniably, but then we all have some regrets. I'd done my best to give them a good a start in life and had enjoyed all those precious years. Of course, I would still be on hand to help them if needed, but realistically they would now turn to their partners first for support and comfort.

Paula came into the living room looking thoughtful.

'It'll just be the two of us soon,' she said quietly, sitting beside me.

'And Tilly and Jackson,' I pointed out.

'I won't leave you,' she said, and gave me a big hug.

I held her close. 'One day you might, when the time is right, and that will be the correct thing to do. It's what happens in families. Children grow up and move on.'

'But it's sad,' she said. 'I liked it when we were little and all together.'

'So did I, love. But we'll visit Adrian and Kirsty and they'll come here, just as we see Lucy and Darren, and Nana,' I said bravely.

Yet, like Paula, I too felt it was the end of an era and wished I could turn back the clock to recapture some of those precious moments. But that's life, and we have to make the most of every day, for it slips by so very quickly.

CHAPTER TWELVE

ABUSED

On Friday afternoon Isa, Tilly's social worker, arrived earlier than expected, so I was able to spend fifteen minutes with her and Tilly before I had to leave to collect Jackson. We sat in the living room and discussed how Tilly's contact with her mother and gran was going, as well as school, her routine, and general health and wellbeing. There weren't any major issues, so I left them talking while I collected Jackson. Isa would want to look around the house as part of her visit, but Tilly would see to that.

As I pulled up outside Jackson's house I wondered how he'd been with them. It was very up and down at present. Kayla answered the door, looking tired as she often did. She hadn't packed any more of Jackson's belongings, but she did tell me Mr Burrows had spoken to her at the end of school and said Jackson had had another good day.

'Jackson seems to be better with Mr Burrows than he was with his last teacher,' she said, and I agreed. I didn't know if Mr Burrows had told Kayla he had been in care, and it wasn't for me to tell her, but I felt this played a part in helping Jackson's behaviour in school. He knew he had an ally in his teacher as well as the support of Mrs Bryant, although he never mentioned her.

Kayla had to call Jackson a few times before he came to the door. I said goodbye to Kayla and the girls and confirmed I'd drop off Jackson for contact tomorrow at twelve o'clock as arranged.

In the car going home I reminded Jackson that Tilly's social worker might still be there when we arrived.

'She's not my social worker,' he said moodily. 'I don't have to talk to her.'

'True, but it might be polite to say hello.'

'Don't want to.'

When we arrived home Isa had just left, so Jackson's politeness wasn't put to the test. He watched television until dinner was ready, and after we'd eaten I suggested he did some of his school work as he was out tomorrow and Sunday.

'I've got all weekend,' he said.

'That's what I used to say,' Tilly said. 'Then suddenly you find it's Sunday evening and you can't get it all done in time.' While this was true, it wasn't the only reason Tilly had fallen behind at school. It had been largely due to the impact of her traumatic home life before coming into care.

Jackson left the table and went upstairs to his room, but then ten minutes later I found him poring over a school book in the front room. 'Good boy,' I said. 'If you need any help, let me know.'

He was only there a short time, but at least it was something. I told Tilly well done. I needed all the help I could get at present when it came to Jackson.

* * *

On Saturday Jackson spent two hours with his mother and sisters, and it didn't go well. Kayla looked exasperated when I collected him. She said he hadn't wanted anything to do with them and had spent most of the time sulking in his bedroom. The girls had wanted him to play and kept going into his room until he'd lost his temper and thrown the first thing that had come to hand – a china football mug Connor had given him. It hit the wall and broke. Jackson was upset and blamed the girls, shouting at them. Kayla, already stressed, had screamed at him, saying things she now regretted. I said I'd talk to him on the way home and explain we all said things in the heat of the moment we regretted and that his mother loved him. I also said I'd try to find out why he'd spent the whole time in his room when the point of contact was to see his family. She thanked me.

I tried talking to Jackson in the car as I drove, but he said rudely it was none of my business. My concerns about taking him to my mother's on Sunday grew. At her age, Mum didn't need the upset of Jackson's angry outbursts, but he had to come – there would be no one to look after him if he didn't. Adrian would be out, Tilly would be seeing her mother and grandmother, and Paula was coming with me – although I wouldn't have left Jackson with them anyway while he was so volatile.

On Sunday morning as we were about to set off, Jackson said he didn't want to come with me to see my mother, and I couldn't make him. Paula sighed, exasperated.

'OK,' I said to him. 'If you really don't want to come, I'll make arrangements to leave you with another carer for the day.'

'You can't do that!' he said. 'I live here.'

'Of course I can,' I replied. 'That is the correct proce-dure. I'll phone another foster carer now.' I picked up my phone.

'No, I'll come,' he said.

'Sure?'

He nodded.

It had been a bluff on my part, for I doubted I would have found someone at such short notice who was free to look after him, but it had worked. He got into the car and we left for my mother's, although I was anxious all the way there, imagining him shouting at her or running away.

As it turned out, nothing could have been further from the truth. Mum welcomed him and then went out of her way to include him. But instead of ignoring her as he did us, he responded. To our amazement, he answered her questions in a polite and respectful manner and even agreed to a game of cards when Mum suggested it. He offered his hand to help her out of her chair even though she didn't need help. Paula and I looked at each other, amazed. Was this the same child?

'You're a good lad,' Mum said.

'My brother and me used to help the old couple who lived next door,' Jackson told her, which explained it. Although I wasn't sure she appreciated being called old.

'That was very kind of you,' Mum said. Paula and I agreed.

We'd had an insight into a different Jackson – sensi-tive, compassionate and caring. The child he was before his brother had committed suicide and his father had died. I hoped we could find him again.

Although Jackson's behaviour was exemplary at Mum's, I decided not to push our luck by staying longer than we'd planned, so at four o'clock we said our good-byes and left. Jackson kissed Mum's cheek on the way out, as Paula and I did, but he was quiet in the car and looked very thoughtful. I wondered if being with Mum had opened the door on other feelings. Later, in the light of what happened next, it seemed that way.

Once home, Jackson wanted to watch television, so I left him in the living room while I went into the front room to Skype Oskar, who I'd fostered a while before and was still in touch with. I tell his story in *Too Scared to Tell*. As I spoke to him and his family, Tilly returned home and, seeing that I was busy, made a thumbs-up sign to say all was well, and then went to her room.

Paula came to say hi to Oskar and, once we'd finished, I closed the screen and Jackson appeared.

'Who were you talking to?' he asked.

'A boy I used to foster,' I replied.

'Why did you foster him?'

'His mother couldn't look after him and then we found out he'd been abused.' Jackson didn't know Oskar, so there were no confidentiality issues. I thought hearing about another child might help him – just as knowing that Mr Burrows had been in care seemed to have helped Jackson in school.

'What's abused?' Jackson asked.

'When someone is hurt physically or mentally,' I said. 'Sadly, a lot of the children I've fostered have been abused.'

'I haven't,' he said.

'No. Good.'

There was a long pause and then Jackson said, 'But I think my brother was.'

I met Paula's gaze. Appreciating the enormity of what Jackson had just said and that we should be alone, she left the room. I looked at Jackson.

'What makes you say that, love?' I asked.

'Someone hurt him.'

'What did they do?' For this could be anything. Perhaps Connor had been in a fight with another lad, which was unlikely to be abuse.

'I can't tell you. Connor said I mustn't,' Jackson replied. He'd said similar before.

'Was Connor hurt physically?' I asked. 'To his body?'

Jackson nodded.

'Can you tell me how he was hurt?' I needed to gather as much information as possible while he was willing to talk, so I could decide what to do for the best.

Jackson thought for a moment and then said, 'No, I can't tell you how Connor was hurt. He told me not to.'

'Why? If he was hurt, it wasn't his fault.'

'He said he was partly to blame because he let it happen.'

'Was he being bullied?' I asked, aware that some victims of bullying feel they are to blame and have invited the bullying, which of course isn't true.

'No. He wasn't bullied,' Jackson said.

'Was he hurt by another child his age?' I asked.

'No. A man.' My heart missed a beat and I went cold. 'I wanted to tell Mum,' Jackson continued, 'but Connor made me promise not to. But it's making me very unhappy. If I tell you, will you promise not to tell anyone else?'

'I can't do that,' I said. 'If Connor was hurt by an adult, I will need to tell your social worker. She will decide what to do.'

'She can't do anything now,' Jackson cried. 'It's too late. Connor is dead.' His lips trembled and his eyes filled.

'Oh, love, come here and sit down.' I took his arm, drew him to the chairs and sat next to him. I passed him a tissue. Tears slipped down his cheeks as all the months of pent-up emotion finally found a way out. 'I know this is very difficult for you, love, but telling will help. You've been very brave. When did this happen?'

'When Dad was ill,' Jackson said, wiping his eyes. His father had died over two years ago – a long time in a child's memory. How accurate was his recollection?

'Who was the man?' I asked.

'A friend of Mum's. He was supposed to help us, but he didn't. He hurt Connor and it made him so miserable he killed himself.'

If Jackson was remembering this correctly, it was horrendous.

'And you haven't told anyone this before?' I asked.

'No, because it was my fault Connor killed himself. It wasn't because Dad had died like Mum thinks. It was because of what Jerry did to him.'

'Jerry,' I said, remembering the name from Kayla. 'He's someone your mother knows?'

'Dad knew him too. He lives further down our road. Dad thought he was nice, so did Mum. But they don't know. He's horrible.'

'Does your mother still see him?' I asked.

'Yes.' Fear gripped me.

'Did Connor tell you how Jerry hurt him?' I asked.

He nodded.

'Can you tell me? It's important because if Jerry hurt Connor, it's possible he could be hurting other children, and he needs to be stopped.'

'I can't say the words. But what Jerry did to Connor was bad. It was to do with his private parts.'

My worst fears were confirmed. Connor had been sexually abused by Jerry, who was still seeing Kayla and the girls.

'It's Jerry's fault Connor killed himself, and mine for not telling Mum what Jerry did before it was too late,' Jackson said, and he collapsed against me, crying.

I held and soothed him as best I could, stroking his hair and reassuring him it wasn't his fault. I passed him fresh tissues. Little wonder he'd been so angry, I thought. What a terrible burden of misery and self-blame to carry all this time. Bad enough to lose your father and brother, but to then have to live with the guilt that perhaps you could have prevented your brother's suicide was horrendous. It would take a long time and a lot of therapy for Jackson to recover from this. But in the meantime, I had to decide what to do next.

The decision was made as Jackson dried his eyes and, looking at me sadly, said, 'I nearly told Mum yesterday, but I didn't know how. So I shut myself in my bedroom and kept away from him.'

'Jerry was there yesterday?' I asked, horrified.

'Yes. He came upstairs to use the toilet. I kept my door closed.'

'Has Jerry ever abused you?'

'No, Connor told me to keep away from him. Mum tells me off for being rude to him, but I don't care.'

'You've been very brave telling me this and now I need to phone the social services,' I said. I called Paula and asked her to come and sit with Jackson.

'Am I in trouble?' he asked me.

'No, love. You've done the right thing.'

What Jackson had told me couldn't wait until morning, when I would be able to speak to Frankie, his social worker. Jerry seemed to be a regular visitor to their house and had been there yesterday. It was possible he was there now. I shuddered at the thought. The girls were in danger.

As Paula sat with Jackson in the living room, I found the number of the emergency duty social worker and called it. I hadn't had to use the number in years, as most matters that needed the social worker could wait until normal office hours. It was preferable to speak to the child's social worker if possible, as they knew the child and the family situation, but this was an emergency.

The duty social worker answered after a few rings and asked for my name and contact details. I explained I was fostering Jackson Heartman and gave a brief résumé of the circumstances that had brought him into care, then I told him what Jackson had just disclosed. I assumed the duty social worker was taking notes as he stopped me every so often to clarify a point. I knew I was gabbling in a rush of emotion to get it out.

'So the child who was abused is now deceased?' he clarified.

'Yes. Connor. He was Jackson's older brother, but his sisters are still at home and Jackson has contact again tomorrow.'

'Jackson is with you now?'

'Yes.'

'Do you know Jerry's surname and address?' he asked.

'No. Shall I ask Jackson?'

'Yes, please.'

I went into the living room where Paula and Jackson were sitting quietly. They both looked at me expectantly. 'I'm still on the phone,' I said. 'Jackson, do you know Jerry's surname?'

He shook his head.

'What about his address?'

'He lives further down our road.'

'Do you know the number of the house?'

'No.'

'OK, love.'

I left the room and relayed this to the duty social worker.

'I'm going to speak to my manager now,' he said. 'If I need any more information, can I call you on this number?'

'Yes.'

'If I don't phone you back then expect Jackson's social worker to contact you tomorrow,' he said, and wound up the call.

I felt that he hadn't shared my sense of urgency, but there was nothing more I could do now. It would be for him and his team manager to decide how to proceed. Perhaps it wasn't as urgent as I thought and could wait until tomorrow. But I'd never have forgiven myself if I hadn't reported it and in the interim Jerry had abused Jenna and Grace.

It was nearly seven o'clock, still light, and a fine evening. We hadn't been out at Mum's and I now felt in need of some fresh air. I went into the living room and suggested to Jackson and Paula that we go for a walk. For once, Jackson didn't object.

'Can we go to the park?' he asked, clearly wanting some distraction.

'If it's still open, otherwise there are some alternative walks we can do. I'll tell you what the duty social worker said as we go.' At his age he had the right to be kept informed, age-appropriately of course.

Paula said she'd come, but Tilly, having walked to and from the bus stop when she'd visited her gran, said she'd had enough exercise for one day and also had some homework to finish. Adrian was still out with Kirsty. How distant the wonderful news of his marriage now seemed in the light of what Jackson had told me. I felt the weight of Jackson's suffering and guilt. How had he coped all this time? The children who come into care are true heroes. I'm sure I'd never have coped with what many of them have been through.

Shoes and jackets on, we left the house and I set a brisk walking pace. The park gate was closed so we continued along our road to the high street. Most of the shops were closed now, so there weren't many others out. As we walked, I told Jackson that the duty social worker was treating what he'd said very seriously and was discussing what to do for the best with his manager. I said either he or Frankie would call us tomorrow.

'Do I still have to go to school tomorrow?' he asked cutely.

'Yes. I think it's better you are kept busy.'

He pulled a face, as many children his age would have done from missing the chance of a day off school, but he didn't protest further.

We walked for an hour and by the time we returned home the street lamps were on and Adrian was home. He came into the hall when he heard us. 'Tilly said you'd gone for a walk because Jackson was upset,' he said when Jackson was out of earshot.

'Yes. Have you had a good day?' I asked him.

'We have. Kirsty sends her love.'

I wasn't going to sully Adrian's day by telling him what Jackson had told me. I shared information with my children on a need-to-know basis, although the child often told them anyway.

Satisfied that we were all OK, Adrian said he had something he needed to prepare for a meeting at work tomorrow and went to his room, where he had a desk and laptop. Tilly was in her room with music on. Paula said she was going to prepare for the interview she had in the morning for a permanent position.

Jackson had a drink and a snack and then went to bed. He was quiet, and when I asked him what was wrong he said, 'I hope Mum's not angry with me for telling.'

'No, of course not. Why should she be angry with you?'

'Because Jerry is her friend.'

'She'll be pleased you have told me,' I said. 'So don't worry.'

Later, those words came back to haunt me.

CHAPTER THIRTEEN

EVIL

The emergency duty social worker didn't call back that evening, so I assumed that, having discussed Jackson's disclosure with his line manager, they were referring it to Frankie to deal with the following day. It was their decision, although I didn't necessarily agree with it. I was very tired and went to bed soon after ten o'clock. I'd just dropped off to sleep when I was awoken by my mobile phone buzzing. I reached out and answered it. The time showed 10.45.

'Mrs Glass?' a female voice asked.

'Yes, speaking,' I replied, bleary-eyed.

'It's Police Constable Jaz Straighte here. I understand you are fostering Jackson Heartman?'

'Yes, that's right.' I sat bolt upright and, for a moment, still half asleep, I thought Jackson had run away in the night and the police had found him.

'I'm at their family home,' she continued. 'I understand Jackson has made an allegation of abuse against a friend of his mother's.'

'Oh, I see. Yes,' I said. I switched on my bedside lamp. 'It was me who alerted the social services.'

'We are bringing his sisters, Jenna and Grace, into

care under an Emergency Protection Order, but the social services haven't got a foster carer free to take them. Can we bring them to you?'

I was wide awake now. 'No, I'm sorry, I haven't any spare beds.'

'Not even put-you-ups?'

'I have a sofa bed downstairs, but I'm not approved to foster any more children.' I think she thought I was being unhelpful, but it was true. At present, I was approved to foster two. 'Are the girls all right?' I asked.

'They're upset, as is Mrs Heartman. I need to get back to the social services to find someone to take them. They can't sleep in the car.' She ended the call.

My heart was racing. So the social services *had* acted on Jackson's disclosure but no one had told me. I wasn't surprised as the foster carer is sometimes the last to know. It seemed the only reason I'd been told now was because the police needed somewhere to take Jenna and Grace. If they'd found somewhere, they wouldn't have called and I would have taken Jackson to school as usual in the morning, completely unaware. I would have been told eventually, but maybe not before Jackson had been told by one of his classmates who lived close by. Not good.

Sleep was impossible now and my thoughts were with Grace and Jenna. They would be distraught at having to leave home, although it was for their own safety. The Emergency Protection Order is only used when a child or young person is in danger of imminent significant harm. It lasts a maximum of eight days, after which a new care order has to be applied for. My thoughts were with Kayla too, the poor woman. But if what Jackson had told me was true (and I had no reason to doubt him), she was letting a paedophile into her home who had already abused one of her children.

What I'd told the police officer about not being allowed to look after any more children was correct. Foster carers are approved by panel to foster a set age range and number of children. I hoped they found somewhere soon so Jenna and Grace could get settled. It was now after eleven o'clock and I sat in bed staring, unseeing, across the room, worrying about them as the rest of the household slept.

Eventually I began to doze but was woken again by the buzz of my phone on the bed beside me. It was the duty social worker I'd spoken to earlier. 'We're bringing Jenna and Grace into care, but we haven't got a foster carer free in the area.'

'I know. The police called me.'

'They told me you said you weren't approved to take more children, but as this is an emergency I can authorize it for tonight. Then we'll find somewhere for them tomorrow, but it will be out of the county.'

'You know I have Tilly here as well?' I checked.

'No. How old is she?'

'Fourteen.'

'Jackson is ten, Jenna seven and Grace five,' he said, thinking aloud. 'I'll need to check. But if it's all right, will you take them? They can sleep on your sofa bed.'

'If you're happy with that, yes.' Usually children over eighteen months have to have a bed and a room of their own. 'It will mean I have four looked-after children here.'

'I'll speak to my manager and get back to you.'

As he ended the call my phone rang again. It was PC Jaz Straighte. 'I understand Grace and Jenna are coming to you after all.'

'I'm just waiting for confirmation from the social services.'

'What's your address?'

I told her.

'We'll be leaving soon and should be with you in half an hour.'

'All right.'

She was certain the confirmation I needed would come through, as indeed I was. There was nowhere else to take the girls and it was very late. But I wouldn't let them sleep downstairs on the sofa bed; they would have my bed. I got up. Light-headed and queasy from worry and being suddenly woken, I drank the glass of water I kept by the bed. Then I quickly dressed, ran a brush through my hair and set about changing the bed linen, ready for the girls. My phone buzzed again. It was the duty social worker confirming that I could take the girls for tonight as it was an emergency. 'Thank you,' he added.

I took a spare duvet from the storage compartment beneath my bed and, with adrenaline pumping, I went downstairs, where I switched on the hall light and unlocked the front door. I pulled out the sofa bed in the front room and arranged the duvet on it ready for me. As I did, I heard a car draw up outside. I went into the hall and, opening the front door a little, saw a police car. Pushing my feet into my shoes, I went out. Two little faces, wide-eyed and tearful, looked at me from the rear seat. PC Jaz Straighte was in the back with them and she got out as her colleague opened the driver's door. He said good evening to me, even though it was nearly midnight. I shivered from the cold. PC Straighte and I helped the girls out of the car. They were in their pyjamas and dressing gowns.

'I want my mummy,' Grace said, fresh tears forming.

'I know, love. You'll see her soon,' I reassured her.

'Is Jackson here?' Jenna asked as we steered them to the front door.

'Yes, he's asleep in his bed.'

'Mummy is upset. She's crying,' Jenna said, her bottom lip trembling.

'A social worker is with her,' PC Straighte said.

We guided the girls through to the living room, while the other officer remained in the hall, having just taken a call on his mobile.

'Where are they sleeping?' PC Straighte asked, glancing at the sofa in the living room.

'In my bed,' I said. 'They'll be more comfortable. I'll take the sofa bed in the front room.'

She nodded.

'Can Mummy live here too?' little Grace asked. Bless her.

'Can we see Jackson?' Jenna wanted to know.

'He's asleep, love,' I said. 'You'll see him tomorrow, and I expect you'll see your Mummy tomorrow too.'

'They haven't got any clothes with them,' PC Straighte told me. 'Their mother was too upset to pack any.'

The girls were looking even more anxious now. 'Don't worry, I've got plenty of spare clothes,' I told them. 'I like your dressing gowns,' I added, trying to raise their spirits. They were wearing matching pyjamas and dressing gowns decorated with pictures of fairies.

The other police officer came into the living room. 'We're needed elsewhere,' he said, and smiled at the girls.

'Best get them off to bed,' PC Straighte said to me.

'I will.'

The police officers said goodbye to the girls and saw themselves out. As the front door closed, I heard Paula's bedroom door open upstairs.

'Who's that?' Jenna asked nervously.

'My daughter, Paula.'

She came down and into the living room.

'Meet Jenna and Grace,' I said. 'Jackson's sisters. They are staying for tonight – or what is left of it.'

Despite Paula being woken, she said hello to the girls and managed a smile. 'I wondered what was going on. Do you want some help?' she asked me.

'No, you go back to bed. You've got an interview in the morning.' But Grace had already slipped her hand into Paula's.

'Do either of you want a drink before you go to bed?' I asked them. I assumed they'd had dinner.

Grace shook her head, while Jenna said a quiet, 'No, thank you.'

'Let's get you into bed then.'

Grace kept hold of Paula's hand and I took Jenna's as we went upstairs. I asked them quietly if either of them wanted to use the toilet. Jenna said she did and took Grace with her, while Paula and I waited on the landing until they'd finished. Holding hands again, we took them to my bedroom.

'You're going to sleep in my bed, and I'll be downstairs if you need me,' I told them.

Jenna looked worried. 'We haven't got any clothes for the morning.'

'Don't worry, love. I've got some spares you can wear.'

Foster carers always keep spare clothes of most sizes for emergencies, as children often arrive with just what they are wearing.

'Can we go home in the morning?' Jenna asked. I swallowed hard.

'We'll see what your social worker says,' I replied.

Paula and I helped them into my bed.

'Can Jackson sleep with us?' Grace asked.

'He's asleep in his bed,' I said. 'You'll see him in the morning. Come on, snuggle down.'

They lay down and I pulled up the duvet.

'You can go now,' I told Paula. 'Thanks for your help.'

'Where is she going?' Grace asked anxiously, clearly having taken a liking to Paula.

'I'm going to my bed to sleep,' she said. 'It's very late. I'll see you tomorrow.'

Paula said goodnight and returned to her bedroom. It was a wonder no one else had been woken by the commotion. PC Straighte's colleague hadn't been very quiet when he'd spoken on his phone in the hall. I dimmed the light and then sat on the edge of the bed.

'Are you going to stay with us?' Grace asked, her little face peeping out from over the duvet.

'Would you like me to?'

She nodded.

'OK. I'll stay until you're asleep and then I will go to my bed downstairs. I'll leave this door open so you can call me if you need me.'

'What's your name?' Grace asked.

'Cathy,' Jenna replied with a yawn. She seemed the more tired of the two.

'That's right, Cathy,' I said.

'Can we see Mummy soon?' Grace asked.

'Quite soon,' I said. When a child first comes into care, contact is usually arranged for the next day.

'Will you tell Mummy we're here?' Jenna asked, her eyes beginning to close.

'She knows where you are, love, so don't worry.'

'Why can't we go home now?' Grace asked.

'The social worker wants to make sure you're safe first. I'll explain more in the morning.'

'Jackson was naughty, but we haven't been naughty, so why can't we stay with Mummy?' Grace said.

'That isn't the reason Jackson came to live with me,' I replied. 'Your mummy just needed some help.'

'Does she still need help?' Grace asked.

'Yes. Now I want you to go to sleep. Jenna is nearly asleep.'

She looked at her sister to see if I was right and then snuggled down beside her.

I stayed sitting on the edge of the bed and soothed Grace's forehead until gradually her eyes closed. Her last comment before she fell asleep was, 'I wish my daddy was still alive.' My eyes filled. They'd had so much to cope with in their short lives.

Once I was sure both girls were asleep, I tiptoed from the room, leaving the door open and the light on low. It was now after 1 a.m. I didn't bother changing into my nightclothes again. I went downstairs and into the front room, where I lay on the sofa bed with the duvet over me. I was exhausted, but I couldn't sleep. My thoughts were racing with the events unfolding, and I knew tomorrow was likely to be even more taxing.

The girls wouldn't be returning home, at least not straight away. There had been enough concern to remove them – not a step ever taken lightly – so the social services would need to be sure that if they were returned, they would be safe. That could take some time to establish. It's felt that if one child in a family is at risk then so too are the others. I also knew that, whenever possible, when siblings are brought into care they are placed together. Having Jenna and Grace sleep in my bed while I slept downstairs on the sofa was only a temporary measure for tonight. Tomorrow the social services would try to find a carer who had room to take all three of them, even if it meant moving them out of the area. It would mean more disruption for the children, another home, a new school, just when Jackson was starting to settle.

The only reason I could think of for leaving Jackson with me and just moving the girls was his behaviour. If it's felt that siblings are managed better separately then sometimes they are split up. Thankfully it wasn't my decision, but I knew it would need a highly experienced carer – probably a two-parent family – to successfully look after all three of them if they were to stay together. Otherwise the placement would break down, resulting in another move for the children. It does happen, and some children have multiple moves – for various reasons – which is obviously very unsettling for them.

My thoughts then returned to Kayla. PC Straighte had said a social worker was with her, but they wouldn't stay all night. They would have tried to find a family member, good friend or neighbour to stay with her while she was distraught. What Kayla was going through couldn't be underestimated. It was truly the stuff of nightmares. To lose your husband to cancer, have your teenage son commit suicide and then have your other three children taken into care was unimaginably upsetting. She'd only just been coping before, and now this. From what Jackson had told me, Jerry had struck when the family had been at its most vulnerable – when their father had been terminally ill. On the pretence of helping them, he'd wormed his way into their lives and abused Connor and possibly the other children too. Paedophiles can spend months, even years, befriending a family before they strike. It seemed that's what Jerry had done, and it was pure evil.

CHAPTER FOURTEEN

CONFUSED AND UPSET

At some point in the early hours I must have dropped off to sleep, but I was wide awake again at 6 a.m. I'd heard noises and movement on the landing. I shot off the sofa bed and rushed upstairs in time to see Jenna and Grace scuttling back into my bedroom. I went in. They were sitting in bed, and looked at me anxiously.

'It's all right,' I told them. 'It's nearly morning. You had some sleep.'

'Can we see Jackson now?' Jenna asked.

'It's very early, he's still asleep, love. We'll wait until he's awake.'

But at that moment I heard his bedroom door open and he went into the toilet.

'Is that him?' Grace asked hopefully.

'Yes.'

'I want to see Jackson,' Grace said loudly.

I heard the toilet flush and then Jackson's voice, heavy with sleep and disbelief. 'Gracey, is that you?'

'You stay here while I speak to him.'

Leaving the girls in my bed, I went round the landing to Jackson. 'Jenna and Grace are in my room. They were brought here late last night.'

Only half awake, he rubbed his eyes and looked stunned. 'Because of what I told you about Connor?' he asked.

'Partly. The social services have to make sure they're safe. We'll learn more today. Are you going back to sleep?'

'Jackson!' Grace called from my room.

'Can I see them?' he asked.

'Yes, of course. But quietly.'

We went round the landing to my room. As soon as the girls saw him their faces lit up. Little Grace threw herself at him and hugged him hard.

'The social worker said we had to come here,' Jenna told him. 'They made us. Mum is upset.'

Immediately I saw Jackson's face darken. This had the potential to add to his feelings of guilt.

'We all want to keep you safe,' I explained. 'If you are not going back to sleep, put on your dressing gowns and we'll go downstairs.' Where hopefully there was less chance of them waking Adrian, Paula and Tilly.

Jackson went to fetch his dressing gown, while Jenna put on hers and I helped Grace into hers. 'Quietly,' I said, as I led the way downstairs and into the living room. Suddenly it seemed I had a lot of children with me.

Jackson collected his phone from the table in the kitchen-diner and joined us in the living room.

'Mum's tried to phone,' he said anxiously, which I thought might happen. 'She's left a message.'

I watched his expression change as he listened to it. 'She's angry with me,' he said, devastated. 'You said I'd done the right thing.'

'You have. Let me listen.'

He passed me the phone and I listened to Kayla's message. I could see why he was upset. She was hysterical and blaming Jackson for 'making up lies about Jerry'.

'It's not your fault, love, honestly. You did the right thing. Your mother was very upset last night. It was a shock, but I expect she will feel a bit better today. I'll tell your social worker so she can have a chat with her.'

'What did Mummy say?' Jenna asked.

'Nothing,' Jackson replied, and tucked the phone into the pocket of his dressing gown.

'Don't return the call,' I told him.

The girls were looking at me questioningly, but they didn't have to know what their mother had said. I got out a selection of books to distract them, but Jackson asked for the television. I put it on and found a children's programme that was suitable for all three.

Jenna and Jackson began watching it, while Grace kept asking questions.

'Where's my mummy?'

'I expect she is at home,' I said, for I didn't really know.

'Why are we here?' she asked.

'To keep you safe,' I replied.

'Have we been naughty?'

'No, love.'

'I want my mummy.'

'I know. Come and sit beside me.'

'No. I don't want you.'

She went over and snuggled up to Jackson on the sofa. 'Why are we here?' she asked him.

'Because of Jerry,' he replied, not taking his eyes from the television.

'I like Jerry, he gives me sweets,' Grace said.

'I don't,' Jackson replied, and eased her away.

'I don't either,' Jenna said.

'Why?' I asked.

'He bought me a doll. But I didn't want it.'

'Why not?'

She shrugged. 'It was babyish. I didn't like it,' was all she said. That might be true, but it was also possible that the doll and sweets had been used by Jerry to groom the girls in preparation for abusing them.

I knew the police would interview all three children at some point, but for now I sat with them in the living room in the clothes I'd slept in, trying to reassure them and keep everyone calm. At 7 a.m. Paula came down, having set her alarm. 'Oh, love, you haven't had much sleep and you've got an interview this morning,' I said, concerned.

'It's fine. I don't have to leave until nine-thirty. Is there anything I can do?'

'Could you stay for a few minutes while I get showered and dressed in fresh clothes?' I asked.

'Sure.'

'Thank you so much.' I was very grateful, for I wouldn't have felt comfortable leaving the girls without an adult present while they were so upset.

I then explained to Jenna and Grace that Paula would stay with them while I went upstairs and got dressed. While this might seem obvious, it wouldn't necessarily be to the girls. They'd experienced so much change and uncertainty recently that if I left the room, they could easily think I'd gone for good and was never coming back. When children first arrive I go to great lengths to inform them of what's happening one step at a time, even saying something like: 'I'm going into the kitchen to get a drink and then I will come straight back.' It's virtually impossible to imagine how unsettling and confusing it is for a child to be suddenly uprooted from home, lose everything that is familiar and dear to them and come to a stranger's house.

I asked Jackson if he was all right and he nodded, so, leaving Paula in charge, I had a quick shower, dressed in fresh clothes and knocked on Tilly's bedroom door to make sure she was awake.

'I'm getting up,' she said groggily. I doubted she was. It always took a few reminders on a school day.

'Jackson's sisters are here,' I added.

'Really? Why?'

'They've were brought into care last night and there was nowhere else for them to stay. Get dressed and come down and meet them before you leave for school.'

I returned downstairs and Paula went to shower and dress, telling the girls where she was going.

'I'm hungry,' Jackson said.

'Let's get you all some breakfast then,' I said, feeling a bit brighter after a shower.

'When can I see Mummy?' Grace asked, looking very sad.

'Later today, I hope. Your social worker, Frankie, will let me know. Now, let's find some breakfast.'

'I want to see Mummy,' Grace said.

'I know, love, but you'll have to wait a bit. I'll tell you as soon as I know what's happening.'

'I want to see Mummy now,' Grace bemoaned.

'Well, you can't,' Jackson snapped.

He switched off the television and we all went into the kitchen-diner, ready for breakfast. I knew today was going to be difficult. The girls had had little sleep, were missing their mother dreadfully and faced another move later. However, I wouldn't mention that until I knew for certain what time they were leaving and where they were going, so I could explain.

Jackson wanted hot oat cereal for breakfast, which was what he usually had. Jenna wanted the same.

'Grace, what would you like?' I asked her.

'Nothing. I want my mummy,' she said, her little face puckering. Jenna put her arm around her.

'She has the same as us,' Jenna said.

'Well, that's nice and easy for me to remember,' I said brightly. 'Would you like a glass of juice too? That's what Jackson has.'

Jenna nodded.

'And Grace?'

'The same.'

I poured their drinks first and then made their hot oat cereal, setting a bowl and spoon in front of each of them. Tilly appeared a lot more quickly than she usually did on a school morning.

'Hi, girls,' she said, beaming at them. 'I'm Tilly and I'm in care too.'

Grace scowled, while Jenna just stared at her. Jackson was busy eating.

'Suit yourselves,' she said crisply, and continued into the kitchen to get the cornflakes she normally had.

'They've only just arrived,' I said quietly to her. 'Remember how you felt when you first came here. And you were old enough to understand what was going on.'

'OK,' she said. Taking her bowl of cornflakes, she sat at the table where she told the girls they were being good, so I thought she'd understood.

Adrian came down dressed for work in his office trousers, shirt and tie. 'I thought I heard voices,' he said. 'Hello, ladies. How are you?'

'This is my son, Adrian,' I told them.

They stared at him, mesmerized. Over six feet tall and sturdily built, he had a quiet confidence and presence about him. Their gaze followed him into the kitchen, where he made coffee and toast.

'Are there any more people living here?' Jenna asked.

'No, love.' I smiled. 'You've met everyone now.'

'Apart from the cat,' Tilly added.

'Yes, that's right. He's outside,' I said. Sammy had shot out through the cat flap when I'd first come down with the children. 'Now eat up,' I encouraged the girls.

Saying goodbye, Adrian took his breakfast to his room to eat while he finished getting ready. He had a meeting first thing this morning. Once Tilly had finished, she left the table to get ready for school and I sat with Jackson and the girls. Grace had hardly eaten anything, while Jenna had eaten about half. She gave the rest of her cereal to Jackson to finish. I tried coaxing Grace into eating, but she wasn't interested.

'Would you prefer something else?' I asked her.

'I want Mummy,' she said.

'No, to eat, silly,' Jackson said, short-tempered, which I ignored.

At least they'd had their drinks, and I now said we should go upstairs and get ready. Jackson stood and went up first. He knew I always laid out his school uniform the night before. He went to his room, while I took the girls to my room to find them something to wear. I had an ottoman full of nearly new children's clothes. As I sorted through them, Tilly called goodbye and left to catch the bus to school. Then Adrian called, 'See you later!' and left for work.

I found clothes to fit the girls and took them into the bathroom so they could wash and dress. As I waited, I texted Frankie asking if she wanted the children to go to school – not that I had any school uniform for the girls, but I needed to know if I should take them. She texted back straight away, although it was only 8.15, saying not to take them as she was going to arrange contact at the Family Centre. Because there were now safeguarding concerns at home, the children would have supervised contact there.

'No school for you today,' I told the girls. 'You'll be seeing your mother instead.'

'When?' Jenna asked.

'I don't know yet. Your social worker will tell me.' But it crossed my mind that if the girls were moved out of the area today, they wouldn't have a chance to say goodbye to their school friends. Meaningful goodbyes are important, but sadly, sometimes looked-after children are moved so abruptly they don't have the chance to say them.

Jackson came from his bedroom dressed in his school uniform.

'You don't have to go to school today,' Jenna told him before I could. 'We're seeing Mum.'

'I haven't got a time yet,' I added. 'But you can keep on your uniform or change. It's up to you.'

He shrugged and stayed in his school uniform – dark-grey trousers and light-grey jersey. The girls were now washed and dressed, so all I had to do was keep three unsettled and melancholy children occupied until I heard from Frankie again.

'Let's go downstairs and get some games out of the cupboard,' I said positively.

Without much enthusiasm, they came with me into the kitchen-diner, where I took out a large selection of games and puzzles from the toy cupboard and set them on the table. These held their interest – even Grace's – for about twenty minutes and then they started asking about their mother. I took out some more games, which occupied them for another ten minutes or so. Then I suggested they looked in the cupboard themselves to see what they wanted. Very soon the table and floor were littered with boxes of games and puzzles. Jackson was very quiet, so I asked him if he was all right.

'Yes,' he replied tetchily.

I knew that the message his mother had left on his phone had upset him, although he wasn't saying much. I hoped Kayla was all right with him when they met. I would inform Frankie when I spoke to her.

Just before 9.30 Paula came in to say goodbye before she left for her interview. She did a double take when she saw the entire contents of the games cupboard strewn across the room.

'Good luck,' I told her.

'And you. See you later.' Although whether she would see the children again would largely depend on how quickly Frankie moved them.

All three children soon became restless again, with

Grace repeatedly asking for her mummy, so I suggested we put on our coats and shoes and went into the garden. I couldn't really leave the house and take them to the park until I'd heard from Frankie what time contact was.

Jenna pointed out that they didn't have their coats with them, just the pyjamas and dressing gowns they'd come in. They did have their shoes, though, so I quickly popped upstairs and found a couple of spare jackets in my collection. They fitted, sort of, and we went outside. As we did, I saw Sammy quietly slink in for his breakfast. I didn't draw the children's attention to him. Ears down, he looked a bit stressed from the invasion of children and should be allowed to eat in peace. Afterwards, he'd find a quiet place to sit.

We continued to the bottom of the garden, where I took all the children's outdoor toys from the shed. Bikes, scooters, skateboards, bats and balls. I'd just finished getting them out when my mobile rang. It was Frankie. 'I've arranged contact at the Family Centre from eleven o'clock till twelve-thirty,' she said. 'It was the only free slot.'

'OK. I'll get them there for eleven,' I said. Then I moved away from the children to talk so they couldn't hear. 'Kayla left a message on Jackson's mobile phone last night blaming him for telling lies about Jerry.'

'Oh dear. I'll speak to her,' Frankie said.

'Also, Jenna and Grace made some comments this morning about Jerry giving them gifts – sweets and a doll.'

'Can you write it down and email me, please? I'm really pushed for time at present. I'll be at the Family Centre, so we might have a chance to talk then.'

'All right. See you soon.'

I didn't ask when the children would be moved, as I doubted she would have had a chance to arrange that yet, and she was clearly in a hurry. However, I would need some notice, as I had to pack Jackson's belongings. Although his mother hadn't sent much, I'd bought him what he needed and those things were now his to keep.

I returned to the children. 'You're going to see your mother now,' I said. Then to Jackson, 'Frankie is going to talk to her about her message.'

He nodded, understanding, and his face brightened, as did the girls' at the prospect of seeing their mother again. But I knew it would be short-lived. Being with their mother would be bittersweet and another trauma to deal with, for at the end of contact they would all have to say goodbye again, and it would be heart-breaking.

CHAPTER FIFTEEN

SAY GOODBYE TO MUMMY

As I drove to the Family Centre I explained to the children what to expect. 'It's like a house with lots of living rooms,' I said. 'You will see your mother in one of the rooms. Each room has a sofa, table and chairs, and lots of games and toys. Other children will be seeing their families in other rooms. A contact supervisor will be with you the whole time. They usually sit at a table writing.'

'Why are they there?' Jenna asked.

'To make sure you are all right. Your social worker will probably be in the room for some of the time too.' It was usual for the social worker to be present at the first contact. I glanced in the rear-view mirror. All three children were on the back seat, Grace sitting on a bolster seat between Jenna and Jackson.

'At the end can we go home with Mummy?' Jenna asked.

'I don't think that will happen today, love, but Frankie will tell us more.'

I knew how difficult it was going to be for her and Grace to part at the end of contact. Jackson was used to leaving his mother and returning to live with me, but

Grace and Jenna weren't. This was the first time they'd been separated from their mother. In the past I'd had to carry young children crying and screaming from the Family Centre. It's heart-breaking for everyone, not least for the parents, who are often also in tears. Eventually, if the children stay in care, it becomes a bit easier for everyone.

Another worry I had about today was Kayla's voice-mail message accusing Jackson of lying. I hoped Frankie had had a chance to talk to her before contact, as it was important that Jackson knew his mother believed him. It had taken him a long time to find the courage to tell and now, more than anything, he needed her support. I knew from bitter experience that didn't always happen and sometimes when a child told a parent they had been abused they weren't believed, especially if it was by a family member or friend. It's damaging for the child and they can spend the rest of their lives not only trying to come to terms with the abuse, but also their parent's denial of it happening, sometimes burying their pain in drink, drugs and anti-depressants.

We arrived at the Family Centre with ten minutes to spare. The children had been very quiet for most of the journey. I opened the rear door to let them out. 'Where's Mummy?' Grace asked.

'In the building over there,' I said, pointing.

'Can I see her?'

'Yes, love, soon.'

I offered Grace my hand, but she took Jenna's instead, and we headed for the main gate. Kayla would have been asked to arrive at the Family Centre early so the manager could show her around and explain their house rules. Parents are asked to sign a written agreement that outlines the arrangements and expectations for contact – for example: arrive on time, not under the influence of alcohol or drugs (when contact can be refused), and leave the room tidy at the end.

We went up the path to the security-locked door, where I pressed the buzzer. The closed-circuit television camera overhead allowed anyone in the office to see who was outside. After a few moments the door clicked open and we went in. I said hello to the receptionist sitting at a computer behind a security screen to our right and gave the children's names.

'Their mother and social worker are here,' she said. 'I'll let them know you've arrived. Can you sign in and wait in the waiting room?'

'Where's Mummy?' Grace asked again as I signed the visitors' book.

'Here. You'll see her soon.'

I took the children into the waiting room. It wasn't very large, but like the rest of the building it was brightly painted with colourful pictures on the walls. There were plenty of books and boxes of games, but the children weren't really interested.

'Shall I read you a story?' I asked Grace. She scowled and shook her head, a bit like Jackson did. He picked up a book and then put it down again without looking at it. I could tell he was anxious.

'It'll be all right,' I reassured him, and he shrugged.

'Why are we waiting?' Jenna asked.

'Because it's not eleven o'clock yet.'

As we waited we could hear children's voices and a baby crying in another room. The centre has six rooms and is in constant use during opening times, Monday to Friday. The children having contact now would very likely be pre-school or babies, as most school-age children see their parents after school. The children's voices we could hear now sounded happy, but I'd witnessed some distressing scenes here in the past.

My phone buzzed. The caller display showed Jackson's school number.

'Good morning. It's the school secretary. We're concerned that Jackson isn't in school and neither are his sisters.'

'I am sorry. They are with me. They have contact. Their social worker is aware. I should have informed you.'

'As long as they're all right,' she said. 'We were worried when none of them arrived. Will they be in school tomorrow?'

'I'm not sure. Either their social worker or I will phone you.' I apologized again and said goodbye as footsteps sounded in the corridor.

Frankie came in. 'How are you all?' she asked the children brightly.

'I want my mummy,' Grace said.

'Yes, you can see her now,' Frankie replied. 'We are in Green Room.' All the rooms are decorated a different colour and are known by that colour.

Frankie led the way along the corridor with the girls while Jackson and I followed. 'It'll be fine,' I reassured him again.

As we came to a halt outside Green Room, I said quietly to Frankie, 'Did you have a chance to talk to Kayla about her phone message?'

'Yes. She won't bring it up at contact.' Then, addressing Jackson, she said, 'Your mother understands that the police have been informed and they will investigate your claims. I'll visit you later today to explain what will happen in more detail.'

I could see that this satisfied Jackson, although I thought Frankie had chosen her words carefully and had been guarded in what she said. Perhaps Kayla had taken some persuading not to raise the matter with Jackson during contact, I didn't know.

Frankie opened the door to Green Room and we went in. Kayla was standing in the middle of the room, a tissue pressed to her face. She looked dreadful. Pale, puffy-eyed and wretched. It was obvious she hadn't had any sleep. The girls ran to her with a small cry of delight and she hugged them hard. Jackson hesitated and then also went over and put his arm around her shoulders. It was a touching scene of a family reunited, although it wouldn't be for long.

'I'll come back to collect the children at twelve-thirty,' I confirmed with Frankie.

'Can you wait so we can have a chat once they're settled?'

'Yes. I'll be in the waiting room.'

Leaving the children hugging their mother, I returned to the waiting room and sat down. I checked my phone and then picked up a magazine. Ten minutes later Frankie arrived. 'They're playing a game together now,' she said, sitting opposite me.

'Good,' I said, and returned the magazine to the table.

'I'll need to visit the children later today,' she said. 'I'm not sure what time. I'll let you know.'

'All right.'

'And the police will be conducting video interviews with the children sometime this week. I'll tell you when I have a day and time.'

'Although the girls won't be with me then,' I pointed out.

'I know. The placement team are looking for a suitable foster carer. Thanks for having them last night. How were they?'

'Upset and confused, but they went to sleep eventually. I put them in my bed and I took the sofa bed downstairs.'

She nodded. 'I've spoken to Kayla about the message she left on Jackson's phone. I'm suspending phone contact for the time being. Kayla was very emotional. Not only that the girls were being taken into care, but by what Jackson said. She believes Connor committed suicide because of losing his father. She says Jackson resents Jerry because he thinks he is trying to take his father's place, which isn't true. He's just a family friend.'

'Some friend,' I said contemptuously. 'Jackson has good reason to resent Jerry if he abused Connor.'

'Yes. In the meantime, contact for all three children will be here at the Family Centre, not the family home. I don't know which days yet.'

'How is Kayla coping?' I asked.

'Not very well. A close friend, Sonia, who lives in the same street, stayed with her last night and brought her here today. She's going to collect her later. She wanted to stay for contact, but I had to explain that contact was for the immediate family only.'

'I'm pleased Kayla has someone,' I said.

'It helps. You mentioned that Jenna and Grace said something about Jerry?'

'Yes. Grace said she liked Jerry because he bought her sweets and Jenna said she didn't like him because he gave her a doll, which was babyish. It sounds as though Jerry was a regular visitor to their house.'

'That's the impression I've got. The police are interviewing Jerry now. I'd better go back into the room,' she said, standing. 'The placement team will be in touch when they have any news.'

We said goodbye and I returned to my car, which was parked in the road at the front of the centre. It wasn't worth me driving home, so I switched on the radio and checked my phone again. There was nothing from Paula yet – it was too soon; she'd still be in the interview. As I sat listening to classical music with the sun shining through the windows warming the car, my tiredness from last night caught up with me and my eyes began to close. But only for a few minutes. I was jolted awake by the sound of my phone ringing.

It was Lucy's number.

'Hello, love, how are you?'

'Knackered. We hardly got any sleep last night. I was wondering if you could come round for a bit and look after Emma so I can get some sleep like you did last time.'

Immediately I felt guilty. 'I'm so sorry, love, I can't today. I've got Jackson's sisters with me. They were brought into care last night and they're all in contact now. I could come tomorrow.'

'Yes, please. I'm pretty sure I'll still be knackered tomorrow,' she said with a small laugh.

'I am sorry,' I said again. 'How are you all?'

'Good, but I'll talk to you tomorrow if you're busy.'

'No, I'm not. I'm sitting outside the Family Centre.'

'Why are the girls in care as well?'

'Something Jackson told me,' I said, without going into detail.

We chatted for a while and then Emma began to cry so we said goodbye and that we'd see each other tomorrow. Almost immediately my phone rang again. It was Joy.

'Are Jackson's sisters still with you?' she asked.

'Yes, they are having supervised contact at present at the Family Centre. I'm waiting outside.' I guessed the situation had changed so rapidly that the information had taken a while to reach her. Referrals usually came through the supervising social workers, but the girls coming to me had taken place as an out-of-office-hours emergency.

'Where did they sleep?' Joy asked.

'In my bed. I slept on the sofa downstairs. It was approved by the duty social worker.'

'I see. When will they be moved?'

'I don't know. I'm waiting to hear. But I will need some notice if Jackson is going too, as I have to pack his belongings.'

'I'll speak to their social worker and get back to you.'

'She's in contact now,' I said.

'OK. I'll catch up with you later.'

We said goodbye and I put the radio on again. As I waited, a car pulled up and a young couple in their teens got out carrying a large teddy bear. They went into the centre. Then a car pulled into the car park and a woman

I recognized as a foster carer got out with a baby in a carrier. I'd heard that the parents of the baby she was looking after were young and I guessed they were the couple I'd just seen. What were the chances of them getting their baby back? I wondered. I had no idea. I felt saddened by what lay ahead for them. This or similar was happening at contact centres all over the country. At the time of writing, nearly two thousand babies a year – many of them newborns – are taken into care in this country.

Ten minutes before the end of contact another car pulled up and parked in the road just ahead of me. A woman in her fifties got out and looked in at me as she passed on her way into the centre. Something in her manner made me think it could be Kayla's friend, Sonia, whom Frankie had mentioned, now come to collect her.

Five minutes later I went into the centre, and as I passed the waiting room I saw her sitting in there. I continued to Green Room – I usually collect the children from the room – and stood outside. Frankie would be able to see me through the glass-panelled door. I could see her talking to Kayla. Footsteps sounded in the corridor and then the woman I'd previously seen appeared. 'Are you waiting for Kayla's children?' she asked.

'Yes. I'm their foster carer. Are you Sonia?' I asked, trying to be friendly.

'Yes.'

'I'm Cathy, I usually wait outside the room at the end of contact.'

There was an awkward silence and then she said, 'What a mess! It's disgusting. We haven't had a wink of sleep all night. Those poor kids need to go home. Putting them with a foster carer!' It was said as though she held me responsible.

I had no idea how much she knew, so I replied, 'I hope they can go home soon.' Which was true. No one wants to see a family separated, but children need to be safe.

'It's a misunderstanding – what Jackson told you,' she said. 'Jerry is an odd one, but he'd never do something like that.'

I kept quiet. As a foster carer, I knew that 'odd' ones as well as those who seemed quite normal did abuse children, although of course Jerry was innocent until proven guilty, as all suspects are.

'I told Kayla it was a bad idea putting Jackson into care,' Sonia continued. 'But she said it would be all right because it was voluntary and she could get him back whenever she liked. It seems I was right.'

Thankfully the door then opened and Frankie said, 'Come in.'

As we went into Green Room, Jackson was returning a game to one of the shelves while Grace and Jenna stood either side of their mother.

'I need to dash,' Frankie said, picking up her bag and laptop. 'I'll phone you tomorrow,' she said to Kayla. Then to me, 'I'll see you later.' She left the room.

I looked at the girls and they looked at me, their little faces grim. I knew this was going to be difficult.

'Say goodbye to Mummy,' I said gently.

'Bye, Mum,' Jackson said. While the girls didn't say anything or move from their mother's side.

'You have to go,' Kayla said quietly, her voice trembling.

'I don't want to,' Jenna said.

'I want to stay with Mummy,' Grace cried and, grabbing her mother's skirt, began sobbing loudly.

The contact supervisor looked over but didn't say anything. It wasn't really her job to intervene unless a child was in danger. Although they often included how the family parted in their reports, which were sent to the social worker.

Grace cried and clung desperately to her mother, while Jenna remained where she was, clearly not knowing what to do. Jackson looked on anxiously.

'Give Mummy a kiss goodbye and we'll get some lunch,' I said encouragingly. It was now 12.30 so they should be hungry. 'What would you like to eat?'

'Nothing,' Grace cried, and buried her face further into the material of her mother's skirt.

Kayla, already close to tears, began to cry too. I appreciated how upsetting it was for her, but the onus is on the parent to end contact as positively as they can, devastating though that is. It was clear that Kayla couldn't do that. I offered my hand to Grace, but she drew back. Then Sonia, who'd been standing just inside the door, came forward.

'Kayla, love, the children have to go,' she said gently but firmly. 'We'll sort out this mess, but try to stop crying. You're upsetting yourself and the children.'

Kayla took notice of her and wiped her hand over her eyes. I passed her the box of tissues. It was heart-wrenching, but the children had to leave.

'I want to stay with Mummy,' Grace sobbed, now looking at Sonia.

'You'll see her again soon,' Sonia replied, glancing at me. 'Won't they?'

'Yes. If I take Jenna and Jackson, could you bring Grace?' I asked her. I thought Grace was more likely to leave with her mother's friend – someone she knew well.

Sonia unclenched Grace's hands from her mother's skirt and, taking one in her own hand, we left the centre with Grace crying but walking beside her. Jenna and Jackson came with me. I opened the car door and they got in and then Sonia helped Grace in.

'Good girl,' I said, and buckled her seatbelt. Her little face was streaked with tears. I wiped it with a tissue and then closed the car door.

'Thank you for your help,' I said to Sonia.

She nodded stiffly. 'I'd best be getting back to Kayla,' she said curtly, and returned up the path to the centre.

Despite her coolness I was very grateful for her assistance. I don't know how I would have managed to get all three children into the car without her.

CHAPTER SIXTEEN

A LONG DAY

The children were quiet as I drove us home. Grace had stopped crying and was resting her head on Jenna's shoulder. Exhausted from the upset and having so little sleep last night, her eyes closed. She was still asleep as I parked on our drive. I opened the rear doors, which were child-locked, and Jackson and Jenna clambered out. 'Shall I carry Gracey in?' Jackson asked.

'Can you lift her?'

'Yes, when she falls asleep on the sofa at home I carry her up to her bed.'

'OK, thanks, love.' I was touched by this little glimpse of their family life in happier times, with Jackson helping.

I unfastened Grace's seatbelt and Jackson reached in and carefully lifted out his sister. I went ahead and opened the front door. 'Put her in there, please, so I can hear her when she wakes,' I said, referring to the sofa bed in the front room, which I hadn't had a chance to pack away yet.

Grace was so tired she didn't stir as Jackson laid her on the bed and I took off her shoes. I crept out, leaving the door slightly ajar. Jenna and Jackson were waiting for me in the hall.

'I'm hungry,' Jackson said.

'What would you like for lunch?'

He thought for a moment. 'Chicken nuggets and chips.'

'Jenna, is that OK for you?'

'Yes.'

'And Grace?'

'Yes, we all like it,' Jackson replied. 'With baked beans.'

'Great. That's what we'll have then.' I smiled.

They came with me into the kitchen-diner and Jackson sat at the table playing a game on his phone. I suggested to Jenna that she might like to do a puzzle, but instead she sat beside Jackson, watching him. I could see them both from where I worked in the kitchen. I could also see that outside it had started to rain, so that ruled out going in the garden after lunch.

Grace stayed asleep almost until lunch was ready, and then I heard her call, 'Mummy!'

'I'll go,' Jenna said.

She reappeared a few moments later holding Grace's hand. Grace was rubbing her eyes but not crying. 'Lunchtime,' I said. 'Your favourite – nuggets, chips and beans.'

Jenna took her to the table and they sat next to each other and opposite Jackson. I handed out the cutlery, paper napkins, a glass of water each and then the plates of food. They were all hungry, even Grace, who began eating straight away. I was relieved, for she hadn't had any breakfast.

Sammy came to investigate – the smell of chicken overriding his fear of new children. He sat on the floor near Jackson, who occasionally dropped him a titbit even though he knew he wasn't supposed to.

It was now 1.45 and I hadn't heard anything from the placement team or Joy. Once again, I couldn't leave the house until I knew the arrangements for today. As we finished eating, Paula phoned to say she'd only just left the interview. 'How did it go?' I asked.

'All right, I think. There were others being interviewed.'

'There's bound to be. You did your best and you stand as much chance as anyone. Are you on your way home?'

'Yes, but I was thinking of going to see Lucy. The bus goes past her place.'

'She'd like that, but give her a ring first.'

'Will do. Have the girls left?' she asked.

'No, not yet. They had contact this morning.'

'OK, see you later then.'

I cleared the table and covered it with a selection of games and puzzles, but the children weren't really interested. They were restless, understandably. They knew they were leaving today, so I assumed it had been mentioned at contact – possibly Frankie had told them.

'When are we going?' Jenna asked.

'I don't know yet,' I replied.

'Where are we going?'

'I'll tell you as soon as I know.'

'I want to go home,' Grace said.

'I know, love.'

'Where is Mummy?' Grace asked anxiously.

'I expect she's at home.'

'All by herself?' Jenna wanted to know.

'I'm sure Sonia will be looking after her.' I tried to distract them with a game.

It was unsettling for me as well and I needed to pack Jackson's belongings. Once I knew what was happening and when, I would prepare all three children to leave for their new home.

At three o'clock, when I still hadn't heard anything, I stepped out of the room so the children couldn't hear me and called Joy. It went through to voicemail, so I left a message. 'It's Cathy, I still don't know the arrangements for the children,' I said bluntly. It wasn't fair to keep them waiting, although I guessed the social services were struggling to find a carer who could take all of them.

At 3.30, when Jackson asked if they could watch television, I agreed, and we went into the living room where I found a film that appealed to all of them. I sat with them, my mobile beside me, as the time ticked by, but there was no call from the social services. I began to think we'd been forgotten, then Joy phoned to say she was trying to get in touch with Frankie. At 4.30 I heard a key go in the front door, followed by Tilly's voice and then Frankie's.

'I should have called, but it's been non-stop,' Frankie said as I went into the hall. 'How are they?'

'They're in here, watching some television,' I said.

Tilly went up to her room and Frankie came into the living room. All three children looked at her warily.

'How are you all?' she asked, sitting on the sofa next to Grace, who immediately moved closer to Jenna.

No one replied.

'Would you like a drink?' I asked her.

'Yes, please. Coffee – milk, no sugar.'

'Jackson, switch off the television, love,' I said. 'Frankie will want to talk to you.' I waited until he'd done as I asked and then went into the kitchen to make the coffee. I could hear Frankie talking to the children, reassuring them that their mummy was all right, they'd see her soon and Sonia was looking after her.

'Have the placement team been in touch?' Frankie asked as I set her coffee on the table within her reach.

'No.'

'I'll give them a ring now,' she said. 'Also, I have to phone your supervising social worker. She's left me a couple of messages.'

She went into the hall to make the calls, although we could hear some of what she was saying. 'I see ... Yes ... Oh dear ... OK ... I'll ask her.'

She then called to me.

'Wait here,' I told the children, and went into the hall.

Frankie covered the mic on her phone as she spoke to me. 'The foster carer they had in mind can't take them. Can they stay here tonight?'

'They can, but the girls will be in my bed.'

'That's all right. It's short term.'

'You'll need to tell Joy,' I said. 'And would it be possible to have some of the girls' clothes and a favourite toy?'

Uncovering the mic, she told her colleague from the placement team that the children could stay with me again tonight.

Ending the call, she said, 'Thanks. I'll phone Joy now.'

I returned to the children and we listened again to the one-sided conversation. 'Are we staying with you again?' Jenna asked me.

'Yes. I think so.'

Frankie returned and told the girls they would be staying with me again tonight. Jackson had rather assumed he was.

'I'll ask your mummy for some of your toys,' Frankie said to the girls.

'Do you have a special cuddly toy you take to bed?' I asked them.

'I have a bear and Grace has a rabbit,' Jenna replied.

Frankie made a note. 'Anything else you want?' she asked. It was the wrong question.

'I want my mummy,' Grace said. Her eyes filled and Jenna took her onto her lap to comfort her.

'Do Jenna or Grace have any medical conditions, allergies or special dietary requirements?' I asked Frankie. It was something that would normally have been included on the placement information forms, had there been any.

'Not as far as I know, but I'll check with Kayla.' She made a note.

'Also, do they take any medicines regularly?' I asked. Although I would have expected to be told by now if so, experience had taught me it was best to check.

Frankie wrote again, then said to me: 'The police will probably see the children on Thursday, but I'm waiting for confirmation.'

I nodded. It would only affect me if Jackson was still here, as the girls would be with someone else by then.

When the child's social worker visits – which they are supposed to do at least every six weeks – they usually have a checklist of questions and observations they go through, which includes asking about the child's routine, health, school, hobbies, contact and so forth, but a lot of this wasn't relevant as the girls had only arrived the previous evening and would be moving again tomorrow. Jackson was different, as he'd been with me longer and might be staying. She now wanted to speak to him alone – a usual part of the social worker's visit. I guessed that among other things she would want to talk to him about the allegations he'd made against Jerry. I suggested they went into the front room and apologized in advance for the state it was in – the sofa bed was still down with a ruffled duvet thrown over it.

The girls looked worried as Jackson left with Frankie and I reassured them he wouldn't be long. It hadn't escaped my notice that since coming into care all the bickering that had so stressed Kayla had stopped – at least for the time being – and on the whole they were supporting and comforting in each other.

'Will we be going to school tomorrow?' Jenna asked.

'Good question,' I said. 'We'll ask Frankie when she comes back. Do you want to go?'

She nodded. 'I can see my friends.'

I thought it was a good idea. As well as the children being able to see their friends, going to school was a familiar routine when everything else around them was changing. If they didn't go, they'd face another day of uncertainty, waiting to be moved.

Frankie was in the front room with Jackson for about fifteen minutes and when they returned I put the question to her. 'Jenna has asked if they can go to school tomorrow. Is that all right?'

'I don't see why not,' Frankie said. 'What time will they be home?'

'Around three-forty-five.'

She made a note.

'If possible, can we have Jenna's and Grace's school uniforms?' I asked her.

She wrote again, then put away her notepad and pen. It was nearly 5.30. 'I'll just have a quick look around and then I'll go.' It's usual for the social worker to check the foster carer's home at each visit.

The children stayed in the living room while I showed Frankie around. She'd just been in the front room, so I took her into the kitchen-diner and then upstairs, opening and closing all the doors apart from Tilly's. We could hear her talking on her phone.

'I won't disturb her,' Frankie said.

'She's supposed to be doing her school work,' I said dryly, and led the way downstairs.

Frankie returned to the living room to say goodbye to the children. 'Can I see Mummy?' Grace asked.

'On Wednesday,' Frankie said. Again, I assumed the children would be gone by then and someone else would be taking them to contact.

I went with Frankie to the door while the children remained in the living room. 'I'll phone Kayla now about the girls' clothes and get back to you,' she said.

'Thank you. I'll have to collect them later when the children are in bed and Paula is home.'

Tilly heard the front door close as Frankie left and she came downstairs. 'I'll do my school work after dinner,' she said, seeming to guess what I was about to say. 'What are we having?'

'Something quick. If you would like to sit with the children and keep them amused, I'll do dinner. They can finish watching the film they started if they wish, or see if you can get them interested in a game. Anything to keep little Grace from crying.'

I went with Tilly into the living room and told Jackson and the girls I would be in the kitchen making dinner if they needed me and that Tilly would be staying with them. As I left, Tilly began rummaging in one of the toy boxes, with all three children watching her. It went quiet and when I checked on them I found Tilly on her knees – having lined up all the toy cars and play people, she was inching them forward in a long procession as the children looked on, intrigued. At least they were being kept amused!

'Thanks, love,' I said, and returned to the kitchen.

As I continued making a pasta bake, my mobile rang. It was Frankie. 'I've just spoken to Kayla's friend, Sonia,' she said. 'She's offered to pack some clothes for the girls and bring them to you later. Is it all right if I give her your address?'

'Yes, of course. Sonia knows she mustn't bring Kayla with her as it would be unsettling for the children?' I checked. It would also be unauthorized contact. It was different now there was a court order.

'I'm sure she does, but I'll check,' Frankie said. 'And I've just had confirmation that the police will be seeing the children at eleven o'clock on Thursday morning. Can you email me a copy of your log notes in respect of what each child has said?'

'Yes.'

Paula texted to say she'd left Lucy's and was on the bus coming home. Adrian arrived home from work at six, followed five minutes later by Paula. Dinner was ready, so I thanked Tilly for looking after the children and brought everyone to the table. I served the very large pasta bake – enough for seven – covered in sizzling-hot cheese, with warm crusty bread and salad. As we ate, Paula talked about Lucy and little Emma. She was besotted by the baby, as we all were. Perhaps Tilly felt a bit jealous and it was time she had some of the attention, for she announced very loudly, 'I'm not going to CAMHS any more.'

Conversation stopped.

'Why not?' I asked. 'You've only been going a few weeks.'

'I've had enough of talking about what happened. I think it would be better if I spent the time studying.'

I saw Adrian smile.

'It's only an hour once a week,' I said. 'There's plenty of time for you to do your school work after, and you have every other evening and weekends. If you really are thinking of stopping then you'll need to discuss it with your social worker first.' Tilly was receiving counselling to help her come to terms with her past, just as many children in care do.

'I phoned Gran earlier,' Tilly said, changing the subject.

'Good, how is she?'

'She's fine,' Tilly said. 'I spoke to Mum as well. I said I'd phone again later in the week and then see them on Saturday.'

'Excellent.' I dared to hope that the rift between Tilly and her mother was slowly healing.

Grace didn't eat much, but I wasn't too worried as she'd had a good lunch. After dinner Tilly offered to look after the children again. Jackson said sharply he didn't need looking after at his age. I thanked Tilly and said she'd been a big help earlier, but now she needed to do her homework. She pulled a face but went upstairs to her room to study. I think she knew I had her best interests at heart. I hoped so.

I explained to Jenna and Grace that Sonia was going to bring some of their clothes later and hopefully their soft toys, but I didn't know what time and that they might be in bed when she arrived. They both looked tired out. Paula read them a story in the living room as I cleared up the dinner things and then she helped me take them upstairs for their bath and to get ready for bed. Jackson largely took care of himself.

By eight o'clock all three children were in bed. I reassured the girls I'd bring up their soft toys if Sonia brought them. Jenna asked for the light to be left on low, as it had been the night before. I said goodnight and then checked on Jackson, who was looking at a magazine.

At 8.30, when I looked in on the children, they were all asleep. I finally had time to sit in the living room with a cup of tea. It was tidy now; some kind person had returned all the toys to the toy boxes and cupboard. A few minutes later, as I was sipping my tea and thinking about the day, the front-door bell rang. I rushed to answer it, hoping it hadn't woken the girls. It had, for as I opened the door Grace screamed, 'Is that my mummy? I want my mummy!'

CHAPTER SEVENTEEN

BACK AT SQUARE ONE

'Come in,' I said hurriedly to Sonia. 'Grace has just woken.'

'Here are the girls' bags,' she said, setting them down in the hall.

'Mummy!' Grace shouted again from upstairs.

'I need to settle her,' I said. 'Did you bring her toy rabbit?'

'Yes, and Jenna's bear.'

Sonia and I unzipped the bags and took out the soft toys as Grace shouted again. Leaving Sonia in the hall, I ran upstairs and into my bedroom.

'Where's Mummy?' Grace asked, panic-stricken and sitting up in bed.

'Sssh, love. She's not here,' I whispered. 'It's Sonia. She's brought some of your clothes and your rabbit.' I tucked the soft toy into bed beside her and gently eased her down. She snuggled her face into the velvety fabric of her favourite toy. It would smell of home and be comforting. 'Good girl. Now I want you to go back to sleep. No more calling out or you'll wake your sister, OK?'

She gave a little nod.

I tucked her in and came out, leaving the door open. Hopefully she would settle now. I returned downstairs. Sonia was still in the hall and didn't seem in any hurry to leave, but, aware that Grace would hear us if we talked in the hall, I suggested we go into the living room.

'Just for a few minutes,' she said. 'Then I should be getting back to Kayla.'

As we entered the living room, Sammy, curled up asleep on a chair, raised his head and looked at her inquisitively.

'I've got a cat,' Sonia said, stroking him. 'Similar colouring.' I felt that the hostility she'd shown to me earlier had largely gone now and I sensed she wanted to talk.

'Would you like a drink?' I offered.

'No, thank you. I won't stay long.' She lowered herself into the armchair with a heartfelt sigh. 'The police visited us this afternoon.'

'I thought they would want to talk to Kayla before long. It's usual when an allegation like this has been made.'

'They asked Kayla about her relationship with Jerry. She doesn't have a relationship with him. He's just a friend – or so she thought. They've been questioning him at the police station. He's back home now, but he's not allowed to come anywhere near Kayla or the children.' She paused thoughtfully. 'The police seem to be taking what Jackson said seriously.'

'Yes.'

'What do you think?'

'About what?'

'What Jackson told you. Kayla and I have talked non-stop about what Jackson is claiming. Maybe he's making it up because he's angry. If it is true, why didn't

Connor tell Kayla at the time or let Jackson tell her if he couldn't? You've been fostering a long time. What do you think?'

'In my experience there are many reasons why a child or young person doesn't report abuse at the time,' I said. 'They may have been threatened into silence by their abuser. Or they fear they have done something wrong, that they won't be believed or that their parents will be upset or angry. The children's father was very ill at the time and it's likely Connor didn't want to make matters worse and upset his mother even more. Perhaps in some way he felt responsible for what happened – which, of course, he wasn't. He was a victim.'

'Do you believe it happened?' she asked. She seemed to have had a change of heart since I'd seen her earlier, when she'd claimed it was a misunderstanding and Jerry wouldn't do something like that.

'I have to report any disclosures that the children I foster make,' I said carefully. 'Then it's for the social services and the police to investigate.'

'But do you believe Jackson?' she asked again.

'Yes.'

She held my gaze. 'And what about the girls? The social worker told Kayla that the reason they were being taken into care was because if one child in a family has been abused then the others might have been.'

'That's true, and the social services and the police will look into it.'

'And what about Jackson?' Sonia asked. 'Has he said Jerry did anything to him?'

'Not to me, but I know he felt uncomfortable around Jerry. He was there last Saturday.'

'So why didn't Jackson tell his mother then?'

'Things have been difficult between them for some time. I don't suppose Jackson felt there was ever a right moment to tell her. It's a big thing for a child to disclose abuse. Some are never able to.'

'He was able to tell you,' she said. 'And he hardly knows you.'

'Sometimes it's easier to tell someone you aren't close to, and when you're away from the family home. Even so, it took him a lot of courage.'

Sonia's face clouded. 'What that poor family have been through. Kayla needs her children back. How does she do that?'

'It's probably a good idea for her to get some legal advice,' I said. 'And she needs to cooperate with the social services and the police enquiries.'

'She is.'

I nodded.

Sonia paused, deep in thought. 'The big problem we're having is believing this could have happened at all – in their own home, by someone they knew.'

'Do you know Jerry?' I asked.

'Only to say hello to in the street. He was always polite. It would have been easier to accept if it was a stranger. But to think that someone we knew and trusted could do that to Connor is unbelievable.'

I understood but said, 'Most cases of child sexual abuse are perpetrated by someone known to the child.'

'That's what Frankie said. It's dreadful. If Jerry did do that then he was responsible for Connor's death.'

'Indirectly, yes.'

Sonia stayed for about half an hour, talking. There

wasn't much I could say beyond what I'd already said, but I think listening and empathizing helped. She said she'd help Kayla get some legal advice tomorrow. She had some understanding of the situation and knew that the Emergency Protection Order only lasted eight days and would need renewing if the girls were to stay in care. I pointed out that Jackson's case was slightly different, as at present he was still in care voluntarily, but that could change and all three children could be made the subject of a care order. If, for example, Kayla took Jackson home and he was felt to be at risk then the social services could apply for a care order to return him to care. It was important she knew.

Once Sonia had gone, I checked the girls were still asleep, then made time for the rest of my family. I talked with Tilly, Paula and Adrian, and then unpacked the girls' bags and set out what they needed for tomorrow. There was a set of casual clothes, underwear and their school uniforms.

I made a fresh cup of tea and sat at my computer in the front room, emailing. The last one was to Frankie, who'd asked for details of what Jackson and the girls had told me about Jerry. By the time I'd finished I was too tired to work on my book. Sometimes, if I had a deadline to meet, I got up very early – at 4 a.m. – to write, but I wasn't planning on doing that tomorrow. I was exhausted. It was midnight before I finally climbed into my bed in the front room and switched off the light.

Grace woke once at 3 a.m., shouting out, 'Mummy!' I was awake in a heartbeat and rushed upstairs. I found her soft-toy rabbit had fallen out and was on the floor. I tucked it in again, soothed her, then said she needed to go back to sleep or she'd be too tired to play with her friends at school tomorrow. I waited until she was asleep, then returned downstairs. I didn't hear any more from her or Jenna until 7 a.m. when it was time to get up anyway.

Organized chaos followed as our usual weekday routine went to pieces. Jackson took full advantage of the fact that I was helping his sisters and, without me knowing, quietly went downstairs and got his mobile phone from the table. When I checked on his progress, instead of being washed and dressed he was lying on his bed playing on his phone. I told him to get ready for school straight away otherwise he'd lose some television time. Tilly came out of her bedroom in her dressing gown looking very pale and quietly confided that she'd started a period in the night and had made a mess. I told her not to worry and, while she showered, I stripped the bed and put the soiled linen into the washing machine, trying to pacify the girls at the same time. When I returned upstairs Adrian was waiting outside the bathroom for his turn so he could get ready for work, and Jackson was back on his bed. I confiscated his phone and said he'd have it back once he was dressed and downstairs, ready for school. I knocked on the bathroom door and asked Tilly to be as quick as she could, and then I went to pacify Grace again, who was crying for her mummy.

At 7.45, Paula, who didn't have any temporary work today and had been planning on a lie-in, came out of her room in her dressing gown to see what the commotion was.

'Could you give me a hand please, love?' I asked.

'I will, but there's too many people here.'

'I know. It's just for today.'

Paula took the girls downstairs and started on their breakfasts, while I knocked on Jackson's door again and said if he didn't appear ready in one minute there would be no television at all this evening. It worked.

He ran out of his room, tucking in his shirt as he went. Tilly came out of the bathroom and Adrian went in.

Everyone had some breakfast and miraculously we were only five minutes late leaving the house. I thanked and praised everyone, including Jackson.

'You're just like my mum,' he grumbled as we got into the car. 'She gets in a state too.'

'With good reason,' I said. 'She has my sympathy. I needed your cooperation this morning, but I didn't get it.'

'Don't care,' he said. Jackson needed firm and consistent boundaries and I hadn't been able to deliver those this morning, so he'd played up. Which is presumably what had happened at home, albeit for a different reason.

I parked in my usual place a little way from the school and opened the rear door, pavement side. Instead of waiting for me as I'd asked, Jackson ran off. I thought he was going to keep running past his school, but at the last moment he veered off into the playground. I had intended to take the girls in first, but I wasn't going to leave Jackson without adult supervision in the playground in his present mood.

As luck would have it, Mr Burrows was on playground duty. He didn't seem surprised to see I had the girls with me, so I guessed he'd been told that they were in care as well now.

'Could you keep an eye on Jackson, please, while I take the girls into school?' I asked him.

'Sure,' he said. 'Looks like you have your hands full.'

'You could say that.' I smiled. 'Thank you very much.'

Jackson was standing with another boy and I took the girls over to say goodbye, but he ignored us. 'He can be so rude,' Jenna said.

We continued into the infants' playground. I didn't know if the infant school had been informed that Jenna and Grace were with me today. I hadn't had a chance to phone, so I went into reception and introduced myself to the school secretary, explaining that I was Jackson's foster carer and I'd been looking after his sisters for a couple of days. The secretary knew the girls and asked how they were. 'Confused,' I said. 'But doing all right, considering.'

She decided I didn't need to complete the form that was normally used when a child moved house, as the girls were only with me for today, but she took my mobile-phone number. The junior school had my full contact details, should they be needed. I then waited with the girls in the playground for the start of school.

'Are we going home with you?' Grace asked, worried.

'I'll be collecting you, yes,' I said. Further than that I didn't know.

Once the girls had gone into school, I went home. Paula was rushing to get ready as she'd just received a call for temporary work – on reception at a garage she'd worked at before. I offered to take her in the car, but she said she'd be OK, so I cleared up the kitchen instead. I then phoned Lucy and asked if it was still all right for me to visit her today. 'Yes, I'm looking forward to it,' she said. 'Come as soon as you can.'

'I can come now if you like.'

'Great. See you soon.'

It was eleven o'clock when I arrived at Lucy's. I was so pleased to see her and little Emma, as Lucy was to see me. I looked after Emma while Lucy showered and washed her hair – something she hadn't had a chance to do that morning. It was a lovely warm, sunny September day outside so I suggested we went to a local park for lunch. It wasn't far away and had a nice café.

'I'll have to make up bottles first,' Lucy said. 'Can you change Emma?'

'Yes, of course.'

Lucy packed the baby bag with everything that could possibly be needed. She kept the pram downstairs in the lobby, so she carried Emma down the flight of stairs and I brought the baby bag – it was rather heavy. She settled Emma in the pram and tucked her in, and I pushed her to the park, about a fifteen-minute walk away. She gurgled happily and then fell asleep. We chose a table outside in the sunshine and I went in and ordered for us both – jacket potatoes with cheese, baked beans and coleslaw, and a pot of tea.

We talked as we ate, and Emma slept. It was wonderful – a complete change of scenery and spending quality time with Lucy. She said that she and Darren had spoken to Nana and were planning on visiting her soon, as well as Darren's grandparents. I told her our news, and that I was expecting a call any moment to tell me the arrangements for the girls and that Jackson would possibly be leaving too. Emma kindly waited until we'd finished eating before she woke. Lucy fed her and then gave her to me.

'Adrian thinks I should just foster little ones,' I said, gazing adoringly at Emma.

'Yes, I know, he told me. Will you?'

'Not sure. I think the social services will want to place older children with more complex needs with me as I'm experienced.'

'You could refuse to take them,' Lucy pointed out.

'I could.'

'But you won't.'

I smiled. 'We'll see.'

I had my phone on the table throughout lunch, but no call came through from the social services. I changed Emma's nappy and then we set off for Lucy's flat. As we left the park, we passed the play area where the children's apparatus was. Lucy said she was looking forward to the time when Emma was old enough to play there and be pushed on the swings. So was I.

On the way back we stopped at a small grocery store, where Lucy bought what she needed. It was two o'clock when we entered her flat and I still hadn't had a phone call from the social services. I stayed until 2.45 and then had to leave to collect the girls and Jackson from school. We'd both had a wonderful day and said we'd do it again soon. I felt recharged and Lucy said she did too.

But as soon as I'd left, my thoughts returned to the girls and Jackson. Time was passing. Would the children be staying for dinner? If so, it would be late when they were moved. It's usually considered better to move children early on in the day so they have time to adjust to their new surroundings before they have to go to bed. Obviously if it's an emergency (as it was when Jenna and Grace came to me) then the children are moved immediately and can arrive at the foster carer's at any time. But this wasn't an emergency. It was a planned move, so someone must know what was happening.

I parked outside the school and phoned Joy. 'I'm still waiting to hear the arrangements for the children,' I said.

'I thought they were staying with you tonight,' she replied.

'I haven't heard.'

'I'll check with Frankie, but I'm sure that's what she said.'

Not pleased, I went into the playground to wait for the girls, whose school came out ten minutes before Jackson's. My phone buzzed with an incoming call and it was Joy.

'They *are* staying with you tonight,' she said. 'Frankie sends her apologies. She meant to phone you but hasn't had the chance. She says it's all right for them to sleep in your bed again.'

'Thank you,' I said tightly. 'And what's happening tomorrow?'

'They don't know yet. I've asked to be told as soon as a decision is made.'

We said goodbye. There was no point in making a fuss. I'd experienced similar breakdowns in communication before. I sometimes felt that because the children were safely with a foster carer, there wasn't the same urgency to pass on information as there was in front-line child-protection work.

Jenna's class came out first and she told me that Grace had been upset during school and had spent some time out of lessons with the welfare lady. Then Grace came out with a woman Jenna told me was her teacher. They came over and her teacher told me the same thing. 'Poor Grace is very confused about where she's living,' she said kindly. 'She's been asking for her mummy all day.'

I thanked her for looking after Grace and said I'd be bringing the children to school in the morning and could be collecting them tomorrow too, but I didn't know for sure. As we left the playground, I was half expecting Jenna or Grace to comment on what I'd just told their teacher, but neither of them did. I think their worlds were so upside down at present that they just accepted another change in arrangements. Grace asked when she would see her mummy again.

'After school tomorrow,' I said.

Frankie had previously told me she was arranging supervised contact at the Family Centre on Monday, Wednesday and Friday. At the time I'd assumed the children would be with their new foster carer by then, but that was looking increasingly unlikely now. I made a mental note to phone or email Frankie to confirm she wanted me to take all three children to contact tomorrow and at what time.

When Jackson came out of school he was with Mr Burrows, who came over. Unfortunately, this time it wasn't to tell me Jackson had had a good day.

'I'm afraid Jackson lost some of his playtime today for poor behaviour in the classroom,' he said, but didn't say exactly what.

I apologized, but of course all the change and uncertainty was having a negative impact on Jackson's behaviour.

'I'm sure he will have a better day tomorrow,' Mr Burrows added.

'Yes,' I agreed, and thanked him. He was always so positive, and I knew that whatever Jackson had done had merited the sanction.

As we walked to the car I asked Jackson what had happened.

'None of your business,' he replied rudely.

'It is my business while you are with me,' I said. 'And please don't be rude.'

'Can if I want,' he retaliated.

And I felt the progress we'd made to date evaporate. We were back at square one.

CHAPTER EIGHTEEN

DECISION

Tuesday evening was pandemonium, and the feel-good factor I'd had from spending the day with Lucy and Emma quickly vanished. Jackson was rude and uncooperative – 'No, why should I? You can't make me,' he said tirelessly. He tried to wind up Jenna and Grace. 'You don't have to do what she says,' he told them whenever I asked them to do something, like wash their hands as we got in from school. 'She's not our mother.'

Then I found him jumping on the sofa bed in the front room after I'd asked him not to. I hadn't bothered packing it away as I needed it again that night, but I had closed the front-room door. The bed was only designed for occasional use and as I went in to stop him for the umpteenth time I heard one of the springs snap. I told him to get off, and that if he wanted to jump, he could use the trampoline in the garden.

'Don't want to,' he said moodily and roughly pushed past me. He went into the living room where the girls were.

I followed and waited until he'd found something to do, then I returned to the kitchen to continue preparing our evening meal. It was quiet for a few minutes and I thought he'd settled, then I heard footsteps on the stairs. Removing the sauce I was cooking from the stove, I went upstairs. My bedroom door was open and Jackson was jumping on my bed while the girls watched. It wasn't their fault. They didn't know this wasn't allowed, but Jackson did.

'Get off, now,' I said firmly. 'You know you're not allowed in my bedroom.'

He continued defiantly and then said, 'It's not your room any more. Jenna and Grace are sleeping here.' Which wasn't the point.

'Off, now,' I said. The girls were looking at me, worried, and I reassured them they weren't in trouble.

'That's fifteen minutes lost from your television time,' I told him. He bounced on.

Then Jenna said, 'You're so naughty, Jackson. It's because of you we're here and not with Mum.'

That wasn't strictly true, but it had the desired effect, and with a flying leap Jackson came off the bed and landed heavily, hurting his ankle.

'Ouch!' he cried dramatically, clutching it.

'That's exactly why I asked you to stop,' I said. 'It's dangerous.'

I checked his ankle. It didn't look damaged and I helped him to his feet. He hobbled off, but by the time he was downstairs and in the living room he'd forgotten about it. However, I would have to record the accident in my log notes, as foster carers have to record all accidents and injuries – even minor ones.

I'd set out lots of toys and activities in the living room, but Jackson wanted the television on. I thought he was watching too much television, but after the fifteen minutes I'd taken away as a sanction had passed, I let him switch it on. I couldn't be in two places at once and I needed to get dinner ready. The girls were quietly playing with some toy farmyard animals, so I returned to the kitchen, leaving the door wide open.

All was quiet for a few minutes, with just the hum of the television, but when I checked on them I found Jackson wasn't watching television but was on the floor, huddled in a corner. He quickly hid something behind his back.

'He's phoning our mummy,' Grace said.

'Tell-tale,' Jackson snapped at her.

I asked for his phone and, after a lot of refusing, he brought it out from behind his back and placed it in my hand. I looked at the call log. Grace was right: he had been trying to phone his mother, although she hadn't answered. He knew he wasn't supposed to phone her, but the girls didn't. I explained to them that we had to keep to the contact their social worker, Frankie, had put in place, so they would see their mother tomorrow but couldn't phone her now. Then the phone began ringing and the caller display showed *Mum*.

I stepped outside the room to speak to Kayla, where I explained what had happened and apologized. She was upset. 'I thought because he called me I was allowed to talk to them,' she said with a sob. I felt bad and apologized again.

Returning to the living room, I told Jackson I would be keeping his phone until his behaviour improved. He was angry and said I couldn't do that. But when he saw I meant it and wouldn't be bullied into returning his phone, he finally settled down. Years of fostering and raising my own children had taught me that if you issue – or warn of – a sanction, you have to carry it out. Children can see through idle threats and you quickly lose credibility. But generally, I find it's better to try to ignore negative behaviour and concentrate on the positives. (I share what I've learnt about parenting in my book *Happy Kids*.)

Tilly arrived home at five o'clock slightly later than usual because she'd been talking to her friend Abby after school. She poured herself a glass of juice and went to her bedroom, where she phoned Abby. I wondered what they found to say as they'd been together at school all day, but then I seemed to remember my father saying something similar to me.

Paula returned home from work just before six o'clock, followed by Adrian, so we all ate together. Jenna and Grace ate a reasonable amount but were very quiet. Adrian was quiet too, so I asked him if he was all right. He said he was but needed to talk to me later. I felt another lecture coming on about fostering and me overdoing it. I knew I was 'overdoing it'. Four looked-after children with one foster carer was too much – no one was getting their fair share of my time – but I didn't have much of a choice at present.

After we'd finished eating Tilly offered to help with the girls, but I said she needed to do her school work, and I asked Paula to give me a hand instead. She sighed; she'd been at work all day and was looking forward to spending her evening relaxing, but she did help. She read Grace and Jenna a story in the living room so I could sit with Jackson at the table in the kitchen-diner while he did his school work. He was still working towards earning back his phone, so did his homework, otherwise I don't think he would have in his present mood. Once it was complete, I praised him and said he could have his phone back, but he must not call his mother as it put her in a very difficult position.

I took the girls upstairs for their baths and then got them into bed while Jackson played on his phone and texted some friends in his bedroom. Grace and Jenna weren't as tired tonight as they had been last night and had a lot of questions, many of which I couldn't answer.

'When can we sleep in our own beds again?' Jenna asked, her soft-toy bear on the pillow beside her.

'I don't know, love.'

'Is Mummy all by herself?' Grace wanted to know, her face sad.

'I expect Sonia is with her.'

'How long do we have to stay with you?' Grace asked.

'I don't know.'

Eventually they were settled enough for me to leave them to hopefully drop off to sleep. It was Jackson's bedtime, but now that he had his phone back he was no longer in a cooperative frame of mind. It was the best part of an hour before he was washed, changed into his pyjamas and in bed, with his phone downstairs on the table.

I now had time to talk to Adrian, who was in the living room.

'I'm free,' I said lightly, going in.

'Good.'

'What's the problem, love?'

'No problem, or there shouldn't be,' he said. 'Kirsty's parents have invited you for supper on Saturday evening to discuss our wedding plans, but who will you ask to babysit?'

Adrian had anticipated my problem. Even with the girls gone, I wouldn't feel comfortable leaving Paula in charge of Jackson and technically Tilly as well. Although Tilly was fourteen, she was still a minor. It was possible that Jackson and his sisters would have been moved by then, in which case I could leave Tilly with Paula, but I couldn't count on it.

'Could Kirsty's parents come here instead?' I suggested. 'I'll make us supper. They won't mind, will they?'

'Probably not, but that's not really the issue, is it, Mum?'

I felt suitably chastised. 'I know, love, and I'm thinking carefully about what you said about just fostering babies and young children.'

'*A* baby or *a* young child,' Adrian emphasized. 'Not a house full. Mum, I love you and I worry you're taking on too much.'

'I know, I love you too. Will you ask Kirsty's parents if they can come here?'

'Yes, of course.'

Later, as I was standing in the kitchen waiting for the dryer to end its cycle so I could go to bed, I thought more about what Adrian had said. It wasn't just him who was affected. I couldn't give anyone the time they deserved. While Adrian, Paula and Tilly could weather the storm, Jackson clearly couldn't. He'd found the courage to tell me that Connor had been abused by Jerry, but I hadn't had a chance to help with the issues arising from that –

his anger, sorrow, regret, remorse and then guilt that he hadn't told his mother, which could have saved Connor's life. Little wonder his behaviour was deteriorating.

As the dryer finished, I shook out the girls' school uniforms and made a promise to myself. First thing in the morning I would phone Joy and Frankie and make it clear that the girls had to go by the end of the day and that Jackson needed an urgent appointment at CAMHS. Sometimes in fostering ultimatums are necessary to get things moving for the sake of the looked-after children, the carer and their family.

Grace woke twice during the night, calling out, 'Mummy!' I got to her before she woke the rest of the house and soothed her back to sleep, telling her she would see Mummy tomorrow.

Both girls were a bit brighter the following morning because they knew they were seeing their mother that afternoon after school. I'd yet to be told what time. Jackson was more cooperative than he had been the day before. Although there was still a lot of us to use the bathroom and toilet and leave the house on time.

As I drove to school Jackson said, 'I'm not waiting in the infants' playground with you.'

'No. I'll see you in first and then I'll take Jenna and Grace into their school.'

'Mum lets me wait by myself.'

I hesitated. The last thing I needed was Jackson doing a runner, yet I should give him some responsibility. 'Can I trust you to wait nicely and go in with your class?' I asked, glancing at him in the rear-view mirror.

He shrugged non-committally.

I parked outside the school, got out and opened the rear door.

'I can wait by myself,' Jackson said. 'It's embarrassing having you there.' Which I'd guessed.

'All right. We'll give it a try. But you are not to leave the playground, and make sure you go in on time.'

'I will, and you'd better take this,' he said. Delving into his trouser pocket, he took out his mobile phone and handed it to me. In all the kerfuffle of leaving the house, I hadn't noticed him sneak his phone into his pocket.

'Thank you,' I said. 'Sensible decision to give it to me.'

'If I take my phone into school, I promise I won't use it,' he said, pushing the boundaries.

'Jackson, I think we both know that is asking rather a lot of you at present.' I smiled and saw the faintest glimmer of a smile on his face too. 'Good boy. Would you like a kiss goodbye?'

'No! Ugh!' He pulled a face.

'I'll see you later then.' I watched him go along the pavement and into the junior-school playground. He was a good kid at heart and I really liked him. He had personality, but a lot of problems that needed addressing quickly.

I took the girls into the infant-school playground and waited until it was time for them to go in. I said goodbye and that I'd see them at the end of school, then returned to my car, my resolution of the previous evening to phone Frankie and Joy still intact.

It was just gone nine o'clock, but I needed to make the calls now or they would hang over me. Taking a deep breath, I phoned Frankie first. It went through to her voicemail, so I left a message. 'It's Cathy Glass. Jackson,

Grace and Jenna are in school. If you want me to take them to contact this afternoon, I'll need to know what time. Also, after much thought, I will need the children moved by the end of today. I can't give Jackson the attention he needs with the girls here too. I am happy to keep Jackson, but he will need to see a therapist as a matter of urgency. Thank you.'

As I ended the call I felt hot and clammy and my heart was racing, but at least I'd said what I had to. Steeling myself, I now phoned Joy. She answered straight away and I told her what I'd just told Frankie.

'I agree with you,' she said. I was relieved. 'You took the girls as an emergency for one night and now it's stretched to three. It's not fair on Jackson, his sisters or the rest of your family. To be honest, I'm not sure a single carer is supposed to be fostering four children. The exception was made for one night because it was an emergency. I'll speak to Frankie and the placement team and get back to you.'

'Thank you, Joy. The children have contact tonight – can you find out what time they have to be there, please?'

'Yes, of course. Leave it with me.'

As the call ended I felt exonerated. I had acted in the best interests of us all and Joy was backing me.

I now continued to the supermarket. With seven of us to feed we were going through a lot of food. An hour later, as I was transferring the bags from the trolley into the boot of the car, my mobile rang. It was Joy.

'I've spoken to Frankie. She's sorry she hasn't been in touch. Contact is from four o'clock to five-thirty today. She'd like you to take and collect them. I said you would.

'Yes, of course.'

'The placement team have found a carer who should be able to take all three children on Friday,' Joy continued. 'Frankie is asking if you can keep them until then?'

'All right. So the day after tomorrow?'

'Yes. Also, can you take them to the police station tomorrow at eleven o'clock for their interviews. Frankie will meet you there.'

'Yes. I'll let their school know they won't be in tomorrow.'

'Thank you. As Jackson is leaving I didn't ask about therapy, but Frankie did say she's making a referral for him and also for family therapy,' Joy said. 'Kayla is now accepting that Jerry could have abused Connor and is obviously in pieces.'

'I can imagine, the poor woman.'

We said goodbye and I finished unloading the trolley into the boot of my car. Now I knew the children would be going to their new home on Friday, the interim seemed manageable. I would have happily kept the girls or Jackson, but realistically I couldn't foster all three with Tilly there as well. It was too much. Then, as if to prove the point, Tilly texted: *Just to remind you I have CAMHS straight after school so I'll be late home.*

I'd forgotten with all the worry about Jackson and his sisters, so I was pleased Tilly had remembered and had decided to go after all. I texted back: *Well done. Thanks for reminding me. See you later. Cathy x*

I drove home, where more good news awaited me. As I parked on the drive and got out of the car, the front door burst open and Paula came out, beaming. 'I've been offered the job!' she cried ecstatically. 'They just phoned. I start in two weeks.'

'Fantastic! Well done!' I hugged her. I was so pleased. All those months of applying for jobs had finally paid off. 'I'll unpack the car and you can tell me all about it.'

CHAPTER NINETEEN

ARE WE GOING TO PRISON?

Paula's job offer was for an administrative position in a manufacturing firm only a short bus ride away. It involved general office work and had a modest starting salary, but with the opportunity for promotion. I helped her compose a letter of acceptance and she also emailed the agency she'd been temping for, handing in her notice.

'When the manager offered me the job he said that having the temping and student work on my CV helped,' Paula told me.

'Excellent.' Like many parents, I'd encouraged my children to take on a Saturday job as soon as they were old enough. As well as giving them some extra pocket money, I felt it helped teach them the value of money, and that things we wanted had to be saved for. I'd been really touched when they'd spent some of it on a small gift for me or each other. I can still remember the pride on their faces at being able to buy it with their own money.

Paula and I had lunch together and then she went out to meet a friend who was also struggling to find work – like so many others. I spent an hour on my computer and then left slightly earlier than usual to go to school so I had time to go in to let them know the children wouldn't be attending tomorrow.

The secretary in the junior school made a note of Jackson's absence and said she'd inform Mr Burrows, while the secretary in the infant school asked, 'How are the girls?'

'Coping as best they can,' I replied. I think she was expecting more, but it would be for Frankie to tell the school what they needed to know, as I wouldn't be involved after Friday. Also, the girls might not remain at this school if the new carer lived too far away.

I waited in the infants' playground for the end of school. Grace came out first and then Jenna. Both girls looked very unhappy, their faces a contrast to most of their classmates, who were overjoyed at seeing their parents again and to be going home.

'Grace was upset at lunchtime,' Jenna told me as we walked towards the main gate. 'I looked after her.'

'That was kind of you. What was the matter?'

'She wanted Mummy.'

I looked at Grace walking beside me, the picture of sorrow. If ever a child looked like she needed her mother, it was Grace.

'You're seeing Mummy soon,' I told her gently. Her bottom lip trembled and she let me take her hand.

We only had to wait in the junior-school playground for a few minutes and then the classes started coming out. Jackson was at the front of his. He looked over, saw us, then, putting his head down ran full tilt across the playground and out the gate.

'Stop now!' I called after him.

'Come on, quickly,' I said to the girls, and, holding Grace's hand, we swiftly crossed the playground.

I looked up and down the street for any sign of Jackson. The pavement was full of parents and carers leaving with children. It took me a few moments before I spotted him crouched down by my car further up the road. As we drew nearer I saw he was grinning.

'It's not funny,' I said firmly. 'Do not run off like that again. There's a busy road there, and you could have easily bumped into one of the little children and hurt them.'

So,' he said shrugging dismissively as if he didn't care.

'That's ten minutes off your television time,' I said, and opened the rear car door.

I waited until the children were in with their seatbelts on before I got into the driver's seat and started the car.

'Where are we going?' Grace asked, although I'd already explained what was happening.

'To see your mother,' I replied.

'Where?'

'At the Family Centre.'

'Is that where we went before?' Jenna asked.

'Yes.'

I could understand why they were confused and not retaining information even from a few minutes before. It's a sign of stress, and I knew it wasn't going to be helped by having to move again on Friday.

'Why can't we see Mummy at home?' Jenna asked as I drove.

'Because your social worker, Frankie, thinks it's better if you all see her at the Family Centre for now,' I said.

Which was what I'd told them before when they'd asked the same question.

'Can we go home with Mummy after we've seen her?' Grace asked.

'Not today, love. I will collect you at the end of contact and you will come home with me, like you did on Monday.'

'Will Sonia be there?' Jenna asked.

'I expect so.'

They fell silent as we approached the building. I parked in the small car park to the side. It only held six cars, otherwise visitors parked on the road outside. I opened the rear door and Jackson shot out, ignoring my request to wait. He bolted across the car park and then up the path to the Family Centre, where he continuously pressed the bell. By the time the girls and I arrived, the secretary was peering through the window at Jackson with a mixture of worry and concern.

'Sorry,' I mouthed as we joined him. Then to Jackson I said, 'I told you not to run off. That's another ten minutes off your television time.' I was only docking it in small amounts because experience had shown me that if a child was really testing the boundaries you soon ran out of sanctions.

'Not fussed,' he said, with one of his shrugs.

The door opened and Jackson shot in first. 'Wait there!' I said.

'I know where the room is,' he returned over his shoulder, and was about to run along the corridor.

'The rooms can change so wait there,' I said.

He stopped and I signed us in the visitors' book and then asked the secretary which room contact was in.

'Green Room,' she said.

'Told you!' Jackson shouted and ran down the corridor.

'That's another ten minutes of television time lost,' I called impotently.

As we turned the corner we saw Jackson disappearing into Green Room. We followed him in. Kayla was there with the contact supervisor, who was sitting at the table. Jackson hugged his mother. She looked taken aback. The girls went over for a cuddle and she wrapped her arms around them. Having brought the children, it was time for me to go.

'Have a nice time. I'll come back at five-thirty.' I said and left, closing the door behind me.

Kayla had looked pale and drawn, I thought, even more than she had on Monday. It would take time before she started to come to terms with what was happening, if she ever did. As I returned along the corridor, the door to the waiting room opened and Sonia came out. 'I thought I heard Jackson,' she said.

'Yes, they're all in Green Room now.'

'Are you waiting for them?' she asked.

'No, I've got some things to do at home.'

She looked disappointed, as though she would have liked company. 'It's a lot for you,' she said. 'Is that why they're moving the children?'

'Partly.'

'Kayla and I saw a solicitor this morning, and he thinks the children should be returned home – the girls at least.'

I nodded but didn't comment. There's a big difference between a solicitor thinking a child should be returned home and it actually happening. The social services would need to be satisfied first that Kayla could look after them and they weren't in any danger.

'I'll see you later then,' I said politely, and left.

I had just enough time to go home and start preparing dinner for later before I had to leave again to return to the Family Centre. Sonia was already waiting outside the door of Green Room, having spent the whole time in the waiting room. At exactly 5.30 she opened the door and we went in. As soon as the girls saw me they began to cry, while Jackson stood sombrely to one side.

'Time to go,' I said gently. But parting was no easier for them now than it had been on Monday. Sonia stepped in and again helped me get the children to the car. I thanked her and she returned to the centre to collect Kayla.

Jackson and Jenna were quiet and withdrawn as I drove home, while Grace rubbed her eyes and sniffed.

'You'll see Mummy again on Friday,' I said, which seemed to make matters worse.

'I want Mummy now,' Grace sobbed.

'I know, love.'

Jenna put her arm around her and comforted her until she stopped crying.

Paula and Tilly were home just ahead of us and looked after the girls while I finished making dinner. A few minutes passed and Jackson, who'd been in the living room checking his phone as he always did when he returned home, came to find me. He was carrying a school book and, to my astonishment, he sat at the table, opened it and, frowning studiously, began to read.

'Good boy,' I said, wondering what had brought this on.

'Mr Burrows said I could do well if I worked harder,' he said, his gaze still concentrated on his book. 'He said when he was going through a bad time as a kid he could forget his problems by reading a good book.'

'Very true,' I said and left him to it as I continued with dinner.

He sat at the table poring over the book for a good five minutes, then asked, 'Have I earned my television back now?'

'Cute,' I smiled. 'You can watch some television after dinner, yes,' I said. 'It won't be long.'

The girls ate a little and Jackson, as always, had a good appetite. Adrian wasn't with us as he was having dinner with Kirsty. Once we'd finished, Paula stayed with the children in the living room and Tilly helped me clear the table. I finally had the chance to ask her how her appointment at CAMHS had gone. I never asked for details. What took place between her and the therapist was private. But I always made a general enquiry as to whether it had gone well.

'I guess,' she said, never overenthusiastic. 'We talked a bit about me living with Gran and Mum.'

'I see,' I said, surprised. That had been the care plan at one time, but it had been changed after her relationship with her mother had broken down.

'We talked about me forgiving Mum,' she added.

'Good.'

'I phoned Gran on the way home and spoke to Mum too.'

'Excellent. How did that go?'

'All right. I'm seeing them again on Saturday. Gran wants me to stay the weekend of my birthday.' Tilly's fifteenth birthday was in a little over two weeks and I'd asked her to think about what she wanted to do by way of a celebration.

'What did you say?' I asked.

'That I'd think about it. Would you mind if I went there?'

'No, of course not, love, if that's what you want. But discuss it with your social worker first.'

She nodded. 'You know you asked me what I wanted for a present?'

'Yes.'

'If it's OK, I'd like money so I can go shopping with Abby.'

'Sure.' I'd put something with it, a surprise, and I knew the rest of my family would buy her a gift too. 'And what about us celebrating? If you go to your gran's, we could do something on the Friday – your actual birthday.'

'It's half-term that week so there's no school. I was thinking of seeing my friends on my birthday,' she admitted, a little embarrassed.

'That's all right. Whatever you want to do. It's your birthday. How about you and your friends come back here for a piece of birthday cake?'

'Yes, great. Thanks. I'll text them now.'

'And then do your school work,' I reminded her, sounding like a broken record.

* * *

I didn't tell Jackson, Jenna and Grace that evening that they had a police interview the next day, as I thought it would play on their minds and keep them awake. I waited until the following morning. As I laid out their casual clothes rather than their school uniforms, I explained we were going to see a nice police officer who wanted to ask them a few questions about home. I said Frankie would be there and there would be toys to play with in a room that looked like a living room.

'Are we going to prison?' Grace asked.

'No, love. The police station. The room has a sofa and chairs and dolls and colouring books.' I'd taken other children to this interview suite. There was also a camera, situated unobtrusively, to record the interview. They would be told about that at the time.

'What do we have to say?' Jenna asked, worried.

'You just answer the police officer's questions.'

'Will they make me cry?' Grace asked.

'No, love, they won't make you cry.' Although, given that Grace was close to tears most of the time, it was quite possible she would cry. In which case, the interview would be terminated. The officers are specially trained in techniques for questioning young children and would never continue an interview if the child was in distress.

'Will Mummy be there?' Jenna asked.

'No. She has already spoken to the police.' Which I knew from Sonia.

I left the girls to get dressed while I went to Jackson's room, where I explained to him what was happening. He looked more worried than his sisters. 'Will I have to tell them about what Jerry did to Connor?' he asked anxiously.

'Yes.' I then spent some time reassuring him. He was worried he would be blamed for not telling about Jerry sooner. I said repeatedly that no one would blame him. He seemed a bit happier when I'd finished.

'Do I have to go to school after?' he asked, finally getting out of bed.

'No. You've got the afternoon off.'

'Can we go to the park?'

'Yes.'

'And have a McDonald's?'

'If that's what you and your sisters want.'

'Cool,' he said. 'Sometimes you're not so bad.'

I smiled. 'Good.' Although I knew that before the treat of McDonald's and the park, he was going to have to talk candidly about Jerry sexually abusing his brother, which would be devastating.

CHAPTER TWENTY

A WORRYING WAIT

I parked as close as I could to the police station and, telling the children again there was nothing to worry about, we walked along the pavement to the side entrance, where I pressed the security buzzer. The interview suite had a separate entrance to the main police station. We were admitted by a kindly officer who showed us into the interview room – the one I'd described to the children.

'I'll tell DS Forbes you're here,' he said. 'She's with the social worker.'

'Thank you.'

'Do you want a drink and a biscuit?' he asked the children.

Grace stared at him, while Jackson and Jenna shook their heads glumly.

'No, thanks,' I said. 'I've got some packets of juice in my bag if they're thirsty.'

'Okey-dokey. Won't be long,' he said cheerily, and left the room.

'I want to go home,' Grace said, rubbing her eyes.

I drew her to the sofa and put my arm around her. 'There's nothing to worry about.'

'I want Mummy,' she said, and rubbed her eyes some more.

Jenna sat on the other side of Grace and took her hand, while Jackson knelt on the floor by the toy boxes and began taking out their contents. He didn't give them much time – they were for younger children. I think it was just a distraction to keep him occupied. Once he'd taken the toys from the box, he began returning them one at a time. I picked up a picture book from the table and opened it on Grace's lap so both she and Jenna could see. A few minutes passed and then the door opened and Frankie came in with the officer we'd previously seen and another one, both in plain clothes.

'Hi, I'm Cary Forbes,' the second officer said brightly and sat on one of the children's chairs so she was at their height. The other officer waited to one side. It was clear Cary wanted to talk to all three children, so I called Jackson over. He perched on the arm of the sofa.

'So, you've got the day off school,' she began, trying to put them at ease. 'Aren't you lucky? You must be Jackson,' she said to him. He managed a small nod. 'Now let me guess, you're Jenna and you're Grace.'

'Yes,' Jenna said, while Grace stared at the officer suspiciously.

Cary then chatted generally to them about school, their friends and what they liked to do in their spare time, preparing them for talking about the real reason they were here. Gradually Jackson and Jenna began to relax and answered her questions, while Grace remained quiet and watchful. 'There's nothing to worry about,' Cary said, seeing her expression. She then talked them through what was going to happen.

'Frankie will be in the room with me, but Alf, my colleague here, will be behind that window over there working the camera. We all looked to where she pointed, but all you could see was a reflection of the room in the glass. I'd been shown the room behind the glass once and it was very small, with just enough space for the equipment and the officer working it.

'Because there are three of you, I'm going to see you one at a time,' she said. 'And the other two will wait with Cathy in another room. I've put some crayons and paper in there.' Then, looking at Frankie, she said. 'I think Grace should go first, don't you?'

'Yes,' Frankie agreed.

I thought that was sensible, to avoid her having to wait and worry, although whether she'd be able to answer any questions was doubtful.

'I'll show you where to go,' Cary said to me, standing.

'See you in a few minutes,' I said to Grace and kissed the top of her head. As I stood, Frankie took my place on the sofa next to Grace.

Cary then showed Jackson, Jenna and me along the corridor and into the room where we were to wait. It just contained a table and four chairs. There was a packet of felt-tip pens, a stack of plain paper and some plastic cups containing water on the table.

'If you need the toilet, it's down the corridor on the left,' Cary said as she left.

We sat at the table. I hadn't been in this room before and compared to the interview suite we'd just come from it wasn't comfortable or child-friendly. But I appreciated why they needed to interview each child separately, otherwise it could be said they'd colluded, which would render their evidence inadmissible. Before, I'd only brought one child and had stayed with them during the interview.

'What shall we draw?' I asked Jackson and Jenna positively, picking up the packet of felt-tips.

They both shrugged.

'Can you play noughts and crosses?' I asked.

'Of course, that's easy,' Jackson said.

'What about you, Jenna?'

She nodded.

'Good.' It was a simple game that didn't require much concentration but would keep us occupied while we waited. As only two people could play at a time, I said, 'You two go first and the winner plays me. Best out of five games.'

We helped ourselves to a felt-tip pen each and Jackson drew the boxes.

'I'm going to be the cross,' he said to Jenna. 'And you can be the nought.'

The first game didn't last long, Jackson beat Jenna easily. I didn't think she was concentrating, as Jackson made a strategic error that could have cost him the game if Jenna had noticed. He won the second game too, but Jenna won the third. Then the door opened and Frankie came in, holding Grace's hand. Grace was rubbing her eyes. Only fifteen minutes had passed since we'd left her. Frankie looked at me and shook her head, so I guessed Grace hadn't been able to answer any questions or had been too upset, so they'd terminated the interview.

'Come on, love, would you like a drink?' I asked and brought her to the table. She looked hot – her cheeks were flushed – so I gave her one of the cups of water.

'Jenna, your turn,' Frankie said to her.

Jenna dutifully stood and left the room with Frankie.

'I can't play with her,' Jackson said, referring to Grace. 'She's too young.'

'We'll play together,' I said.

I waited until Grace had finished her drink and then let her choose a felt-tip pen. Jackson drew some more boxes and put a cross in one. I suggested to Grace where to put her nought. Jackson won a game and then Grace and I won the next two, and so it continued. Half an hour later, when the door opened, the table was littered with sheets of paper covered in noughts and crosses, and the score was four to Jackson and six to Grace and me.

'Ready?' Frankie asked Jackson as Jenna came over and sat quietly beside me at the table.

Jackson stood and left with Frankie. He was more relaxed now, having been involved in the game.

'Everything all right?' I asked Jenna after they'd gone.

Grace was looking at her too.

'Cary asked me about Mum and Jerry,' Jenna said. 'I told them he was a friend who helped her, but I didn't like him. Was that the right thing to say?'

'If that's how you felt, yes.' She'd said similar to me before.

'Cary asked why I didn't like him.' I was now expecting Jenna to say it was because he'd given her a babyish doll, which was what she'd said to me. But what she did say turned me cold. 'He used to try to come into the toilet when I was in there. And when he used the toilet he never closed the door. One day, when we ran out of milk and Mum had to go to the shop, he stayed with us and he wanted to give Grace a bath to save Mum the trouble. Grace didn't want a bath and Mum came back in time.'

'You told Cary this?' I checked, horrified.

'Yes.'

'Good.'

'She asked me if Jerry ever touched me in a way that made me feel uncomfortable – you know, my private parts. I said he hadn't, but I didn't like it when he was in the house. When I went upstairs he always needed to use the toilet so he could come too. I'm sure he left the door open on purpose because he wanted me to see him wee. Cary asked if I told Mum about this, but I didn't. Mum was so upset when Dad died and then Connor, I didn't want to make it worse.'

'I understand.'

Neither Jackson nor Connor had told their mother of the abuse either, because they hadn't wanted to upset her. But in trying to protect her they had carried the burden of their suffering alone. It must have been crippling and had almost certainly played a part in Connor's suicide, and Jackson's subsequent behaviour. Not telling had also left the family wide open to more abuse – and possibly other families too.

'I don't like Jerry,' Grace said, having heard what Jenna said.

'Did you tell Cary?' I asked her.

She shook her head. 'Jerry gave me sweets.'

'I know, love.' How confusing for her – a five-year-old.

I would be noting all this in my log and letting Frankie know. I'd looked after children in the past who had disclosed more abuse after a police interview. It was as though the flood gates opened and memories they'd previously suppressed or hadn't been able to talk about came pouring out. Conversely, some children never wanted to talk about it again and found that the police interview gave them some closure.

I now asked Jenna if she wanted to continue to play noughts and crosses or do something else. I had some puzzle books in my bag.

'I'm going to make Mummy a card telling her I love her,' she said and took a sheet of paper from the pile.

'I want to make Mummy a card,' Grace said, copying her sister.

Jenna took another sheet of paper and folded them in half so they opened like cards and gave one to Grace. Sharing the felt-tip pens, they began drawing flowers on the front and colouring them in, then they both wrote inside. I helped Grace with the spelling. *I love and miss you loads*, Jenna wrote, and Grace wanted to write the same. Having made a card each for their mother, Jenna now said, 'I'm going to make a card for Daddy and Connor and leave it on their graves.'

My eyes immediately filled and it was a moment before I could speak. 'That's a lovely idea,' I said. 'Do you visit their graves often?'

'We go with Mummy on Sundays, but Jackson won't come,' Jenna replied.

I made a mental note to pass this on to Frankie so their new carer would know. If the girls were visiting their father's and brother's graves regularly then they should continue to do so if possible.

The girls made two more cards each, for their father and brother, taking time to colour in the hearts they drew on the front. Grace copied Jenna's drawing. *We still love you*, Jenna wrote inside hers, while Grace put, *Love from Gracey*. Which she could spell.

'Did Daddy call you Gracey?' I asked. I'd only heard Jackson do so.

She paused for a moment and looked thoughtful. 'I can't remember if Daddy did, but Connor used to.'

'She was only little when Daddy died,' Jenna said.

I nodded. The girls now began doing other drawings while my thoughts went to Jackson, and I wondered how he was getting on. Hopefully he was able to answer Cary's questions and speak openly about what had happened.

Jackson was gone for over an hour. When he returned he was tense and angry. He didn't say anything, but his anger showed in his face and body language.

'All done, thank you, you can go now,' Cary said to us. 'I'll see you out.'

I quickly cleared up the table as the girls picked up their drawings and cards.

'I'll phone you with the arrangements for tomorrow,' Frankie said to me.

'They'll be in school,' I said. 'Shall I take them to contact?'

'Yes, please.'

Cary saw us out while Frankie remained behind, presumably to discuss the children's interviews with Cary and her colleague. As we walked to the car I could see that Jackson was still tense. I asked him if he was all right and he shrugged me off. I waited on the pavement as all three children climbed into the car and fastened their seatbelts, then I got into the driver's seat.

I was about to start the car when Jackson's anger exploded.

'I fucking hate Jerry!' he shouted at the top of his voice, and kicked the back of the seat. He beat his head with his fists, letting out a long moan that was heart-wrenching.

I quickly got out and opened his car door. 'Take a deep breath and calm down,' I said, placing my hand lightly on his shoulder. 'Breathe, Jackson,' I said as his face clenched in anger. A passer-by looked over.

Grace was holding on to Jenna and looking scared.

'You'll be all right,' I told him. 'Take deep breaths. Slowly in and out. In and out.'

I eased his hands away from his head while gently talking to him, encouraging him to calm down and breathe slowly. Gradually he recovered.

'You're all right now,' I told him.

He looked at me, slightly surprised and bewildered, as if he'd come out of a trance, which in a way he had. Real anger can result in loss of control, which is why it's so frightening and a very unsafe place to be.

I waited with the car door open until I was sure Jackson had recovered, then I asked him, 'Do you still want to go to McDonald's and the park or would you rather go home?'

'I want to go to McDonald's,' he said.

'OK, love.'

As I drove I glanced in the rear-view mirror to make sure he was all right. Grace was no longer keeping close up to Jenna and was holding Jackson's hand, which was nice. A few minutes later I heard Jenna ask him, 'What did you tell Cary?'

'About Jerry,' Jackson said quietly. 'But I don't want to talk about it any more.'

'That's fine,' I said, meeting his gaze in the mirror. 'But if you do want to, you know you can talk to me or Frankie. Now, what does everyone want to eat?'

'Chicken nuggets Happy Meal,' Jenna said.

'Same for me,' Grace said. 'You get a toy in it.'

'Jackson?' I asked.

'A Big Mac meal with a strawberry milkshake.'

So I thought he was feeling a bit better, for the time being at least.

CHAPTER TWENTY-ONE

THE REASON I FOSTER

The children were tired on Thursday night from the emotional turmoil of the police interview and spending the afternoon in the park, so they all had an early night. Grace slept through, but it didn't stop me listening out for her in case she woke upset. The following morning Jackson was quiet but less tense. As I dropped the children off at school, I reminded them that they would be seeing their mother later, not that they needed reminding. Grace had talked about nothing else since getting up.

Having seen them in, I went straight home. Frankie had said she would be in touch about the arrangements for moving the children today so I assumed it would take place after contact. Would they need dinner first? I wondered. I didn't know. It wasn't ideal, moving them late in the day, and I hoped they didn't have far to travel to their new carer.

The first thing I did when I arrived home was pack away the sofa bed in the front room, as it was no longer needed. I was looking forward to sleeping in my own bed again and changed the sheets in readiness, then put the washing machine on.

Returning upstairs, I looked in on Paula who was relaxing on her bed reading a novel, making the most of her leisure time before she started full-time permanent work. We talked for a while and then I went into my room again and packed the girls' belongings into the bags Sonia had brought, making sure I included their soft toys. They would be comforting the girls tonight when they spent their first night in a strange bed.

Leaving the bags in my room, I went into Jackson's bedroom. He had many more belongings than the girls, but I hesitated packing and decided to wait for confirmation from Frankie that he would be going with the girls. Instead, I folded his clothes into neat piles so they could easily be packed when I got the call. It was now lunchtime and Paula and I decided to have soup and a sandwich, which we had at the table in our kitchen-diner, chatting as we ate.

Having been a foster carer for many years, I'd learnt to expect the unexpected and be prepared for most eventualities. But what happened next took me unawares. Paula and I finished lunch and were about to leave the table when my mobile rang from the kitchen where I'd left it. As Paula cleared away the plates, I took the call. It was Frankie.

'How were the children yesterday after the police interviews?' she asked. 'Sorry I couldn't speak for long after.'

I told her how they'd been, including what the girls had said to me about Jerry and Jackson's angry outburst in the car. 'He really does need an urgent referral to CAMHS,' I added.

'It's in hand,' she said. 'I am right in assuming you can keep Jackson?'

'Yes.'

'Good. The girls are going home after contact this afternoon, but Jackson will remain with you for the time being.'

'Oh, I see. Well, that is good news.'

Paula looked over and I mouthed – the girls are going home. She gave me the thumbs-up sign.

'Jackson gave a good interview yesterday,' Frankie continued. 'So did Jenna, although she didn't have much to say. We're satisfied that Kayla didn't play a part in Jerry's abuse and didn't know anything about it. Jenna and Jackson both said they hadn't confided in her as they didn't want to upset her.'

'Yes, they told me that,' I said.

'Cary and I have spoken to Kayla and she accepts that what Jackson is saying is true – that Jerry abused Connor, and he also behaved inappropriately around Jenna and Grace. She's very remorseful and understands she must not allow him anywhere near her children ever again. We are satisfied she won't. She has agreed that it is in Jackson's best interests to stay in care for the time being. Sonia will move in with the family for a while to help Kayla, and we will monitor the situation. Can you take the girls' belongings with you to contact? But please don't tell the children what is happening. I shall be there at the start of contact to explain it to them.'

'All right. What's happening about Jackson seeing his mother and sisters in the future?'

'He will have contact at the family home on Mondays, Wednesdays and Fridays for an hour and phone contact on the other nights and at the weekend.'

'So he's not going there on Saturdays?'

'Not for now. We'll review it in a few weeks. I'll see you at four o'clock then.'

Of course I was pleased Jenna and Grace were going home, but I was worried how Jackson would take the news. I guessed Frankie was too, which was why she wanted to explain what was happening to them herself. Clearly the girls returning home and leaving Jackson in care had the potential to make him feel even more rejected, upset and angry. I felt for him. He could view it that having found the courage to talk about Jerry's abuse – to me and the police – he was being punished by having to stay in care. Although Frankie hadn't said so, I guessed Kayla had agreed to him remaining in care as she knew she'd struggle to look after him as she had before. And of course, for my part, with the girls gone I would have the time to give him the help and support he needed, but would he see it that way? I doubted it.

I hid my concerns as I collected the children from school and drove to the Family Centre. I asked them, as I usually did, if they'd had a good day and Jenna said she had, while Grace kept saying, 'We're going to see Mummy now.'

'That's right, love,' I replied, as I had before.

'Grace, you keep saying the same thing,' Jenna said, though not unkindly.

'That's because she's happy,' I said, and I thought how happy she was going to be when she learnt she was going home.

Jackson, on the other hand, was still looking pensive.

'Are you all right, love?' I asked him, glancing in the rear-view mirror.

'No,' he said. 'I lost playtime and it wasn't even my fault.'

'Oh dear, that doesn't sound right. What happened?'

'Nothing,' he retorted, meaning I don't want to talk to you about it.

I guessed I'd find out in time, but I wasn't surprised there'd been another altercation after the unsettling day he'd had at the police station.

'Frankie will be at contact for a while,' I said as I parked the car outside the Family Centre. I always liked to let the children know when someone else was going to be there if I was told in advance.

I opened the rear car door on the pavement side to let everyone out, reminding them to wait for me. Jackson not only waited but hung back, and then followed the girls and me up the path. I thought his reluctance to see his mother again might be because of what he'd told the police. He'd tried so hard to protect her in the past and now it was all out in the open.

'If you have any questions or concerns, ask Frankie,' I reminded him as we went into the centre.

He waited beside me and the girls as I signed the visitors' book. I could see that Sonia, Kayla and Frankie had signed in fifteen minutes before, so I assumed Frankie had wanted to speak to them first before the children arrived. The secretary said we were in Green Room again, but Jackson didn't rush on this time; he walked with us to the door. It was open and Kayla, Sonia and Frankie looked over as we entered. The girls ran to their mother and wrapped their arms around her as they usually did, while Jackson waited hesitantly at my side. Kayla hugged the girls and then looked at him. Her eyes glistened. 'Come here, son,' she said. 'Give me a hug. You poor boy, keeping all that to yourself.'

It was what he needed to hear. He ran over and, encircling his mother in his arms, cuddled her for all he was worth. Frankie looked at me and smiled.

'I'll go then,' I said, 'and come back at five-thirty.'

'Yes, please.'

'Have a good time,' I said as I left.

Sonia followed me out. 'Have you brought the girls' bags with you?' she asked.

'They're in the car. I'll let you have them now if you like.'

We went outside to my car and as I opened the boot Sonia said curtly, 'It's right and proper the girls are going home.'

'Yes, it is,' I agreed.

'They should never have been taken in the first place. I told the police Kayla had no idea what Jerry was like. It nearly killed her when they went. It'll be ages before she recovers.'

I could sympathize, but Sonia was wrong when she said the girls shouldn't have been removed from home. Jerry had been a regular visitor to their house and the girls had been in danger. Indeed, I thought Kayla was lucky they were being returned so soon. Another social worker might have been more cautious and applied to the court for an extension of the Emergency Protection Order to keep them in care longer. But I didn't tell Sonia that. Having handed her the bags, I said I'd see her at the end of contact and left.

As I drove, my thoughts went to Jackson and his family and the moving scene that would be unfolding in Green

Room. I could picture the joy on the girls' faces as Frankie told them they were going home with their mother. But what about Jackson? How was he feeling? Confused, upset, angry? Probably a mixture of all three. I hoped Frankie was explaining the reasons for the decision. Then selfishly I thought of tomorrow evening and Kirsty's parents, who were coming for supper. I hoped Jackson behaved himself then. I'd fostered children before (as many carers have) who'd tried to sabotage a family gathering through very challenging behaviour. As he'd tried to do when he'd first met Lucy and family. It wasn't the child's fault, but it was nerve-racking and embarrassing for all and could ruin a social occasion. Some carers stop socializing completely while fostering, as they find it too stressful. I preferred to try to teach the child how to behave in company and include them when possible.

I had enough time to return home and do a few jobs before it was time to collect Jackson. I approached the Family Centre with some trepidation, wondering how he had taken the news. It could have a bearing on his behaviour over the weekend. As I signed in the visitors' book, I saw that Frankie had left half an hour before, which I took as a good sign. If Jackson had really kicked off, I assumed she would have stayed and probably phoned me.

The door was open to Green Room and it was quiet inside. Sonia was already there and everyone had their coats on, ready to leave. The girls were smiling unreservedly and Jackson – while not smiling – wasn't looking cross.

'We're allowed to live with Mummy again!' Jenna cried as soon as she saw me.

'I know. That's great!'

'I'm not coming home with you,' Grace said, and poked out her tongue.

'Don't be rude,' Sonia said.

I smiled and then looked at Jackson. 'Are you OK?'

He nodded, but I couldn't tell what he was thinking.

'Say goodbye to your brother,' Kayla told the girls. 'We'll phone him tomorrow.'

'Bye,' Jenna said, and gave him a hug, which he returned.

'Bye, Gracey,' Jackson said, and hugged her.

'Have a good evening,' I said, and Jackson and I left. He fell into step beside me. 'Did Frankie explain the reasons for the decision?' I asked him.

'I guess. Mum says we'll all be together before long, just as soon as she is up to it.'

'Good.'

I thought he was taking it very well and Frankie and Kayla must have done a good job of explaining things to him. However, I soon found out they'd had help, although they probably weren't aware of it.

'You know I said Mr Burrows talks to me sometimes at break?' Jackson said as I started the car.

'Yes.'

'Last time, he told me when he was in care he couldn't live with his brothers and sisters. There were five of them and they had to be split between carers. He didn't see some of them again until he was an adult.'

'That is sad,' I said. 'The social services try to place brothers and sisters together, but it's not always possible, especially if it's a large group, and sometimes contact is lost.'

'Mr Burrows said I was lucky to see my sisters regularly and I think he's right,' Jackson concluded positively.

Well done, Mr Burrows, I thought – not for the first time. A few kind words and a shared experience were proving invaluable. The next time I saw Mr Burrows I'd thank him and make sure he knew how much his talks with Jackson were helping.

On Friday evening, once we'd had dinner, I telephoned my mother and said I'd visit her on Sunday, then I spent some time helping Jackson with his homework. Mr Burrows' influence was having a good effect here too, as Jackson wanted to do well for him. I wondered if Mr Burrows had ever thought of fostering, as I felt sure he'd be good at it.

Once Jackson was asleep in bed, I left Paula and Adrian in charge and went to the supermarket to shop for the weekend, including what I needed for supper tomorrow. Thank goodness for late-night openings! Tilly came with me. She volunteered, having got 'bored with doing homework'. She promised to do some more when we got back, although I had doubts about how much she'd actually done as she seemed to have spent most of the evening on her phone. Pity Mr Burrows' influence didn't extend to her, I thought.

As well as enjoying Tilly's company while shopping it gave me the chance to talk to her one to one, first about her school work and then other things, including her gran and mother. She wanted to buy a bunch of flowers to give to her gran when she saw her tomorrow.

'I'd better get one for Mum too,' she added, picking up a second bunch.

As we walked up and down the aisles and I spent time choosing the items I needed for supper tomorrow, I explained why I wanted to create a good impression and give the evening a sense of occasion. I'd met Kirsty's parents briefly before, but tomorrow we'd be planning our children's wedding – an important and exciting occasion. Tilly said she was less angry with her mother and admitted therapy was helping. At the checkout she wanted to pay for her flowers separately, so I checked my goods through first. Once outside, she presented me with a bunch of flowers. I hadn't seen her pick up a third bunch. I was touched and delighted.

'Thank you, love. They're beautiful. That is kind.' I kissed her cheek.

'You've been good to me,' she said, which made me tear up.

Tilly was very different now to the angry young person who, fearing for her safety, had fled home and put herself into foster care. It's moments like this that reaffirm why I foster.

That night, it was strange being in my own bed again after nearly a week of sleeping downstairs on the sofa bed. I lay awake thinking about Jenna and Grace, also back in their own beds. I was pleased Sonia was staying with the family. Although she could be brusque at times, she was strong, level-headed and generous. I felt she should be able to give Kayla the support she needed to get her life back on track.

It had been a very hectic and emotional week for me and the diary was already filling up for next week. But before that we had the weekend. Whether it would be a relaxing one or not would depend largely on Jackson and what frame of mind he was in.

CHAPTER TWENTY-TWO

LIFE AFTER

On Saturday morning I took Jackson to our local leisure centre, where he spent two hours jumping on a trampoline, which he enjoyed and I hoped would also burn off some of his energy. As I drove home, I explained Kirsty's parents were coming for supper and we would all be on our best behaviour, but I didn't make too much of it. That afternoon Adrian played football in the garden with Jackson. Later Kayla and the girls phoned and then Jackson watched some television. So far so good, I thought.

Kirsty arrived with her parents, Andrea and Malcolm, as arranged at seven o'clock and they expressed surprise that the house wasn't in chaos.

'The girls went home yesterday,' Adrian explained. 'So we just have Jackson and Tilly with us.'

'I'm sure that's plenty,' Andrea said.

She'd arrived with a folder tucked under her arm, which she said contained literature about wedding venues. Adrian suggested we looked at it after we'd eaten. He poured drinks and sat in the living room with them, talking, while I put the finishing touches to supper. Tilly returned from seeing her gran and mother and joined us for dinner, as did Jackson, although he'd already eaten at six o'clock when he'd complained of being hungry. There were eight of us at the table in the front room, which we used for special occasions. Jackson behaved pretty well until it was time for him to go to bed. We'd finished eating – main course and pudding – and were now going to discuss the wedding. Tilly and Paula went to their rooms and I took Jackson up while Adrian made coffee.

I waited until Jackson was in bed and I joined Adrian, Kirsty and her parents at the table, which was now littered with literature about wedding venues, cars, dresses and so forth. A few moments later Jackson was out of bed, running around the landing and making silly noises. I excused myself and went upstairs and saw him back into bed. I was then up and down the stairs like a yo-yo trying to settle him, apologizing each time I left the table. I felt bad that I wasn't giving the wedding arrangements my full attention. When Jackson began repeatedly flushing the toilet Paula came out of her room, told him to stop and took him back to his room. But then a few minutes later he was running up and down the stairs. At that point Tilly must have had enough, for she came out of her room and shouted, 'Shut up! Stop behaving like an arsehole! How old are you?' Andrea looked shocked.

While not included in the foster carer's handbook, it worked. Jackson went quietly to his room and we heard his bedroom door close. Five minutes later, when I checked on him, he was in bed asleep. I returned to the table and poured myself a glass of wine, and we continued in peace – not only planning the wedding, but the engagement party that Andrea was throwing next month. Kirsty and Adrian also gave us an update on how the purchase of their flat was going. The surveyors report was in and a copy of it had been sent to their solicitor, who was going through it and also checking the draft contract. While it would be some weeks before the flat was theirs, it was progressing well.

We finally said goodnight just before midnight. As Andrea left, she asked anxiously, 'You won't be bringing that boy with you to the engagement party, will you?'

'No. I'll make some other arrangement for him.' I appreciated why she was worried, having seen him being disruptive, but I leapt to his defence, just as I did all my children. 'He's a good kid at heart,' I said. 'But he's had a lot to deal with. He's doing OK.' Telling the children off in private was one thing, but I was fiercely loyal to them in public.

Andrea looked sceptical, but after they'd gone Adrian thanked me for all the trouble I'd gone to and said everyone had had a good time and he was proud of me. I was relieved. Adrian appreciated that as a family who fostered, challenging behaviour was something we had to deal with and then move on from. Most of our visitors understood this too, and if they didn't, we tended to see less of them.

Having got through Saturday evening, I was looking forward to seeing Mum on Sunday and having a more relaxing day. Jackson had been well behaved when he'd seen her before, so I wasn't envisaging too many problems. Paula came with me. Tilly was going to come but then changed her mind and said she was going to see her gran instead. I told her to phone her first to make sure it was all right, as she'd been there yesterday as well. I'd also inform her social worker. Contact with younger children is more rigorously controlled and monitored, but older children often make their own arrangements – ideally with their social worker's and foster carer's knowledge and consent, but not always. There were no safeguarding issues that would have stopped Tilly from going, so I agreed and suggested she took her school work with her to finish there. She said she would and left at the same time we did. Adrian was seeing Kirsty and would visit Mum another day.

Sunday didn't turn into the relaxing day I'd hoped for. Jackson's behaviour deteriorated almost from the minute we walked in. Mum had lots of games ready, which she kept for the children we fostered, but he refused to even look at them, preferring to run up and down the stairs making silly loud noises, much as he'd done the evening before. Mum got some felt-tip pens out and for a moment we thought he'd settled, then I discovered he'd been drawing on the table he was sitting at, and it wouldn't wash off. He knew that was wrong, so I stopped some television time and tried to enlist his help in the kitchen. It was raining hard outside and cold, so I was making us lunch at Mum's rather than going out. Jackson didn't want to help and began running around the living room, eventually knocking over and smashing a glass vase Mum had had for years. She made light of it, but I felt bad and was annoyed with him. I stopped some more television time.

He sat at the table to eat, but as soon as he'd finished, he was off again. I found him upstairs going through the drawers in Mum's bedroom, which he knew wasn't allowed. I could see his behaviour was stressing Mum, so I took him out for a walk. Just the two of us, in the rain. It gave Paula and Mum the chance to spend time together without being continually interrupted and gave me the chance to talk to Jackson. I couldn't get out of him what was bothering him – I'm not even sure he knew. We walked for over an hour in the rain and included a brief visit to the park. Unsurprisingly, we were the only ones there. He seemed calmer as we returned.

'Did you have a good walk?' Mum asked him.

He ignored her, and going into the hall began running up and down the stairs again and in and out of the bedrooms.

'He'll hurt himself,' Mum said, worried.

I kept trying to find him different things to do, but he wasn't interested. I could see Mum and Paula were growing more and more anxious, so I packed away all the toys and we left earlier than planned. Mum was very forgiving and made excuses for him, but once in the car I gave him a good telling-off.

'You know how to behave at my mother's. You told me you and Connor used to help the elderly couple next door. I'm sure you didn't behave like that with them. Not good, Jackson. My poor mother.' I looked at him in the rear-view mirror. 'Whatever got into you?'

He was quiet for a moment and then said, 'I want to go home and be with my family.'

'Is that what all this is about?'

He nodded glumly. 'It's not fair. Jenna and Grace have gone home, but I can't.'

'Yes, and Frankie explained why when she saw you on Friday,' I said.

'I know, but I still want to go home.'

'I understand that, but you don't take out your frustration on my mother, please. It's not fair.' As protective as I was of my children, I was also protective of my dear mum.

'I'm sorry,' he murmured.

'Good. Don't ever do that again.'

Once home, I stopped his television as I'd told him I would. Although I appreciated why he'd behaved as he had, allowing his bad behaviour wouldn't do him any good long term. Society expects us to conform to certain behavioural norms, which includes having respect and consideration for others.

I phoned my mother to make sure she was all right and she said she was, just a bit tired, and she was pleased to see us all. But that's Mum, loving and forgiving as always.

On Monday morning, when I took Jackson to school, we caught sight of Sonia taking Jenna and Grace into the infant school, but they didn't see us. Jackson was disappointed and I reminded him he would be seeing her and his sisters after school. I hadn't heard anything to the contrary, so I assumed I was collecting him at the end of school and taking him home, unlike previously when she'd taken him. He wanted to wait by himself in the playground, as he had been doing recently, so I said goodbye on the pavement and watched him go in. I didn't immediately drive off, though; I waited in my car until the start of school. Jackson was unsettled again and if he had plans to run away now was a good opportunity, but he went in with his class.

At eleven o'clock I was at Tilly's school for her PEP (Personal Education Plan) meeting. Tilly, Miss Jenkins – the deputy head (with responsibility for looked-after children) – and I were arranged around a desk in a small office that wasn't being used. Tilly's social worker, Isa, wouldn't be coming, but she'd receive a copy of the PEP. I'd met Miss Jenkins many times before in connection with Tilly. She was aware of her background and had been very supportive when Tilly had gone through a really bad time. Her manner was sometimes stern and when she spoke it was often forthright, but I knew she always had her students' best interests at heart. I'd learnt to read her expressions in my dealings with her over the last year, so it was no surprise when, having read out Tilly's recent test results, she said, 'Tilly could do so much better if she applied herself.'

I agreed.

She then gave Tilly (another) lecture on the importance of working hard this year in preparation for her exams next year.

'You are more settled now,' she said. 'You have somewhere quiet to work at home. And I know Cathy encourages you to study, so no excuses, please.'

'No, Miss,' Tilly agreed.

'Your future is in your hands, Tilly.'

'Yes, Miss.'

As well as basic details about the student, the PEP sets out their achievements, aims and goals. It now included a timetable of study that Miss Jenkins had drawn up. It wasn't so different to the advice I'd been giving Tilly: study for an hour before dinner and two hours after with a break halfway through, and study three subjects a night, an hour each. I hoped that, as it was now coming from the deputy head, it might carry more weight. Ultimately, though, it was up to Tilly.

At the end of the meeting Miss Jenkins asked Tilly how her mother and grandmother were.

'Gran is keeping well and my mum is doing OK,' Tilly replied. 'I'm seeing them again at weekends.'

'That's good. I am sure they will want you to do well too.'

'Yes, Miss. I want to be a police officer.'

'Excellent. Then you'll need to work hard.'

Tilly had decided on this career when she'd seen first-hand what a good job they did when she'd reported abuse.

After the meeting Tilly returned to her lessons and I went home.

Two hours later it was time to collect Jackson from school and take him home for contact. We didn't see Jenna and Grace as their school came out ten minutes earlier. Jackson had spoken to them and his mother briefly on the phone on Saturday and Sunday, but like many children he'd found it awkward making conversation on the phone. He was now looking forward to seeing them again. The last time had been on Friday at the Family Centre.

Sonia opened their front door and said they'd only just got in from school, so it appeared she'd collected the girls as well as taking them that morning.

'How is Kayla?' I asked as Jackson shot in.

'A bit weepy. I've made an appointment for her to see a doctor tomorrow. How has Jackson been?'

'All right at school as far as I know, but up and down over the weekend.' It was reasonable for her to know, as she was helping the family.

'Same with Jenna and Grace,' she said. 'Especially Grace – she kept crying for no reason, which upset Kayla. I think the whole family is traumatized.'

A loud noise – which sounded as though something had broken – came from inside the house, together with a shout from Jenna.

'I'd better go,' Sonia said quickly. 'I'll see you later.'

When I returned an hour later to collect Jackson, Kayla came to the door. She looked tired and drawn but gave Jackson a big hug as she said goodbye. We began down their front garden path when he suddenly stopped and turned. 'Mum, will you be at school tomorrow to pick up Jenna and Grace?' he asked her.

'I'm not sure, love. I'll see how I feel. Otherwise Sonia will be there.'

He pulled a face. 'But I want you to come.'

'We'll see,' she said, and appeared close to tears again.

'That's fine,' I said, and steered Jackson to the car. Their front door closed.

'I know you like seeing your mum at school,' I said as we got in. 'But she needs Sonia's help at present. I'm sure she'll start going again as soon as she feels up to it.'

I thought Kayla was probably worried that when she returned to the school playground some of the other parents would know that Jenna, Grace and Jackson had been in care. Emotionally fragile at present, it would be another hurdle for her to cross.

The consultation forms for Jackson's review, scheduled for Friday, had arrived. After dinner I explained to him what the review was – a meeting about him to make sure everything was being done as it should to help him while he was in care. He also had his PEP tomorrow. It wasn't a coincidence, as the Personal Education Plan should be completed before the review. It forms part of the care plan and is checked and updated at the review. He didn't have to fill in any forms at home in advance for the PEP, just for the review. As usual with a child's review there were two sets of forms: one for me as his carer to fill in, and one for Jackson. I'd completed mine that afternoon. It was a standard form that asked about the child's health, education, hobbies and interests, contact with family and friends, how the child's cultural and religious needs were being met, and their general wellbeing. The child's was a smaller, more child-appropriate booklet designed to elicit the child's views and feelings on being in care. As a foster carer I had a duty to encourage Jackson to fill it in.

'I'll do it myself,' Jackson said.

I gave him a pen and, telling him to let me know if he needed any help, I left him at the table to get on with it.

The questions included whether the child knew why they were in care. What they liked about living with their foster carer and what they didn't like. What was going well for them and what wasn't. Some questions included emojis with various expressions, ranging from happy to sad to angry, and the child had to tick the one that best applied to them.

Once Jackson had finished, he slid the completed form into the envelope provided and sealed it.

'I'll post it tomorrow,' I said.

I wondered what he'd written. I might be told at the review if Jackson wanted his form read out. Otherwise it would be seen by his social worker and the reviewing officer, then put on file.

At bedtime, when I went into Jackson's room to say goodnight, he said, 'You know that review form I filled in?'

'Yes, love.'

'Do you want to know what I wrote?'

'Only if you want to tell me.'

'It was nothing bad about you.'

'Good.'

'The last question said, "Is there anything you want to add?" I put I wanted to go home and it to be like it was before my dad and Connor died.'

My heart clenched. 'Oh love, if only that was possible. I'm afraid the review can't do that.'

'I know that really,' he said, sitting on the bed. 'Not even God can bring back dead people. But I want my mummy back. The old one I had before Dad got ill and Jerry hurt Connor and made him die. My mummy was happy then. We all were.'

With tears welling in my eyes, I sat beside him.

'I think you will have your mummy back one day,' I said. 'But she, like you and your sisters, has been through some really upsetting times. You've all had to deal with so much. Now it's out in the open and you are all talking about it, I think it will start to get better.'

'I hope so. My dad would be so angry if he knew what Jerry did to Connor.'

'Yes, he would,' I said. 'I'm angry and your mother is too, as well as being upset. But we all show our feelings in different ways. I think that's why you get naughty sometimes – to let out your feelings.'

'Do you think Connor is with Dad now?' he asked. I swallowed hard. 'Mum says they are together in heaven, watching over us.'

It was a moment before I could reply.

'Yes, love. I'm sure she's right.'

'Mum says she can feel them near her sometimes, in a nice way. When I'm in my bedroom I sometimes think Connor is still there. We used to share a bedroom. I think I can still hear him. It's not scary. Just nice.'

'I can understand that. I feel the same way about my father. He died a few years ago, and although I can't see him, I have moments when I can feel his warmth as if he's giving me a big hug, like he used to.'

'My dad used to hug me,' Jackson said. 'I miss his hugs.' He rested his head on my shoulder and I put my arm around him. I held him close as his tears began to fall.

'It's all right,' I said.

As I sat there comforting Jackson, I suddenly had the feeling that my father was close by, loving and protective as he had been in life. If there is a heaven then I'm sure my dad is up there now with Jackson's father and brother, and all the other good people who have left this world. It was a warm, reassuring feeling and a sign that there is probably more to life and death than any of us realizes.

CHAPTER TWENTY-THREE

TWO CHILDREN, DIFFERENT NEEDS

Jackson's PEP meeting on Tuesday afternoon went well. Mrs Bryant, the SENCO, who was also providing Jackson with pastoral support, was there, as was Jackson. Sometimes the parents and the social worker are present at these meetings, but not always. They would receive a copy of the PEP.

Mrs Bryant led the meeting, having previously spoken to Mr Burrows for feedback on Jackson's progress, and also to Ms Gainsborough, the deputy head. Overall Jackson was a good average academically. His maths and science were better than his literacy skills, but he had managed to keep up, despite all the turmoil and time off school. This was good news and Mrs Bryant and I praised him. What wasn't so good was his behaviour, which often involved angry outbursts, so some of his goals and targets for the PEP were around him managing this.

'You know you can see me or Mr Burrows at any time,' Mrs Bryant reminded Jackson as she closed the meeting.'

* * *

We didn't see Jenna and Grace leave school that after-noon, but the following morning Sonia was looking out for me. She was waiting with the girls on the pavement. As Jackson and I got out of the car, they came over.

'What's all this about a review?' she asked me, puzzled. 'Is it something Kayla should go to?'

'Yes, it is. All children in care have regular reviews,' I said. 'It will give Kayla the chance to voice her views and ask any questions she might have. Frankie will be there, so will someone from the school. I come and usually my supervising social worker does too. All children in care have a care plan and the review will make sure it's up to date and meeting the child's need. Jackson will be there for at least some of it.'

'I see,' Sonia said. 'Frankie told Kayla, but she didn't seem to understand. I'll pass it on.'

'It's important Kayla goes if she can,' I emphasized.

'I'll tell her. Frankie said I can go too.'

'Can we come too?' Grace asked.

'No, it's just for me because I'm in care,' Jackson replied, with a touch of pride.

We said goodbye and Sonia took Jenna and Grace into the infant-school playground, while I watched Jackson go to the junior school. Mr Burrows was on playground duty again and gave a little wave with a thumbs-up sign, signalling he'd keep an eye on Jackson. I waited for a short while in the car, watching Jackson, then returned home to collect Paula. We'd arranged to go shopping and have lunch out. She wanted to buy new office clothes for when she started work.

The day is short when you're doing a school run, and all too soon I was dropping Paula off back at home. It was 3 p.m. and I went straight to school to collect Jackson and take him home for the hour's contact. Sonia had collected the girls and was in just ahead of us. I wished them a nice time and returned to my car. Before I had a chance to start the engine, my mobile rang and Nancy's landline number showed on the display. Tilly's grandmother hadn't been in touch for a while, so I wondered what she now wanted.

'Hello, how are you, Nancy?' I asked.

'Very well, and yourself?' She sounded upbeat.

'Good, thanks.'

'I've just spoken to Tilly's social worker, so has Heather.' Heather was Nancy's daughter – Tilly's mother. She was living at Nancy's bungalow permanently, having fled an abusive partner.

'I've told Isa Tilly is coming here for her birthday weekend, and I said from then on she should stay every weekend with a view to coming here permanently by Christmas.'

'I see. What did Isa say?'

'That she didn't think Tilly was ready for that yet. But I don't think she is doing enough to encourage Tilly. Can you talk to her?'

'I could, but I'm not sure it will do any good. Tilly's nearly fifteen and she knows her own mind. It's what she feels comfortable with. To be honest, if you put her under pressure, it could have the opposite effect.'

Nancy fell silent. Like Jackson, Tilly was in care voluntarily – accommodated, as it's sometimes known – so in theory she could move home at any time, although if she did and the social services had concerns, they could apply for a court order to bring her back into care.

'What's Tilly been saying to you then?' Nancy asked.

'That she loves you both and is happy to stay for her birthday weekend but isn't sure about any more yet.'

'So when will she be sure?' Nancy asked. 'This is dragging on. She should be at home with her family.' Which Nancy had said before. She was a kind and caring woman who loved and cherished her family, but she couldn't see why Tilly needed to take this at her own pace, instead of just putting the past behind her and moving on – as Nancy had had to do with her own daughter many times before.

'Tilly has important exams next year,' I said. 'She needs to be able to concentrate, so we should keep her life as calm as possible. I was at a meeting at her school on Monday to revise her Personal Education Plan and she still has a lot of catching up to do.'

'She can study here. She has her own bedroom,' Nancy said.

'I know. But it has to be up to her and her social worker.'

'When is her next review?' Nancy asked.

'Not until next year. Now Tilly is in care long term, the reviews are less frequent.' I knew straight away it was the wrong thing to say.

'Long term!' Nancy exclaimed. 'Oh no she's not. Her mother and I want her home by Christmas. I'm going to speak to that social worker again. No offence to you.'

'None taken.'

With an abrupt goodbye, Nancy ended the call. I liked Nancy. She was fiercely protective of her family, but the problem was she believed she knew what was best for

Tilly. Tilly had her own views. If she did agree to live with her grandmother and mother permanently, she needed to feel it was right. When you foster you don't just look after the child; you're usually working with the family as well.

It wasn't worth me going home now, so I moved my car around the corner to wait for Jackson's contact to end. I texted Paula and asked her to start dinner, and then I phoned Lucy for a chat. At five o'clock I returned to collect Jackson. Kayla answered the door.

'I'm going to Jackson's review on Friday,' she said. 'Sonia said I should. Thanks for explaining what it's about.'

'You're welcome. I'll see you there, if I don't see you at school before.'

She called Jackson, but he didn't come. She called him again and then Sonia brought him to the door. He said goodbye, but once in the car he was quiet and with-drawn.

'Are you OK?' I asked as I drove.

He nodded but remained looking thoughtful and downhearted.

'Jackson, I've known you for long enough to spot the signs when something is wrong. What is it?'

I saw him frown, then gaze through his side window. 'Mum's going to the cemetery on Sunday and she wants me to go.'

'I see. Do you want to go?'

'Maybe. I'm not sure.' I remembered Jenna telling me that she and Grace went with their mother to visit the graves of their father and brother, but Jackson would never go.

'It's up to you, love. I'm sure your mother will understand if you don't want to go.'

'Do you go to your dad's grave?' he asked.

'Yes, sometimes. Not as much as my mother does. It's nice. Peaceful. There is nothing to be afraid of.'

'Mum takes flowers.'

'Yes, we do.'

'I haven't told her yes or no.'

'If you don't feel ready to go this Sunday then maybe another time?'

'Maybe,' he said.

Fostering two children from different families meant that I was continually switching between one set of issues, needs, wants and problems and another. We hadn't been home long before Tilly arrived, having attended her weekly therapy session at CAMHS.

'I am not pleased,' she announced, coming into the kitchen. 'Has my gran phoned you?'

'Yes, a little while ago,' I replied.

'What did she say?'

'That she wanted you there permanently.'

'And what did you say?'

'That I didn't think you were ready yet.'

'She phoned Isa and my school! She spoke to Miss Jenkins. She's got no right telling everyone my business.'

This was rather an overstatement, as her social worker and the deputy head already knew her family situation, but I appreciated why she might feel that way.

'It won't go any further, and you know your gran,' I said. 'She means well, but she's struggling to understand why you can't just move in.'

'I phoned her from the bus and told her off. I was cross when I found out she'd called my school, but I feel bad now.'

'Give her a ring and clear the air, or I can,' I said.

'Isa is going to talk to her first.'

'OK. Leave it for now then.'

But later that evening Tilly came downstairs. She'd been in her room 'studying'. 'Gran's just phoned and apologized,' she said, clearly relieved. 'I said I was sorry too.'

'Good. I'm pleased you've made it up. Your gran is a wonderful lady, but no one gets it right all the time. The most loving families have disagreements. It's knowing how to put it right that counts. It shows strength of character to apologize. Well done, both of you.'

Nancy and Tilly were similar in many ways: both strong characters, more so than Tilly's mother, Heather, who relied on them quite heavily.

Jackson's review was at 11 a.m. on Friday at his school. Joy, my supervising social worker, was there, having phoned on Thursday for an update on Jackson. Also present was the Independent Reviewing Officer (IRO), who would chair and minute the meeting. The IRO is usually a qualified social worker with extra training, and acts impartially, independent of the social services. Frankie was there, so was Mrs Bryant, Kayla and Sonia. Mr Burrows arrived last with Jackson, who met us all with a small, self-conscious nod. He sat at the table between his mother and Mr Burrows. Joy was on my left. We'd taken over the staff room for the meeting as it wouldn't be needed until lunchtime.

'Welcome, Jackson,' the IRO said, opening the meeting. 'This is your first review. It's usual to start these meetings by introducing ourselves. Would you like to go first and give us your full name?'

'Jackson Heartman,' he said in a small voice.

'Thank you, and you are ten?' the IRO confirmed as he typed.

'Yes.'

'This meeting is about you, to make sure that we are doing what we should to help you while you are in care. Perhaps you'd like to start by telling us how things are going for you?'

'OK,' Jackson said, with an embarrassed shrug. I think we ask a lot of our looked-after children, expecting them to come to these quite formal meetings and speak in front of a group of adults.

'Thank you for completing your review form,' the IRO said. 'I see you wrote "Private" on it. So you don't want me to read it out?'

'No.'

'That's fine. But it's all right if your social worker reads it later?'

'Yes.'

I saw Kayla and Sonia exchange a glance, clearly wondering what Jackson had written. Perhaps Frankie would let them know, I wasn't sure.

'So, Jackson, are you healthy?' the IRO asked. It was a standard question.

'Yes.'

'And enjoying school?'

'Sometimes.'

'What are your favourite subjects?'

'Maths and science.'

'And what do you like doing when you're not in school, in your spare time?'

'Watching television and playing games on my phone,' Jackson replied.

'Do you play any sports or attend after-school activities?'

He shook his head.

'Would you like to?' the IRO asked.

'I wanted to go to football, but it's on a Friday and I see my mother then,' Jackson said. I'd encountered this problem before – most contact for school-aged children is directly after school when extra-curricular activities are held.

'I'm starting an athletic club after the half-term holiday on a Thursday,' Mr Burrows said to Jackson. 'You may like to come along and see if you like that?'

Jackson's face lit up. I'm sure he would have signed up to anything Mr Burrows – his hero – was organizing.

'Yes, please,' he replied.

'Fantastic,' I said, and made a note as the IRO typed.

'How is school going generally?' the IRO now asked him. It was another standard question.

'OK,' Jackson said.

'And friends? Do you see them outside of school?'

Jackson shook his head and the IRO glanced at me.

'I have asked him if there is anyone he would like to invite home or meet up with, but he hasn't wanted to yet.'

'What about Mitchel?' Kayla asked. 'He's in your class and you used to play with him.'

'Not fussed,' Jackson said with a shrug.

'No one is going to force you to see your friends. But if you change your mind, tell your foster carer,' the IRO said.

Jackson nodded.

'Do you understand why you are in care?' the IRO asked. Another question usually asked at reviews.

'To help my mum,' he replied.

'How is it going at your foster carer's home?'

'OK.'

'Any complaints?'

'No.'

'Excellent.'

'Is there anything else you would like to tell this review?'

'No.'

'Any questions?'

Jackson thought for a moment and then said, 'When is Jerry going to prison?'

'The sooner, the better,' Sonia said.

I could tell from the IRO's expression that he didn't know who Jerry was. He would have been sent information on Jackson prior to the review, but I wasn't sure if details like this would have been included.

'Jerry is being investigated for allegedly abusing Jackson's brother,' Frankie told him. Then to Jackson she said, 'The police are still investigating. I'll tell you when there is any news.'

'Does that answer your question?' the IRO asked Jackson.

He nodded.

'Anything else you would like to say?'

'I hope he goes to prison for a long time.'

'So do we all,' Sonia said.

CHAPTER TWENTY-FOUR

BECAUSE I DIDN'T TELL ...

I was asked to speak next and I kept it positive. I said Jackson was healthy, eating and sleeping well, and he'd had no accidents or illnesses, which the IRO would want to know. I said I was helping him manage his behaviour at home and he was going to school each day and doing his homework. I briefly covered the week when his sisters had stayed and continued to say that Jackson came with us on family outings, including visiting my elderly mother. I said he'd had a lot to cope with and had been referred to CAMHS, and I hoped the appointment would come through soon. I finished by asking if Jackson could have a photograph of his family for his bedroom. I'd mentioned it before to Kayla and Frankie, but I thought it had been forgotten.

'Why does he need a photograph?' Sonia asked. 'He sees them.'

'It's a nice connection with home for when he doesn't see them,' I said. 'I usually frame the photo and stand it on a shelf in the child's bedroom, so they can see it last thing at night and first thing in the morning.'

'I'll find one,' Kayla said.

'Thank you. Also, Jackson mentioned you'd asked him about going to the cemetery on Sunday.' I'd made a note to cover this. 'He's not sure yet.'

'Jackson knows he doesn't have to come,' Kayla said. I nodded.

'How would he get there and back?' Frankie asked.

'I could take him,' I said.

'Is this every Sunday?' Frankie asked Kayla.

'The girls and I go most Sundays, but he doesn't have to come each time. Once would be nice.'

'When Jackson wants to go will you organize it with Kayla?' Frankie asked me.

'Yes, of course.'

The IRO then asked me if I could keep Jackson for as long as was necessary, and I confirmed I could. The question is usually asked. He then asked Frankie to give her report.

Frankie said Jackson was settling in well with me and he was accommodated under a Section 20. She said his sisters had been the subject of an Emergency Protection Order but had now been returned home, which was also the care plan for Jackson. Frankie didn't really say anything I didn't already know. When a child is present at their review our reports and comments tend to be qualified, as clearly there are some issues that can't be discussed in front of the child, especially if they are young. Frankie concluded by confirming Jackson was attending school regularly now, and she'd made an urgent referral to CAMHS that she would chase up.

The IRO thanked her and asked Mrs Bryant to go next. She went through Jackson's PEP that we'd drawn up on Tuesday, then praised him for his hard work. She said she was available for pastoral support, but he preferred to talk to his form teacher, Mr Burrows. She ended by telling Jackson, 'Well done.' He managed a small smile.

'Let's hear from Mr Burrows next,' the IRO said.

'As Mrs Bryant has covered Jackson's progress in his school work I won't go over that again,' Mr Burrows said. 'So I'll say a few words about Jackson the person. He's a good kid who has experienced huge sadness and turmoil in his young life, having lost his father and brother, and then having to go into foster care. Jackson is astute, intelligent and sensitive. He feels things deeply, although he doesn't always know how to express his feelings. Sometimes he needs a cooling-off period and we have a quiet room here where he knows he can go if necessary. He's a lively member of the class and a pleasure to teach. Overall, I think he is coping remarkably well. I admire his strength of character and resolve. Keep up the progress you have made,' he said, turning to Jackson.

I could see him grow with pride from the praise of his wonderful teacher.

'Thank you,' the IRO said, and was about to move on when I interrupted.

'Can I just add a few words?' I asked.

'Yes, go ahead.' Everyone looked at me.

'Mr Burrows is being very modest and has understated the amount of help he has given Jackson. He may not be aware of it, but making time to talk to and listen to Jackson is having a huge impact, as is sharing his insights and experiences. I'd like to take this opportunity to thank him for all he is doing for Jackson and for going that extra mile. If ever he thinks of fostering, I am sure he would be great.'

'Well said,' Joy added, while Mr Burrows smiled self-consciously.

I purposely hadn't included that he'd told Jackson about his experiences of being in care because I wasn't sure how many people knew that.

The IRO thanked me, minuted what I'd said and then asked Kayla to go next. She hesitated and I wondered if she was up to it.

'She's got something to say,' Sonia said. Then to Kayla, 'Go on, say what you want to.'

I saw Jackson looking at her carefully, wondering, as I was, what she was going to say.

'I'd like to thank Cathy for looking after my son,' Kayla began in a small, faltering voice. 'But I hope she won't have to for much longer.' Then, looking at Jackson, she said, 'I'm sorry I've let you down. I wasn't there for you when you needed me, but I promise things will get better. From Monday, I shall start taking Jenna and Grace to and from school and bringing you back for contact as I used to. I also want you to start coming home again on Saturdays and staying for the weekend. So we can all be together again before long.'

Jackson stood and, throwing his arms around his mother, kissed her. But I could see the IRO had concerns, as indeed did I. 'Has the weekend contact been agreed?' he asked Frankie.

'Not yet,' she replied, then, clearly not wanting to discuss it in front of Jackson, she said to Kayla, 'Can we talk about this after the meeting?'

'I'm not sure there's anything to talk about,' Sonia said.

'It's all right, I'll see Frankie after,' Kayla said.

'So the care plan remains unchanged?' the IRO confirmed with Frankie.

'Yes, but I will review contact with Kayla after this meeting.'

He nodded and made a note.

Having checked with Kayla that there was nothing else she wanted to say, he asked Joy if she would like to speak.

She looked at those present as she talked and spoke confidently. 'My role is to supervise, support and monitor our foster carers. Cathy is one of our most experienced carers. I visit and phone her regularly, when we discuss the child's needs and progress. She keeps me updated by email too, and I have no doubt she would ask for help if necessary. She is providing an excellent standard of care for Jackson, and I have no worries. I would like to add a special thank you for taking Jackson's sisters at very short notice. Otherwise they would have had to stay with a carer out of the county.'

'Noted,' the IRO said as he typed. 'So, no complaints from anyone?'

The IRO always asks this, and those present either said 'no' or shook their heads. He wound up the meeting by setting the date for the next review and thanked us all for coming.

Mr Burrows waited for Jackson to say goodbye to his mother and then they left with Mrs Bryant.

'I'll see you later,' I said to Kayla and Sonia. They were still seated at the table, waiting to talk to Frankie. I left with Joy.

'Frankie will need to be sure that Kayla can manage Jackson as well as the girls for the whole weekend,' Joy said as we made our way out of the school. 'Otherwise it could set back the family's recovery and do more harm than good.'

I completely agreed.

That afternoon Frankie phoned to say that she and Kayla had decided Jackson would go home for two hours on Saturdays and they would monitor it with a view to him staying for the whole weekend in future.

'He's going to be disappointed,' I said. 'He thought he would be staying for the weekend straight away.'

'I know, it's a pity Kayla gave him that impression at the review. Can you explain to him why we think it's best to take it gradually?'

'I'll try.'

I knew Jackson wouldn't be pleased. He came out of school in good spirits, looking forward to seeing his mother for an hour straight away and then returning the next day for the whole weekend.

I waited until we were in the car before I broke the news as gently as I could.

'That's not fair! Mum promised!' he thundered and kicked the back of the seat. I hadn't started the car yet, so I turned to face him.

'She wants you home as soon as possible, but we all think it would be better if you began slowly, going home for two hours on a Saturday first.'

'I hate you!' he said. Folding his arms across his chest, he glowered at me. I wasn't going to take him to his mother's in this mood.

'Calm down, Jackson. Take a few deep breaths. What

does Mr Burrows tell you to do when you are angry or disappointed?'

'I'm going to be late seeing my mother!' he said, ignoring my question.

'No, you won't. We're usually early. Breathe deeply and think of nice things.'

'No.'

But eventually he did and calmed down enough for me to take him to his mother's.

Sonia answered the front door and Jackson went in, pushing past her without saying hello.

'What's the matter with him?' she asked me.

'He's annoyed he can't stay for the weekend yet.'

'So am I.'

'In my experience it's best to take it gradually,' I said. 'Is Kayla all right?'

'She'll be down in a minute. She had a rest while I fetched the girls from school.'

We said goodbye and when I returned to collect Jackson, Kayla answered the door.

'How's Jackson been?' I asked.

'A bit angry at first but then OK. He's been playing with the girls.'

'Good.'

'I've got the photo you wanted,' she said. 'It's already in a frame. I've wrapped it so it doesn't get broken. Jackson knows he has to look after it.' She took a package measuring about eight inches by six inches, wrapped in newspaper, from the hall table and handed it to me. 'I used to have it in my bedroom, so it will be nice knowing Jackson is looking at it as he goes to sleep.'

'I'll make sure it goes in a safe place,' I said.

She called Jackson and he came reluctantly on the third call. 'See you tomorrow, love,' Kayla said, and kissed his cheek.

'Bye,' he said, still a bit disgruntled at having to leave.

I carried the photo carefully to the car and put it safely on the passenger seat. Only once we were home did I give it to Jackson. I waited as he removed the paper, then showed me the photo. Immediately my eyes filled. I think I'd been expecting a photograph of Kayla and the girls, but this was of the whole family before their father and brother had died. The children looked much younger and it was clear that their father was ill, but they were all together, smiling.

'That's lovely,' I said, my voice catching. 'Who took it?'

'One of the nurses who came to our house to look after Dad.'

'Did he die at home?' I asked, feeling it would do Jackson good to talk about it.

'Yes, during the night. This was taken about two weeks before he died. It's the last one of us all together.'

I stood quietly, the photo in my hand, gazing into the eyes of the man who only had a few short weeks to live, then Connor. Had the abuse happened by then? Quite likely, but of course it was impossible to tell anything was wrong from the photograph. His suffering was buried deep within him. Sorrow and grief rose up within me. That poor boy, I thought. If only he'd been able to tell his mother or another adult. It could have saved his life.

'It's a beautiful photo,' I said, swallowing hard. 'I'll put it safely in your bedroom, shall I?'

'Yes. Can I watch television?' Jackson asked.

'Until dinner is ready.'

He disappeared into the living room while I went upstairs to his room and placed the precious framed photograph on a shelf where he could see if from his bed. I then took a picture of it on my phone just in case it got damaged. I'd looked after children in the past who'd flown into a rage and, wanting to hurt everyone – including themselves – had destroyed precious things, including ripping up family photos. Now, if anything happened to it, I could print a reasonable replica. I stood for a moment, looking at the family, and then went downstairs. I hoped Jackson found comfort in having the photo in his bedroom as his mother had.

By the time we'd finished dinner Jackson was over being annoyed with me and approached his school work with enthusiasm, saying, 'Mr Burrows will be pleased.' I knew all the good comments Jackson had heard at the review were having a positive effect. Children thrive on praise; it breeds confidence and success. He completed his homework in record time, and I praised him again.

On Saturday Tilly went to see her gran and mother. Paula and I dropped Jackson off at his house and then spent the two hours while he was at contact with Lucy, Darren and baby Emma, before returning to collect him. On Sunday I went to see my mother. Everyone came and Jackson behaved himself this time, so I praised him some more.

Contact on Monday, Wednesday and Friday went well, then the schools broke up for a week's half-term holiday. Paula started her new job and Tilly celebrated her birthday – twice. On her actual birthday she went shopping with her friends and then they all came back for cake. Then that weekend she stayed with her gran and mother and they took her out for a meal. This was a huge step for her mother, Heather, who for a long time had been very reluctant to leave the house at all after years of abuse from her partner. Tilly showed me the pictures she'd taken on her phone – of the three of them at the restaurant, and then at home with her blowing out the candles on the cake her gran had made and decorated.

'You had a good time then?' I said.

'Yes, I might stay next weekend too.'

'I'll let Isa know.'

The schools returned the following week and Kayla began taking the girls to and from school. Jackson and I saw her most mornings and some afternoons. She told me that Sonia had moved out and returned home, but she was still on hand to help if necessary. On the days when Jackson had contact he went straight home with his mother after school, which gave me a few extra hours. He also phoned his family on the nights he didn't see them. On Thursdays he began going to the after-school athletics club run by Mr Burrows. He loved it! 'Much better than football,' he said.

I asked Jackson again if he wanted to invite a friend home or meet up with them, but he didn't.

His appointment at CAMHS came through. The first session was for an assessment to see if therapy was suitable, and if so, what form it should take: one-to-one counselling or art therapy in a small group. The letter asked that a parent, carer or guardian be present for the first appointment, so it was decided I would go. I'd attended similar sessions before with children I'd looked after, so had some idea of what to expect, although they differed slightly depending on the psychologist and the reason for the referral. CAMHS treats a wide range of issues, including depression, bipolar, schizophrenia, anxiety, problems with food, self-harm, abuse, violence and anger. There are clinics right across the UK and ours was in a separate wing at our local hospital.

I'd explained to Jackson that morning where we were going and why, and he'd seemed all right with it then. But when I collected him from school at 1.30 – his appointment was at 2 p.m. – he was surly and negative.

'I'm not going to talk to a stranger,' he grumbled as we left the school. 'And you can't make me.'

'No, and neither would I or anyone else try to. Your social worker, mother and I thought it might help you.'

'Well, it won't,' he said, annoyed. 'You don't know me.'

He remained in the same mood all the way to the hospital, so I thought it was going to be a waste of time. I parked and fed the meter, and then he refused to get out of the car.

'OK, we'll go home then,' I said, and began to get into the driver's seat.

'No. I'll go,' he said. He got out, slamming the car door shut. He then walked some way behind me across the car park until we were in the hospital, where he closed the gap. I led the way to the children's mental-health unit and pressed the security buzzer.

'There is nothing to worry about,' I reassured him.

'I'm not worried,' he snapped, but clearly he was.

'Jackson Heartman and his foster carer Cathy Glass,' I said into the grid when asked for our names and the reason for our visit. 'We have an appointment with Dr Griffiths at two o'clock.'

The door opened and the receptionist asked us to take a seat. The waiting area was gaily decorated with bright collages of birds, butterflies and animals on the walls, and plenty of toys and books for all ages of children. We had just sat down when a woman came in and introduced herself as Doctor Rayne Griffiths. 'How are you?' she asked Jackson.

He managed a sour nod.

'A bit unsure,' I said.

'There's nothing to be frightened about,' Dr Griffiths said. 'Let's go through and have a chat.'

We went with her into a consultation room, which was bright and comfortable. It was carpeted, with lemon-painted walls, and had a desk with a computer, bookshelves, filing cabinets, toy boxes and four chairs around a coffee table, where we now sat. Jackson was alert and watchful, despite Dr Griffiths' easy manner. I wasn't hoping for much. If a child of Jackson's age really doesn't want therapy, they won't have it.

Looking at Jackson as she spoke, Dr Griffiths explained her role and what they did at CAMHS, much as I had done. She then confirmed some basic details from a printout – Jackson's date of birth, my contact details and how long he'd been in care.

She asked him how his mother and sisters were.

'OK,' he said.

'And school?'

'OK.'

'What do you like best?'

'Science, maths and athletics,' he said, finally starting to relax a little.

'Your social worker has suggested you come to see me for some counselling sessions,' Dr Griffiths continued. 'She feels they may help you. Do you know why she might think that?'

I saw a brief flash of anger cross Jackson's face, then it gave way to sadness and he said quietly, 'Because a pervert hurt my brother and I didn't tell anyone.'

CHAPTER TWENTY-FIVE

ANOTHER HURDLE OVERCOME

was taken aback by the frankness of Jackson's reply. I think Dr Griffiths was too.

'I see,' she said. 'So, how does that make you feel?'

'Angry and upset,' Jackson admitted, rubbing his arm agitatedly. Then the words came tumbling out. 'And guilty. Very guilty. I feel it's my fault. I should have told someone what Jerry did and saved Connor. I feel angry because Connor told me not to tell anyone and then left me – like Dad did. I'm not angry with Dad, because he couldn't help dying, but Connor could. He had a choice, and he chose to die and that makes me sad and angry.' His lips trembled and a tear slipped down his cheek, which he quickly rubbed away. I was choked up. I hadn't expected it to come pouring out like this. I touched his arm reassuringly as Dr Griffiths passed him the box of tissues.

She gave him a moment to recover and then said, 'I can understand why you feel angry and sad, Jackson. It's very confusing as well as upsetting when a loved one takes their own life. It leaves us with a lot of conflicting thoughts and emotions. When someone dies naturally, of an illness, like your father did, we are sad and miss them, but eventually we are able to think of all the good times we had with them. We learn to accept our loss and live again with our happy memories. When someone we love takes their own life it leaves us with many unanswered questions. We can feel overwhelmed, helpless, frustrated and guilty, although we have no need to feel that way.'

Jackson was concentrating on Dr Griffiths, taking in every word.

'It can be devastating, Jackson,' she continued in the same calm, even voice. 'We keep asking ourselves, was there something we could have done to prevent our loved one from dying? You said Connor had a choice and I expect you have thought, if only I had done this or said that, perhaps I could have changed his mind and he would still be alive now. But when a person is in a dark place, as your brother was, they aren't thinking clearly. It's not your fault, Jackson. You are not to blame. I hope with the help of counselling you will be able to see that, so when you think about your brother it's in a healthy, loving and happy way. OK?'

Jackson nodded and Dr Griffiths looked at me. 'I hadn't really intended to go into this today, but as it came up it seemed sensible. That's enough for now and we'll continue in the next session.'

'Thank you,' I said.

'Jackson,' she said, 'I'm going to write to your social worker and suggest you come to see me every week for an hour. How does that sound?'

'All right.'

'Good. Your social worker has also suggested family therapy – when you would come with your family – but I'd like to see you for a few sessions first. So, you're happy to come here and talk to me as you have been doing today?'

'Yes,' Jackson said.

'Well done.'

I thanked her again and she saw us off the unit. I came away feeling relieved and impressed that Dr Griffiths had managed to get Jackson talking so easily. It was a hopeful start.

He was quiet in the car as I drove – not moody, but deep in thought. I assumed he was thinking about what Dr Griffiths had said, as indeed I was. I asked him a couple of times if he was all right and he said he was or nodded.

Perhaps it was being able to open up a little and have his feelings acknowledged that allowed Jackson to take the next step, for he suddenly said, 'I want to go to the cemetery on Sunday. Can you take me?'

'Yes, of course, love.'

Jackson had contact that afternoon so we went straight to his house, as it wasn't worth returning to school for the last fifteen minutes of lesson time. I parked and we waited in the car until we saw Kayla and the girls coming down the street. As we got out, Grace ran to him with a cry of delight. He picked her up and hugged her.

I said hello to Kayla and the girls, and we went up their garden path. 'How did it go this afternoon?' Kayla asked me as she unlocked her front door. She knew Jackson had had his first appointment at CAMHS.

'Very well. Dr Griffiths is going to offer him an hour a week.'

'That's good.'

She opened the front door and the children disappeared inside.

'Kayla, in the car just now Jackson said he wants to go to the cemetery.'

'Really?' she said, surprised. 'He's always refused before. He can come this Sunday.'

'I'll take him and meet you there. What time are you thinking of going?'

'I'm always there at eleven-thirty,' she said.

I thought this sounded rather exact and I wondered why she didn't suggest they went on Saturday when he was with her anyway. But then she added, 'I go at eleven-thirty on a Sunday because that's the time and day Connor was born.'

'Bless you,' I said, and gave her a hug. 'We'll be there.'

Contact on Friday and Saturday appeared to go well. Sonia was there on Saturday when I dropped Jackson off, having popped in to see if Kayla needed any shopping. She walked with me to my car and said she was pleased that Jackson was going to the cemetery – as was Kayla – as they felt it was part of the healing process. I agreed.

As I couldn't visit my mother that weekend, Lucy and Darren went. On Sunday Jackson and I left the house at eleven o'clock, which allowed us some time to buy flowers on our way to the cemetery.

I'd been to our local cemetery before, although my father wasn't buried there. He was in the village cemetery near where my mother lived. This one was much larger – fifty acres – and more like a country park with tree-lined drives, footpaths and gardens. It serves the whole of the county and has done so for many years. Some of the oldest headstones bear inscriptions dating back to the 1800s. It's very well maintained by gardeners who are busy all year round, cutting grass, raking leaves, trimming shrubs and trees, and generally looking after the last resting place of our loved ones.

Jackson was walking quietly beside me, carrying the flowers we'd brought to put on the graves. I knew his father and brother had been buried, not cremated, and lay next to each other. We followed the path towards the area that was now being used and contained the more recent graves, just as Kayla had explained. These headstones here were unweathered and their flowers fresh, as I'm sure was the loss of their loved one.

'Over there,' Jackson said as Kayla and the girls came into view.

We left the main path and went along a narrower one. Kayla was kneeling, tending to the graves. Jenna was helping her, while Grace was standing to one side and amusing herself by trying to balance on one foot, apparently at ease in the cemetery.

'Hello,' Kayla said when she saw us, and smiled at Jackson. 'Those are nice flowers.'

He looked away awkwardly.

'I hope they're OK,' I said. 'There's not much choice at this time of year.'

'They're beautiful, thank you.'

'My daddy is there,' Grace said, pointing to her father's grave. 'And that's where Connor lives.'

'He doesn't live there,' Jenna said. 'It's just for his body.'

'That's right,' I said. But I thought what a difficult concept death is for a young child. Grace was too young to have many memories of her father, but she would remember her brother.

'It's a lovely spot here,' I said to Kayla as I glanced around. A bench stood a little way off beneath a large oak tree. The autumn sun shone through the trees, casting gently stirring patterns on the graves and flowerbeds.

'I chose it,' Kayla said. 'I find it very comforting being here. I feel close to them, if you know what I mean. Sometimes I pop in during the week for a few minutes if I'm struggling.'

'Yes, it's very tranquil.'

Jackson was standing quietly beside me, still holding the flowers.

'Would you like to help me put those in the vase?' Kayla asked him.

He nodded and handed them to her. I thought I should give them some time alone, so I said I'd go for a little walk and come back presently.

'Thank you, Cathy,' Kayla said.

I returned to the main path and followed it through the cemetery and then partway around the perimeter. It was peaceful and reflective. Others I passed often smiled or said hello, but it was the elderly I felt sorry for. They looked so fragile and alone, probably having lost a lifetime partner. Yet, like my mother, they bore it stoically, with fortitude and resolve. After my father had died my mother told me: 'Your dad wouldn't have wanted me to mope about. We made a promise to each other that whoever was left made the most of their time before we joined each other.' They were fine words and I sensed many of the elderly people I saw that day felt the same way.

After about fifteen minutes I headed back to where Kayla and the children were, taking a different path that took me by the family vaults, some bearing photographs of the deceased. One was of a young boy, probably the same age as Connor.

Kayla was ready to go as I arrived. The flowers were arranged in the memorial vases and the headstones were shining.

'See you next week,' Grace said to the graves as we moved away and gave a little wave.

'They can't hear you,' Jackson said.

'I wouldn't be too sure, love,' Kayla replied. 'I often talk to your dad and brother when I'm here. Like little prayers.'

'That float up to heaven,' Jenna added, I guessed repeating something her mother had said.

'Yes, that's lovely,' I said.

We left the cemetery together, said goodbye at the gates and that we'd see each other at school tomorrow. In the car I asked Jackson if he was glad he'd come.

'Yes, but I don't want to go every week,' he said.

'That's fine. When you want to visit again tell your mother and me and we'll arrange it.'

'They won't mind, will they?' he asked.

'Not at all, your mum said it was up to you when you went.'

'No, I meant Dad and Connor,' he said.

I glanced at him in the rear-view mirror. 'No, love, they won't mind either. They know how much you love and miss them.'

'Like your dad does?'

'Yes.' And I changed the subject, as I couldn't be misty-eyed while driving.

Jackson didn't mention his visit to the cemetery again and I didn't bring it up. I felt he'd overcome a hurdle in being able to go and he would decide when he felt ready to go again – if he ever did. He started therapy after school on Tuesdays, and with contact on four other days, plus Mr Burrows' athletics club on a Thursday, the weeks were very busy. Tilly was still going to therapy on Wednesdays, although she moaned about it sometimes. She also began staying with her gran and mother every weekend. After the success of her birthday weekend, her gran had encouraged her to stay and Tilly had agreed to give it a try. She caught the bus there on Saturday morning – it wasn't far – and returned to us on Sunday afternoon. Isa, her social worker, was aware. I always asked Tilly if her weekend had gone well and she said it had. She seemed to be more accepting and forgiving of her mother now.

October slipped into November. The air chilled and shops began to decorate their windows for Christmas. Adrian and Kirsty's engagement party was on the second Saturday in November and I'd asked another foster carer, who was also a friend, to stay with Jackson. She had a partner who was able to look after their children while she helped me out. Paula and Lucy were my nominated sitters – all foster carers appoint at least one – but they were coming to the engagement party. Tilly had decided not to come but to see her gran and mother as usual. John, Adrian's father, had been invited but said he had a prior engagement. He did, however, send Adrian money for an engagement present.

My mother was coming to the engagement party and staying the weekend with us. Lucy and Darren were bringing Emma. At three months of age, she was easily transported and would hopefully sleep in the travel cot. I let Kirsty's mother Andrea know, though; I thought I should after her comments about not taking Jackson.

I was still smarting a little about that – it was a niggle that irritated me from time to time. My family, close friends and I are very inclusive and make sure children are invited and made to feel welcome at all age-appropriate family gatherings and events. However, I am aware that others don't feel the same way. Adrian had confided that Kirsty's mother hadn't wanted any young children at his and Kirsty's wedding, feeling they would spoil the recording if they were restless during the service. He and Kirsty had insisted the children of those attending should be invited. It was, after all, their wedding, and Kirsty was a teacher and enjoyed being with children. Eventually her mother had capitulated and agreed. Although the wedding wasn't until June the following year, when the matter of the guest list came up I mentioned to Adrian that Tilly and Jackson needed to be included, assuming they were still with us. I'd have to confirm nearer the time. Adrian agreed and then Kirsty phoned me and said, 'Of course they must come. If Tilly and Jackson aren't with you, you are likely to be fostering someone else, so we'll cater for two and then we can add their names later.'

'Wonderful,' I said. 'Thank you.' This confirmed my thoughts about Kirsty – a thoughtful, warm-hearted and kind young lady.

The engagement party was a great success – as it was organized by Andrea, I thought it would be. It was the first time I'd been inside Kirsty's parents' house and it was rather nice. They'd had an extension built on to the living room, which created a massive open space as big as the whole of the downstairs of my house. It was all decked out with balloons, bunting, streamers and engagement cards. The adjoining room, also large, was the kitchen-diner, where a buffet supper had been prepared by caterers. There was a separate table for engagement presents and that's where we left ours.

Malcolm, Kirsty's father, had organized the music with a playlist to suit most tastes – young and adult. But it was soon drowned out by all the talking as our two families socialized – many of us meeting for the first time. Emma wouldn't settle upstairs and Lucy and Darren were in danger of missing the party, so I suggested we brought her down and I'd look after her. I could see they were relieved. They got themselves a drink and finally joined the party while Paula, Mum and I took care of Emma. She didn't mind all the noise and people; she stared around wide-eyed and mesmerized. She soon became the star attraction and others wanted to hold her. Indeed, Kirsty's father spent half an hour walking around showing her off as she grinned and gurgled.

'Looking forward to being a granddad?' I asked him quietly with a smile.

'Too true,' he replied.

Eventually, exhausted, Emma fell asleep on Malcolm's shoulder and he transferred her to Lucy, who took her upstairs and settled her in the travel cot. She and Darren then took turns to check on her.

Adrian had warned me that Kirsty's parents were going to make a speech, so I had a few words prepared too. I said how lovely it was to meet Kirsty's family, and thanked everyone for coming, and then thanked Andrea and Malcolm for the wonderful party – especially Andrea for going to so much trouble. Everyone clapped. I said what a lovely daughter they had and how pleased I was that Adrian was going to marry her and make her part of our family too. I didn't try to make any jokes or reminisce about embarrassing moments from Adrian's past, as Malcolm had done with Kirsty. I'm not good at that sort of thing. I spoke for a few minutes from my heart and then passed to Adrian, who also thanked everyone for coming and for all the gifts. He said he felt very lucky to have found the woman of his dreams – his soul mate, best friend and life-long partner to be.

'Here! Here!' my mother – who'd had a few drinks – called out.

Malcolm then proposed a toast and we raised our glasses. 'To the happy couple – Kirsty and Adrian,' he said.

I saw my mother's eyes glistening, as indeed were mine. 'To the happy couple,' we repeated.

The guests began leaving round eleven-thirty. Paula, Mum and I left at the same time as Lucy and Darren, and we helped them to their car with the travel cot and all the other paraphernalia that accompanies a baby. Emma slept on. We kissed each other goodnight and then went our separate ways. As I drove us home, I experienced that warm glow that comes from having spent an enjoyable evening with family and friends. But I also thought of all those families who would never enjoy anything close to it. The families of many of the children I'd fostered, living in poverty, with abuse and neglect. It was another timely reminder of how lucky I was to have been given the life I had, and why I continued to foster. I couldn't change the past for the children I looked after, but in some small way I might be able to help them towards a better future, as I hoped I was doing with Tilly and Jackson.

CHAPTER TWENTY-SIX

INCIDENT

The afterglow of the engagement party was still with me on Monday morning, but it vanished when Jackson's social worker telephoned. It was one o'clock and I'd just had some lunch. The house was quiet as Adrian and Paula were at work and Tilly and Jackson were at school. Sammy was curled up by the radiator in the living room, not appreciating the steady drizzle outside of a cold November day.

'I've just been talking to the police officer dealing with Jackson's case,' Frankie said. 'I'm afraid it's not good news. The police won't be prosecuting.'

'Oh no!' I gasped, setting down my mug of tea. 'Why not?'

'There just isn't enough evidence to take the case to the Crown Prosecution Service. It's very disappointing, but I can see their point. In order to proceed they need to have a reasonable chance of securing a conviction in court and they don't. All the evidence is third hand – from Jackson – and that's not sufficient.'

'But I thought he gave a good interview,' I said.

'He did, but it's not enough by itself. There's no forensic evidence and they obviously can't interview Connor.

Jackson isn't claiming Jerry abused him, but that Connor told him he'd been abused by him. It's not enough to bring a case.'

'What about the girls?' I asked. 'I know Grace didn't say much, but Jenna did. I understand she told them that Jerry used to follow her upstairs to the toilet, and when he used the toilet he left the door open on purpose so she could see him.'

'It's most probably true, but it isn't enough,' Frankie said. 'Jerry's defence barrister will claim Jenna was making it up or imagining it, which is what Jerry is saying. He told the police he always closed the bathroom door if he was using the toilet, but the girls used to push it open as a joke. There's no lock on their bathroom door. The police checked.'

I sighed. 'What about Kayla? Couldn't she add anything that might help?'

'No. She believes what Jackson and the girls are saying now, but at the time when most of this happened no one told her. Her husband was dying and she was oblivious to everything else. She has admitted she wasn't really coping, trying to nurse him at home as well as looking after four children. She told the police she was in such a state she had no idea what was going on. The children have said they didn't confide in her at the time, so it's not as if she knew and covered it up. She told the police she hadn't had any doubts about Jerry's integrity and had been happy to accept his help. Of course, she regrets it now and blames herself for not being more aware, but that isn't evidence.'

'What a huge let-down,' I sighed. 'After Jackson was brave enough to tell me and then give a statement to the police.'

'I know, and we need to make sure he understands that he did the right thing and we believe him, but there isn't the evidence to prosecute. Of course, if more evidence comes to light, the police will reopen the case, but realistically that's not likely to happen. Most of this is historic. It happened some time ago, and within the house, so there aren't likely to be any other witnesses. I'll see Jackson after school and explain it to him.'

'He has contact tonight,' I reminded her. 'He goes straight home with his mother after school.'

'What time do they get in?'

'About four o'clock.'

'I'll see them there then. I'm going to phone Kayla now and tell her.'

As the call ended, I stayed where I was, staring into space, angry and upset. Not only for Jackson and his family being let down, but because Jerry had got away with it. I believed what Jackson and Jenna had said, and while I appreciated the reasons the police weren't able to prosecute, Jackson and his family would, I imagined, be gutted. So would Sonia, who'd already said she hoped Jerry got a long sentence.

Now, there would be no sentence at all. Yet I supposed some good had come out of it. I'd fostered children before who'd disclosed abuse and been told there was insufficient evidence to proceed, but they'd still found some closure in being able to tell. It's often cathartic and part of the healing process to be able to speak openly about abuse and have it taken seriously and investigated by the police. Also, Jerry's details would stay on the police computer and if anyone in the future reported him, this allegation would show up and hopefully add weight to their claims and the case against him. Even so, it was a huge disappointment and I worried how Jackson would take it.

Mid-afternoon Sonia phoned. She was with Kayla.

'It's disgusting!' she said. 'He's got away with it. Kayla's just told me. I saw Jerry on my way here. Next time, I'll give him what for.'

'Sonia, be careful,' I warned her. 'I know how angry you must all be, but if you approach Jerry he could report you for harassment. At present he is innocent.'

'Innocent? Like hell he is!' she exclaimed. 'We've got the social worker coming here later and I'll tell her what I think.'

'All right, but not in front of the children or they might think they've done wrong in telling.'

'I'm not silly,' Sonia said, now turning her frustration on me. 'That social worker and the police should have done a better job. And also, just to let you know, Kayla is going to tell Frankie that Jackson will be staying here at weekends from now on.'

'OK, fine, whatever they decide. Frankie will let me know.'

I appreciated why Sonia was upset, but taking it out on Frankie wasn't going to help.

When I arrived to collect Jackson from home at five o'clock Kayla answered the front door looking stressed and anxious.

'How are you?' I asked her.

'Fed up with all of this,' she said. 'Perhaps we should move so we can have a fresh start. But I couldn't face all the upheaval and losing my friends. Yet the thought of seeing Jerry again makes me feel physically sick. I'm bound to see him at some point. He lives further down the street. Sonia's already seen him.'

'Yes, I know. I'm sorry. I don't know what to say. Give yourself some time. Perhaps he'll move away.'

'Perhaps,' she sighed dejectedly.

'Let me know if there's anything I can do. Is Sonia still with you?'

'No. She's just left. Frankie is going to phone you about Jackson staying the weekend.'

'OK.'

She called Jackson and as usual it took a few calls before he came. His sisters were upstairs playing.

'He's got revision homework for some tests tomorrow,' Kayla told me as Jackson picked up his school bag and coat.

'I'll help him,' I said. 'See you tomorrow.'

We went down the path. As we got into the car Jackson said, 'Frankie came to see us. I can stay with Mum at the weekend.'

'Good. Happy with that?'

'Yes.'

But I knew that wasn't the real purpose of Frankie's visit. I started the car and drove off. Jackson didn't add anything but sat gazing through his side window, deep in thought, until I parked at my house. 'Jerry isn't going to prison,' he said, and looked at me, waiting for my reaction.

'I know, love. Do you understand why?' I asked, turning to face him.

'Sort of, but Jerry lied,' he said vehemently. 'I told the police the truth. He did hurt Connor.'

'I know, and we believe you, but because it happened some time ago it's difficult to prove.'

'That's what Frankie said. But it's not fair. It was a waste of time me going to the police station.'

'No. You did right in telling the police what you knew.'

'Can I tell Mr Burrows?' Jackson asked.

'Yes, if it helps you.'

'He said he had to talk to the police once about things that had happened.'

'Did he tell you what?'

'No, just that it was right to tell if you or anyone you knew had been hurt.'

Jackson needed a lot of encouragement to start revising for his tests the next day, and even once he'd begun, I could tell his mind wasn't on it. Many of the answers he got wrong and I hoped his school understood why. So often, what is going on in a child's life impacts badly on their education and learning. Just because a child is in care doesn't mean their problems end – as Jackson's case was showing.

Frankie emailed that evening to advise me that Jackson would go home for the weekend and asked me to take him at 11 a.m. on Saturday and collect him at 4 p.m. on Sunday. She said that if it went well, then he would be going home every weekend. I replied to confirm the arrangements. I then telephoned my mother. With both Jackson and Tilly going home at the weekends, I would have more time to spend with her.

* * *

The following morning I took Jackson to school as usual. We saw Kayla briefly taking the girls into their playground. They all seemed a bit brighter after a night's sleep. Grace made a point of telling me, 'Jackson can stay with us this weekend.' As though she'd just scored a point.

'Yes, fantastic,' I said.

She looked at me suspiciously, expecting a different reply. 'Don't you want him to be with you?' she asked.

'Yes, of course, but we can't both have him and he's your brother.'

Kayla smiled. Grace was quite a character and of the three children probably the least affected by her father's and brother's deaths, simply because she'd been so young.

Jackson went into his playground and I waited in the car until the start of school. He'd said last night he was going to tell Mr Burrows about Jerry not being prosecuted. They seemed to have regular chats and I knew Jackson found them very helpful.

When my mobile buzzed at 1 p.m. and I heard Mr Burrows' voice I assumed for a second it was because Jackson had told him of the police's decision, until he said, 'I'm afraid Jackson has been involved in an incident at lunchtime. The deputy head is insisting he goes home for the rest of the afternoon.'

'Oh no, what happened?' I asked, dismayed.

'It's probably best if I explain when I see you. Are you able to collect him now?'

'I'll be there in fifteen minutes.'

'I'll stay with him in the quiet room until you arrive.'

'Thank you.'

My heart was in my mouth as I grabbed my car keys, bag and coat and headed out the door. Whatever had he done? He'd been doing so well, and now this! Was it connected with Jerry not being prosecuted? I thought so. Jackson had kept it together at home yesterday evening but had then given vent to his frustration at school.

I parked outside the school and walked swiftly to the main gate, which was security locked as the children were in the playground for their lunch break. I pressed the buzzer, then had to wait until someone in the office let me in.

'Are you here to collect Jackson?' one boy asked as I crossed the playground.

I nodded and continued to the main door. How quickly the school grapevine worked! I guessed the incident had been witnessed by other students. I pressed the security buzzer and the door opened immediately.

'I've come to collect Jackson,' I said to the secretary. 'I believe he's in the quiet room with Mr Burrows.'

'I'll let him know you're here.'

She went to the rear of the office and picked up the phone, then turned her back as she spoke. I heard her say, 'Jackson's foster carer is here. Yes, I will.' She returned to me. 'Through the double doors and it's the third door on the left.'

I thanked her and went along the corridor, past classrooms that were empty during lunchtime. As I approached the quiet room, the door opened and Mr Burrows stepped out. He drew the door to behind him.

'Can I have a word with you first? Jackson is calmer now, but I don't want to go over it all again in front of him.'

'Yes, what happened?' I asked anxiously. Mr Burrows had lost his usual sanguinity and looked worried.

'Jackson attacked another boy, quite viciously.'

'Oh no.'

'He was provoked, but I've told him he has to learn to control his anger or it will get him into a lot of trouble.'

'Yes. What led to it?'

'A boy in his class said he wasn't allowed to go to his house again because everyone knew his mother had a pervert for a friend. Thankfully Mitchel's mother was understanding, although she's obviously very concerned for her son.'

'The other boy was Mitchel?' I asked, surprised. 'Kayla said he and Jackson were good friends.'

'That's right. They were. We've informed Kayla of the incident and also Jackson's social worker.'

'I am sorry. I will speak to Jackson. Did he tell you the outcome of the police enquiry?'

'Yes, after the incident, when I'd calmed him down. He said he was angry and Mitchel's comment had made him snap. I understand, but as I told him, we can't go through life attacking people because they've said something we don't like. We have to find other ways to express ourselves.'

'Thank you. He's started therapy so hopefully that will help.'

'He told me he was going.'

'And thanks again for all you're doing,' I said. 'I know he takes notice of what you say.'

'He'll come through it,' Mr Burrows said, trying to lighten my mood. 'I did, and I didn't have the support of someone like you.'

'That's kind, but I thought you were in foster care?'

'I was, for many years, with too many moves and not much love. Not all foster carers are like you.'

'That saddens me,' I said. 'Every child needs a loving home.'

'I suppose it was character building,' he said with a resigned shrug. 'Although I wouldn't want that life for my kids. Now, let's see what Jackson has to say for himself.' He opened the door to the quiet room, where Jackson was sitting in silence, head bowed.

CHAPTER TWENTY-SEVEN

CONNOR

Jackson was very remorseful as his teacher and I spoke to him. He said he was sorry he'd hit Mitchel and let Mr Burrows down.

'It's not just me you let down,' Mr Burrows said. 'But your mother, your foster carer and most of all yourself.'

'I know.'

Mr Burrows and I both told Jackson that while Mitchel's comments had been hurtful, there were other ways of dealing with upset. Now Jackson's fury had gone, he agreed and promised it wouldn't happen again.

I thanked Mr Burrows for all he'd done and we left the school as afternoon lessons began.

Once home, Jackson wanted the television on. I said there was no way he was watching television when he'd just been sent home from school for assaulting a boy. I suggested he wrote Mitchel a letter saying he was sorry.

'Can I text him instead?' he asked. 'He's gone home too.'

I thought for a moment and then agreed. 'All right, but I want to see the text first before you send it.'

I sat next to him on the sofa as he tapped in the short message. *Sorry I hurt you. Can we still be friends?*

'That's fine,' I said. 'But don't be surprised if he doesn't reply or doesn't want to be your friend.'

He nodded and sent the message.

'How did the tests go this morning?' I asked him.

'OK, I guess.'

'Have you got any homework to do?'

'Yes.'

'You can do it now then.'

He was about to fetch his school bag when his phone sounded with an incoming text.

'Mitchel's replied,' he said, delighted, and showed me the message. *We can be friends. Sorry I said what I did.*

'Excellent,' I said. 'Now you can both move on.'

'I wonder if Mitchel's mother really did say that about not coming to my house,' Jackson said. 'Shall I ask him?'

'No, love. Just leave it. You've both apologized, so let it go.'

However, when Jackson phoned his mother that evening, she brought up the subject. She said it was likely Mitchel had passed on what his mother had said, as she'd stopped talking to Kayla and was snubbing her at school and in the street. Previously they'd been good friends. And who could blame her? I thought but didn't say. She was only protecting her son. It was just a pity she hadn't found out all the facts before she'd commented.

Both boys were in school the following day. I didn't know who Mitchel was until Kayla pointed him out. He had a nasty red graze and bruising on one cheek. I felt bad, as did Kayla. But as I sat in my car watching Jackson and waiting for the junior school to go in, I saw Mitchel go up to him, and then the two boys began talking. They were friends again, and hopefully one day his mother would show the same generosity of spirit to Kayla.

Fostering two children, running a home, seeing to the needs of my own family and writing meant the time vanished. By the end of November I was Christmas shopping in earnest. As far as I knew there would be ten of us for Christmas dinner. My mother, Paula, me, Lucy, Darren and Emma (although she'd have her own weaning food this year). Adrian and Kirsty were coming for Christmas dinner and then going to Kirsty's parents' in the evening. Lucy and Darren were seeing his parents during the day on Christmas Eve. I was assuming Tilly and Jackson would be with us for Christmas Day at least. It's usual for looked-after children to experience it with their foster carer, even if they have regular contact with their own family. They either see their parents just before or after Christmas – at home if they are allowed to or at the Family Centre if it's supervised contact.

However, the first week in December Isa telephoned and said that Tilly's mother and gran wanted her home for good by Christmas. Nancy had said that the weekends were going well, which I knew, and Tilly wanted to move back there, which I didn't know. Isa said she'd spoken to Tilly, her mother and grandmother at length and was satisfied they'd reached a stage where it could work. I tentatively agreed, although I was surprised Tilly hadn't told me. I hoped she wasn't just bowing to pressure from her gran.

When Tilly arrived home from school I took her to one side and gently told her that her social worker had telephoned and what she'd said. She looked embarrassed.

'It's OK, love. I know your gran has wanted you there for some time. Isa seems to think you feel it's right too now.'

'I think so.'

'You don't sound very sure.'

'Yes, I am. They're my family. Gran needs me and Mum is making a big effort. I've been talking to my counsellor. I can better understand Mum now – the reasons she behaved like she did and why she didn't do anything to help me.'

'So why are you still uncertain?'

She hesitated and then, throwing her arms around me, said, 'I'm going to miss you guys. This has become my home. You are like my second family.'

'Oh, love. We'll miss you too,' I said. 'But we'll still see each other.' We hugged for some time and then I slowly drew back. 'You can visit whenever you want.'

'I know. But it's so lively here compared to Gran's. There's always something going on.'

'You can say that again!' I said with a smile. 'Come on, cheer up. I know it's a big step, but I agree it's the right one. You can all make it work.'

'Do you think so?'

'Yes. You and your mother have come a long way. You've still got to work at your relationship, but you'll get there, I'm sure. And your gran, well, she's a treasure but she's not going to change, so I wouldn't even try.'

'I know,' Tilly said, finally smiling. 'I love her so much.'

'When are you planning to move? Have you discussed that?'

'Gran wants me to go now, but Isa said I should wait until the end of this term – Friday, the twentieth of December.'

'That's makes sense,' I said. 'So we've got you for a few weeks longer.'

'Yes, and I want to see your mother to say goodbye. Can I come with you this weekend?'

'Yes, of course, that would be nice. She'll be pleased to see you again. I'm going on Saturday.'

'I'll tell my gran that I'll just be seeing her on Sunday this weekend then.'

Over dinner, Tilly told Adrian, Paula and Jackson that she was going to live with her gran and mother at the end of term. Adrian and Paula were pleased for her but said they would miss her. Jackson said, 'I'm going home too. Sonia said.'

'Sonia doesn't make the decisions, love,' I pointed out. 'Your mother and your social worker will decide.' Because Jackson, like Tilly, was in care voluntarily under a Section 20, a court order wasn't needed to return them home, just the agreement of all parties involved.

'Sonia's usually right,' Jackson said.

'We'll see. Your social worker will tell me if there is any change.'

I telephoned my mother to let her know that Tilly would be coming with me on Saturday to say goodbye. Mum knew quite a bit about Tilly's home life as Tilly had often confided in her when we visited. Mum was pleased for them and felt, as I did, that it was right.

The rest of the week passed without incident and on Saturday I dropped Jackson off at his house first and then continued to my mother's with Tilly and Paula in the car.

Mum was quiet and seemed rather tired. She said she hadn't slept well. She still wanted to go out for lunch, but she didn't eat much. Usually she had a good appetite. I suggested she should see a doctor for a check-up, but she replied, 'No, love, I'm fine. Don't you worry about me. You've got enough to do. I'm just feeling my age.'

But I made her promise that if she didn't feel better in a day or so she'd make an appointment to see her doctor.

As we prepared to leave, Mum gave Tilly a goodbye card with money in it for a gift. 'If I don't see you again, all the best,' Mum said, her eyes filling.

They hugged goodbye. Tilly was emotional too.

Although we would see Tilly again, it was unlikely Mum would, unless she was staying with us when Tilly visited. Mum had said many goodbyes over the years to children we'd fostered, but as she was getting older she seemed to find it more difficult. I kept it short, and then phoned her once we were home to make sure she was all right. 'Yes, I'm fine, love,' she said. 'I'll have an early night.'

The following day – Sunday – when Tilly left to spend it with her mother and grandmother, she was carrying a massive holdall full of her belongings. 'You are coming back tonight?' I checked.

'Yes, I thought I would take some of my things each time I go to Gran's so there isn't so much at the end.'

'That's fine, love,' I said, kissing her goodbye. 'Have a good day. Say hi to your gran and mother from me.'

I watched her go to catch the bus, weighed down by the bulging bag. There was no real need for her to start taking her belongings – they'd all fit in my car, and she had plenty of clothes and toiletries at her gran's to see her through. But by taking them piecemeal she would be gradually transferring her attachment from the place she currently called home – my house – to her new home: her grandmother's. We do something similar when a child is moved for adoption. At each visit we take a few of their belongings and leave them in their new home. It makes the transition easier.

On Sunday, while we had the chance, Paula and I put up the Christmas decorations. Usually everyone helps, but with Adrian at Kirsty's, Jackson at his mother's for the weekend, Tilly at her gran's for the day and weekday evenings full, I thought we should do it now. We left dressing the tree until everyone was there. Sammy helped by chasing baubles around the floor and pouncing on garlands as we tried to hang them. But by the time we'd finished the house looked very festive and ready for Christmas.

When I collected Jackson at four o'clock he and his sisters were excited as they too had been putting up Christmas decorations. They insisted I went in to admire their work.

'Wonderful. Very pretty,' I said. Their tree was up and decorated too.

'The children did most of it,' Kayla told me. 'It's the first year we've put up decorations since …' She stopped, took a breath and then continued. 'Since their father and Connor died.'

'It looks very nice,' I said. My gaze went to a family photograph on the wall, now framed by fairy lights.

'Our last Christmas all together,' Kayla said quietly. It was very touching.

Kayla also told me that she was having a meeting with Frankie next week. 'To see about Jackson coming home,' she said. 'Sonia's going. Will you be there?'

'Not as far as I know. Frankie will let me know if she wants me to attend.'

Foster carers are invited to some meetings connected with the child they are looking after, but not all. Which meetings they are invited to can vary from one social services to another and also between social workers. Carers are always present at the child's reviews, but other meetings are discretionary. Frankie would tell me the outcome if I didn't go.

'I told you Sonia said I was going back to Mum,' Jackson said to me in the car on our way home.

'Yes, but like I said, love, it's not Sonia's decision, so don't get your hopes up.' Yet I thought he was probably right and the outcome of the meeting would be that he returned home. That had always been the care plan, and Kayla was coping better now.

That night I had a dream about Connor – just as he looked in the framed photograph I'd seen on the wall in their living room. It was very vivid, almost as if he was there, but not at all frightening. He put his arm around Jackson like an older brother would, protective and reassuring. As I woke, I reached for my phone to make sure I hadn't been woken by a missed call or text. The time showed 11.30 p.m., which struck me as slightly odd; it was the time Kayla visited Connor's grave, although that was 11.30 in the morning, not at night. Stranger was to come. When I saw Kayla at school the following morning I mentioned my dream. Kayla came across as a spiritual person who was able to talk about her husband and son naturally. It was Jackson who hadn't been able to. She wasn't fazed.

'Connor comes to me sometimes at the time he was born,' she said. 'It's his way of reassuring me he's looking out for Jackson, just as he did in life.'

'But I thought he was born at eleven-thirty in the morning?'

'No, at night, but the cemetery is closed then, so I do the next best thing.'

Make of it what you will. The sceptics will say of course I would dream of Connor at that time, having seen his photo illuminated by fairy lights and aware of the significance of that time. But I agree with Kayla, and I was pleased I'd told her, as she'd found it comforting.

Frankie visited Jackson and his family on Friday after school when he was at home for contact. She telephoned me with the outcome. 'Jackson will be returning home to live at the end of term, which I understand is Friday, the twentieth of December.'

'Good. You'd like me to move him?' It's usual for the foster carer to be involved in seeing the child to permanency.

'Yes, please.'

'Tilly is going home at the end of term too, so I suggest we move them both on Saturday, the twenty-first. Jackson in the morning and Tilly in the afternoon, then I can say goodbye properly and it won't be such a rush.'

'That works for me,' Frankie said. 'I'll let Kayla know.'

I was of course pleased both Tilly and Jackson were able to go home, but as the call ended, I felt sad they wouldn't be with us for Christmas. We would be two short – or would we? Once they'd gone, I'd be placed on standby, ready to receive another child. Sadly, some children are brought into care as an emergency over Christmas, even on Christmas Day, although thankfully not often.

The following week we received the good news that Adrian and Kirsty had exchanged contracts on their flat with a completion date of 3 January, when it would become legally theirs. We were delighted. Adrian telephoned my mother to tell her and said that as soon as they'd completed and had the keys, she'd be the first to see it. She said she couldn't wait and also asked him to tell me that she'd been to the doctor for a check-up and had been pronounced fit – although they had taken some blood to be tested to make sure she wasn't anaemic. I phoned her straight back to make sure I was being told everything, and she assured me I was. My mother makes light of her problems and they have to be teased out of her.

Jackson's excitement grew as the end of the term approached. Not just because Christmas was coming and he was getting a new bike from his mother, but because he was going home. Unlike Tilly, he didn't have any reservations about leaving us, although Mr Burrows did. I'd been looking out for his teacher in the playground, and when he was on duty again I went in with Jackson. While Jackson went to his friends, I spoke to Mr Burrows.

'You'll have heard the news?' I asked.

'Yes, Jackson is going home at the end of term. How do you feel about it?'

'It should work,' I said. 'He's made huge improvements – when I think back to the child who arrived. And children should be with their parents if at all possible.'

'Agreed, but he still struggles to control his anger sometimes. I hope Kayla can cope.'

'So do I, or he'll be back in care. But I don't think that will happen. Kayla is in a better place now and has support. I talk to her most mornings outside school and when I take Jackson for contact. There is an optimism about her that wasn't there before. She seems stronger and will ask for help if she needs it.'

'I'll do what I can to help Jackson in school,' Mr Burrows said. 'He really enjoys athletics club.'

'Yes, I know. Pity you don't run a homework club too.'

He smiled. We chatted for a while longer, then I thanked him for all he'd done and said if I didn't see him again I hoped he had a lovely Christmas.

'And you.'

I'd already bought him a gift voucher to go in a thank-you card, which Jackson would take in on the last day of term. I also emailed Jackson's school secretary and Tilly's to advise them of the change in arrangements for the new term: that I would no longer be their carer as they were returning home. Experience had taught me that sometimes the schools records weren't updated.

Now all I had to do was finish the preparations for Christmas and check if my mother's test results had come back yet. They had.

CHAPTER TWENTY-EIGHT

GOING HOME

'I'm not anaemic,' Mum said. 'But the doctor is putting me on some tablets to thin my blood. Apparently, lots of people my age have to take them.'

'Why?' I asked, no less concerned.

'To help my heart. It's working overtime and beating too fast.'

'Mum, have you been diagnosed with a heart condition?' I asked anxiously.

'Only a little. That's why I've been feeling tired.'

'What medication have they put you on?'

'Beta blockers. It's fine, love. Honestly. Nothing to worry about.'

Of course I was worried, and as soon as I'd finished talking to Mum I went online and researched her condition. Atrial fibrillation, where the heart can beat too quickly, is more common in the elderly. Beta blockers are often prescribed, I read, and once the condition is under control it shouldn't shorten a person's life expectancy. I was reassured, but even so I would be keeping a close eye on Mum, especially over Christmas.

We were going to collect Mum on Christmas Eve and then return her home on 27 December, but I now thought that, with no foster children and two spare beds, she should stay for longer. Usually she had my bed and I took the sofa bed downstairs, but now she had a choice of rooms and could stay for as long as she wanted. Indeed, she could come to live with us permanently if she wished. Until now, Mum had been independent, but maybe age was catching up with her and she'd like to live with us. I knew my children would be overjoyed, and if she did come, I would just foster one child, perhaps an infant, as Adrian had suggested, who wouldn't come with the challenging behaviour some older children do. It would be less stressful for us all. I decided I'd talk to Mum about coming to live with us as soon as the opportunity arose.

When Adrian and Paula arrived home I told them that Nana had been diagnosed with a mild heart condition and, while it was nothing to worry about, I was thinking of asking her to live with us. As I thought, they were delighted by the idea. I then telephoned Lucy and said I was going to give Nana her room over Christmas, and also that I was going to see if I could persuade her to live with us permanently. 'You wouldn't mind her having your room, would you?' I asked Lucy. I still thought of it as her room.

'No, of course not, Mum. But I doubt she'll agree.'

'You could be right. But I'll plant the idea, so if she reaches a point where she can't live independently, the offer is already there.'

After school on Friday, 20 December, I gave Tilly and Jackson a little leaving party – 5 p.m. till 8 p.m. Those invited could just drop in for however long they wanted. It's usual when a child leaves for a foster carer to do something special to end their stay. Tilly invited Abby, and Jackson, Mitchel – they were now best friends again. Mitchel arrived with a Christmas card and present for Jackson. Adrian, Paula and Kirsty joined us after work, and Lucy and Darren came with baby Emma at the start. Mr Burrows arrived at 5.30, but Tilly hadn't wanted to invite her teacher. Frankie and Isa came for a while, although they would still be the children's social workers after they'd left me, so it wasn't goodbye for them. Joy wouldn't be involved with them, though, so she came with good-luck cards, each containing a gift voucher. The three social workers spent some time huddled together talking – about office politics from what I could hear. I'd invited my mother, but she said she was saving her energy for Christmas and wished the children well over the phone.

I made a buffet supper with soft drinks and everyone helped themselves. The noise level rose with all the talking and laughing and Jackson got overexcited and started teasing Tilly, and encouraging Mitchel to do the same, until Tilly shouted at him to 'piss off!' I thought it was time to have some organized games and I chose a couple of old favourites: pin the tail on the donkey and Twister. Isa, Frankie and Joy had left by then, but the rest of us joined in, including Mr Burrows. It was great fun, and having the house decorated for Christmas helped with the party feel.

I gave everyone a Christmas chocolate from the tree as they left. Mr Burrows left at seven, Mitchel was collected by his father at half past seven, Lucy and Darren left soon after, but Abby stayed until nine, when her father collected her. Once she'd gone and the house was quiet,

Tilly looked sad and began going around, giving us all a hug. 'I'm going to miss you guys,' she kept saying.

Jackson didn't want a hug and shot up to his room. I think it was the first time he was washed and in bed without repeatedly being asked.

'The sooner I'm asleep, the sooner I'll be going home tomorrow,' he said, snuggling down. He screwed his eyes tightly shut as if forcing sleep.

'It wasn't so bad living here, was it?' I asked him.

'No, but I'd rather be at home,' he replied, eyes still closed.

'Of course you would, love. And remember, you need to help your mother by doing as she says.'

'Yes, I know.'

'Goodnight then.'

'Goodnight.

The following morning Lucy and Darren appeared again with baby Emma for a final goodbye, which was kind of them and unexpected. It was only nine o'clock, but Emma had been up since six. While they were in the living room with Jackson, Tilly and Paula, Adrian helped load my car with Jackson's belongings. As we worked, carrying all the cases and bags from the house to the car, he reminded me of my promise to consider only fostering infants in the future.

'Yes, I know. I'll tell Joy,' I said. 'Although it rather depends on the age of the child needing a home. I can't be too choosy.'

I heard him sigh.

'But if Nana does come to live with us, I will definitely do as you say,' I added, then, sounding just like my mother, 'There's no need for you to worry about me, though. I'm fine.'

Once the car was loaded it was time for Jackson to say goodbye. Suddenly he fell quiet and looked lost. 'Am I going now?' he asked me.

'Yes, love, but we'll see you again soon, I'm sure.'

He said a subdued goodbye to everyone, and I said bye to Lucy and Darren, as they'd be gone by the time I returned. They all waved us off on the pavement, but Jackson was quiet, the euphoria of last night gone. In the boot of my car were two large suitcases containing Jackson's belongings, and there were bags beside him on the back seat and in the footwell. Also, on the passenger seat beside me was a bag of Christmas presents. A child leaving a carer is always sad, no matter how positive the ending, but I was sure Jackson would be all right once he was home – unlike some children I'd fostered, when I'd thought that going home wasn't really the best decision. It's very difficult, but ultimately the carer has to abide by the social services' or judge's decision.

As I drew up outside his house, their front door opened and Kayla and the girls came out. 'Jackson's home!' Gracey shouted at the top of her voice and ran down the path.

Without waiting for me to release the child lock on his door, Jackson scrambled over the back of the passenger seat and let himself out that door, which didn't have a child lock. Normally I would have told him off as it was dangerous, but on this occasion I let it go. I didn't want to end on a negative note. He scooped up Grace and, as he hugged her, I saw the family likeness between him and Connor: the older brother looking after his younger sibling, just as Kayla had spoken of. He set Grace down and everyone helped unload the car, even little Grace. I left the bag of Christmas presents till last and then gave them to Kayla.

'You may want to put these away until Christmas,' I said. 'There's something in there for each of you.'

'Oh, you shouldn't have, that is kind. I've got a little something for you too.'

She went into their front room and returned with a gift-wrapped box. 'A few chocolates for you and your family.'

'Thank you. Have a lovely Christmas. I know you will. Then we'll get together in January.' It's usual to see the child at least a few times after they've left, assuming the family want to, and sometimes they keep in touch for years.

We were in the hall with the front door open and I was about to leave when Sonia appeared, rushing down the path. I don't think I'd ever seen her so animated.

'You'll never guess!' she cried. 'You know Clem, who lives at number forty-two?' Kayla nodded. 'I've just seen her and she tells me that Jerry has been re-arrested. It seems her neighbour's child is saying he did something to him.'

'Oh no, that poor child. I am sorry,' Kayla said, clearly upset.

'So am I, but it should help our case, isn't that right?' Sonia asked me.

'It could,' I said carefully. 'Or your statements might help their case.'

'We'll phone the police first thing on Monday and see what they have to say,' Sonia told Kayla.

I couldn't add anything, so I said goodbye, wished them a happy Christmas and left with a heavy heart. Sadly, it appeared Connor wasn't the only one Jerry had abused. I wondered how many more there were, suffering in silence. I hoped that this time there was enough evidence to prosecute.

It was eleven o'clock when I arrived home. Adrian and Paula had helped Tilly bring down her bags and stack them in the hall. Although she'd been taking some of her belongings each weekend, there was still a lot to go. 'Aren't you going to stay for lunch?' I asked her. She wasn't due to go until this afternoon, but it was up to her.

'I may as well go now,' she said. 'I phoned Gran and said I'd be there when you got back from taking Jackson.'

'OK, that's fine, love.'

I had a quick coffee as Adrian, Paula and Tilly loaded my car. As I went into the hall, ready to go, Tilly gave me a lovely bunch of flowers. 'Thanks for having me,' she said, and kissed my cheek.

I was really touched. 'They're beautiful, love. Lilies – my favourite. Thank you.'

'I got them while you were out. Adrian gave me a lift in his car,' she said.

I thanked her again and put them in some water. It was time for her to say goodbye and I knew it was going to be difficult. She hugged Paula and Adrian and said, 'I'll text. I'm going to keep in touch with Lucy too.' They already had each other's mobile numbers.

Sammy came to see what was going on and Tilly picked him up and cuddled him. 'Gran hasn't got a cat,' she said wistfully. I could see she was becoming fretful, so I said it was time to leave and gently eased her out the door and to my car. Once in, she lowered her window to wave at the others.

'Bye! Love you guys!' she called, her voice breaking. She waved until they were out of sight and then raised the window.

'I'm going to miss you all so much,' she said.

'We'll miss you too, love, but it's right you're going to live with your mother and grandmother. We'll keep in touch and you know you're welcome any time. Perhaps you can persuade your mum and gran to come for a visit?'

'Yes, that would be nice, I'll try.'

It wasn't far to her grandmother's bungalow, but I kept the conversation going, light and easy, talking about Christmas and what she was planning for the New Year. Last New Year she'd been with us and she reminded me how she'd celebrated it with Abby.

I drew up and parked outside the bungalow. Tilly sat for a moment looking at the front door before getting out. Her homecoming was more subdued than Jackson's had been, but no less welcome. The front door remained closed as we took as many bags as we could carry from the car and to the door. Tilly pressed the bell. After a few moments her mother, Heather, answered with a smile. 'Hello, welcome home.'

'Thanks, Mum.'

Her gran came slowly down the hall. 'My, that's a lot of bags,' she said as we took them in.

'There are plenty more where they came from,' Tilly replied with a small laugh, and kissed her gran.

'Heather, can give you give them a hand while I make us a cup of tea?' Nancy said. 'You will stay for a cuppa, won't you, Cathy?'

'Yes, please.'

Nancy went to the kitchen as Heather slipped on her coat and outdoor shoes, then the three of us finished unloading my car. As well as the main bags and boxes, there were lots of smaller ones stuffed full of items in regular use that Tilly had packed that morning. Hair straighteners, make-up, a phone charger, toiletries and a bag of last night's washing. We carried everything straight into Tilly's bedroom. Previously it had been the dining room and I hadn't seen it since they'd decorated. The walls had been painted dusty pink and the old grey curtains replaced by bright pink blinds, the same shade as a new rug. A light-pink duvet cover was on the bed with a couple of scatter cushions. The bookshelves had stayed and there was now a small table acting as a desk. 'No excuse for not studying,' I said to Tilly with a smile.

'That's what Gran told her,' Heather said.

'I will work, I want to do well,' Tilly said. I knew she did, but sometimes other things got in the way.

As I had done at Jackson's, I kept the bag containing their Christmas presents until last, and then handed it to Heather to put away until Christmas. With the car unpacked, we went into their living room, which was festively decorated. A small Christmas tree, already lit, stood on the coffee table in one corner. Heather and Tilly helped Nancy bring in the tea. There was also a plate of homemade mince pies. They were delicious; the pastry light, just as my mother used to make – a skill I've never acquired.

I stayed for over an hour, talking. I'd got to know Nancy and Heather well in the early days when Tilly had first arrived and there'd been so much trauma going on. I hadn't seen them for a while, as Tilly had been using the bus to visit them.

As I said goodbye, I wished them a merry Christmas and Nancy gave me a gift-wrapped box, which looked remarkably like chocolates. 'Thanks for looking after Tilly when things were bad,' she said. 'I didn't appreciate it at the time, but looking back, I do now.'

'You're welcome,' I said, hugging her. 'We got there in the end.'

'And thanks for all you did to help me,' Heather added. 'I don't think I'd be where I am now if you hadn't stepped in.'

I felt quite emotional. I hadn't expected that. 'You did it,' I said. 'Not me. You found the courage to leave and put things right, so well done.'

They saw me off at the door and as I drove away Nancy blew me a kiss. She was such a treasure, the stalwart of her family, and in some ways reminded me of my own mother. They'd both enjoyed long and happy marriages, had grieved when their husbands had died, but then found the strength to move on and enjoy life again with their families. I think we have a lot to learn from their generation.

Once home, I had lunch with Adrian and Paula, then they went out together to do some Christmas shopping while I thoroughly cleaned the two spare bedrooms. I stripped the beds, vacuumed the carpets, wiped the woodwork, then remade the beds. Lucy's room I prepared for Mum's stay at Christmas with a floral duvet, a set of fluffy cream towels and a reed diffuser that gave off a subtle scent of Christmas spice. Jackson's old bedroom I kept neutral to suit a boy or girl of any age, just in case a child arrived as an emergency. I was hoping it wouldn't be used, but unfortunately Christmas, with all its fine promises and high expectations, can be the snapping point for a family already struggling.

Rooms done, I updated my log notes with my final entries for Tilly and Jackson and emailed my last statements to their social workers, copying in Joy.

Our evening was quiet and, dare I say, relaxing – a change from the usual hustle and bustle of a houseful. Adrian was out with Kirsty, so Paula and I ordered a takeaway and ate it in front of the television.

On Sunday I visited Mum and she naturally asked after Jackson and Tilly. I reassured her their moves had gone well. Mum said she wasn't so tired and felt the tablets were helping. She was due to see the doctor again for a check-up in a month. I took the opportunity to talk to her about coming to live with us. She thanked me for my concern but said, 'It's very kind of you all, but I'm not decrepit yet. I'm looking forward to spending Christmas with you all and then I shall be returning to my house.'

I completely understood. Mum had spent most of her married life in the same house. It was where she'd raised her family and it was full of happy memories. Of course she wanted to stay there for as long as possible.

* * *

On Monday Joy telephoned and for a moment I thought she was going to tell me about a child who needed a home, but thankfully it was to confirm she'd received my reports on Tilly and Jackson. She thanked me for looking after the children and said I'd done a good job, which is always nice to hear.

'So, I can put you on standby?' she said, winding up.

'Yes, although one child only, please, if it's over Christmas, as my mother will be with me. And, Joy, I'm thinking I would prefer to foster a newborn or infant in future if possible.'

'Really?' she asked, surprised. 'But you are one of our most experienced carers. You're ideal for fostering older children with complex needs.' I immediately felt guilty.

'I'm just saying it's something I'm considering,' I said. 'My son worries about me.'

'Well, let's talk about it in the New Year, shall we?' Joy said.

'OK.'

Wishing each other a merry Christmas, we said goodbye. At some point I'd have to tell her that Adrian would be moving out next year to get married, but there was no rush. I had little doubt as soon as I told her she'd want me to use that room for fostering too, such is the shortage of foster carers and the high number of children coming into care. But that was all in the future. Christmas was coming, and I intended it to be our best one ever.

CHAPTER TWENTY-NINE

A LIFE LOST

I collected my mother on Tuesday afternoon, and as usual on Christmas Eve we all went to the family service at our local church. Kirsty came with us, and Lucy and family joined us there. We occupied the entire length of one of the long pews. It was a lovely warm family atmosphere. The service was designed for children so there was no long sermon, but lots of joyful carols and a nativity play. It didn't matter if children left their seats or called out. It was, after all, to celebrate the birth of baby Jesus. Emma was enthralled by what was going on around her and lay over Darren's shoulder, grinning at the row behind, much to their amusement. She chuntered loudly when we sang carols as if joining in. It was her first Christmas, so it was special for us all. We saw friends and neighbours there and as we left we wished each other a merry Christmas.

It was a cold but clear night and, walking home, we gazed up at the stars, stopping every so often to try to identify a constellation – Orion, Gemini, the Plough. There was a single star shining brightly ahead of us that Mum said looked like the star of Bethlehem, which had guided the three kings to where baby Jesus had been born.

Once home, we had supper and then Lucy and family and Kirsty went home. We'd see them again tomorrow for Christmas Day. Mum was tired, hardly surprising after the journey here, the walk to and from church and all the excitement. She went to bed at nine o'clock and once she was in bed I went up to make sure she had everything she needed. She looked comfortable, snuggled in Lucy's bed. 'I feel like a teenager,' she said, laughing.

'Well, just make sure you behave yourself. No all-night partying.' I kissed her goodnight.

I stayed up late preparing for the following day, but I didn't mind. It was all part of the fun and joy of Christmas. Once Adrian and Paula were asleep, I tiptoed in and out of their rooms with their Father Christmas presents in stockings, which I hung on the ends of their beds. It was a family tradition that my children had never grown out of. I also hung one on Mum's bed. Lucy's was downstairs under the Christmas tree with all our other presents.

It was midnight when I finally climbed into bed. I hoped I didn't receive a call now for an emergency placement. I always kept a few presents spare just in case, but no one wants to see a child taken from home on Christmas Eve, unless it's absolutely essential and they are in danger.

I was relieved when I woke the following morning and there'd been no call. I slipped on my dressing gown and went downstairs to check on the turkey while the rest of the house slept. I'd set the oven on automatic, and all seemed well. I basted it, fed Sammy and then returned upstairs to shower and dress. I heard Mum get up to use the toilet, then go back to bed. Once I was dressed, I took her a cup of tea. She was sitting in bed, opening her Father Christmas presents just like a child. 'You shouldn't have gone to all this trouble,' she said. But I could tell she was pleased. Like my father, Mum had never lost that child's enthusiasm for life and all it offered. I think it's what kept her young and outward-looking.

Once everyone was dressed, we had a light breakfast and as soon as Lucy and family and Kirsty arrived we began opening presents. We had drinks and savoury snacks around midday and then our Christmas dinner in the afternoon, seated around the table in the front room, which was laid with festive place settings. After we'd eaten ourselves to a standstill, we played games and won prizes from the Christmas tree. There was one for me, quietly put there by my children, which was a lovely surprise. In the evening Adrian and Kirsty left to spend it with her parents, and the rest of us continued playing games and snacking.

We took it in turns to hold Emma, although she spent most of her time on Mum's lap. They were enchanted with each other and we took lots of photographs. When Emma finally fell asleep we got out the Monopoly board. It was nearly midnight by the time we declared it a draw! Lucy and family went home. They could have stayed the night but preferred to settle Emma in her cot at home. We would see them again the following day for a walk.

Like other families, we usually went for a walk on Boxing Day – 26 December – to 'blow away the cobwebs', as Mum said. Or rather burn off some calories from all the eating. We walked for over an hour and when we returned home Mum fell asleep in a chair in the living room. I wasn't surprised or concerned after the late night and long walk. She had a little supper in the evening but didn't want much, and again I wasn't concerned as she'd had a good breakfast and lunch. She had an early night and, once she was in bed, I went up to say goodnight. She thanked me for a lovely Christmas. 'The best ever.' But we always say that. She was due to go home the following day.

'Mum, you know you can stay longer,' I said. 'As long as you want.'

'That's kind, dear, but I'll go as planned. We've had a wonderful time and I'll see you all again soon, won't I?'

'Yes, of course.'

I could see she was exhausted, so I checked she had everything she needed, kissed her goodnight and came out. I was in bed soon after ten, as was Paula. I heard Adrian let himself in around 2 a.m. He didn't have to be up early for work as he and Paula had the whole week off.

I slept well but didn't lie in for long – I never do. I made coffee and drank it downstairs, expecting to hear Mum on the move before long – she was an early riser too. When she slept in I didn't think anything of it. She'd been very tired the night before, so I left her to sleep. Adrian and Paula were still in bed too. But by 9.30, when I still hadn't heard Mum, not even to use the bathroom, I went up to make sure she was all right. I knocked lightly on the door and went in. 'Mum?' I said quietly.

She was in bed, apparently asleep, lying on her back, her head slightly facing away. I went over to the bed.

'Mum?' She didn't respond. 'Mum? Are you all right?' I felt the first stab of fear. 'Mum?' Her eyes remained closed. Her lips were slightly parted as though relaxed in sleep, but I couldn't hear or see her breathing.

'Mum? Are you asleep?'

No movement or reply. My fear stepped up another notch.

I reached out and felt her forehead. She always had such smooth skin. It was warm, but not as warm as it should be. Had she got cold in the night? I thought. But the heating was on.

'Mum?'

I picked up her hand, which was resting on top of the duvet. That too felt colder than it should, and it was limp. 'Mum?' No response. I put my cheek to her lips and couldn't feel her breath. I felt for her pulse. There wasn't one, and in that instant my world fell apart. My dear mother had passed away in her sleep.

With tears running down my cheeks, I rushed into Adrian's room. He was in bed with his earpieces in, listening to music. He took them out as soon as he saw me. 'What's the matter?'

'Nana has passed away in her sleep,' I said.

'Oh my God, no.' He was out of bed in a heartbeat and rushed to Mum's room.

Paula's door opened. 'What is it?'

'Nana has passed away,' I said.

She came with me to where Mum lay. Adrian had checked her pulse too and was now phoning for an ambulance, although I knew it was too late for that. We waited numbly by her bed, hardly saying a word. She looked serene and at peace, as if asleep, and as beautiful in death as she had been in life. I stroked her hair and Adrian and Paula held a hand each, tears streaming down our faces. I left them for a few moments to phone Lucy. She said she'd come straight over and arrived at the same time as the paramedics. They were so kind and sensitive. They pronounced Mum dead and said she'd probably died three to four hours before, so there was nothing we could have done. They explained that, as it was an unexpected death, a post-mortem would probably be required, so they'd take her to the mortuary at the hospital. We had the opportunity to kiss her goodbye before they took her away. My dear mother, the children's grandmother and great-grandmother, so loved, had gone to join her husband. Rest in peace.

We were obviously all grief-stricken at losing Mum but took some comfort from knowing that she'd had a long and very happy life. Connor's life, however, had been cut short in the most tragic way possible. Suicide is on the increase, especially among young men, but help is available to anyone at any time. The Samaritans offer a twenty-four-hour helpline, and they save lives: www.samaritans.org. No matter how bleak you may be feeling, there is another way.

For an update on Jackson, Tilly and the other children in my fostering memoirs, visit www.cathyglass.co.uk.

Thank you.

SUGGESTED TOPICS FOR READING-GROUP DISCUSSION

The book opens with Cathy clearing out Lucy's bedroom. Why does she find this so difficult? Why not just refuse to take Jackson?

Meeting the parents of a foster child for the first time is always difficult. Why is meeting Kayla more difficult than usual? How would you have prepared for that meeting?

What do you see as the main challenges of looking after a child like Jackson, who can be volatile but deep down is hurting? Why does his behaviour deteriorate when Lucy and her family visit?

Why do you think Jackson's teacher was able to reach him?

Jackson has kept Connor's secret. Why? Could Kayla have been more aware of the situation, both when the abuse happened and afterwards?

How would you describe Tilly? Her relationship improves with her mother, so she is able to live with her and her grandmother. From what you know of her story, is it the right time?

Although Jackson loved his family, contact at home was problematic. Why do you think that was?

When Jackson discloses abuse, his sisters are immediately taken into care. What reasons are given? Do you think it's the correct decision? Were there any alternatives?

Frankie, Jackson's social worker, recommends family therapy. What might the family discuss?

One of the reasons for the success of Cathy's books is that they allow the reader to see into the lives of Cathy and her family. Readers often comment that they feel they are in the room with them, feeling what they do. How is this achieved?

The ending of the book is bittersweet. Jackson and Tilly return home, but Cathy's dear mother passes. She has featured in all of Cathy's memoirs. How might her loss affect the family and fostering in the future?

Cathy Glass

One remarkable woman, more
than **150** foster children cared for.

Cathy Glass has been a foster carer for
twenty-five years, during which time she has
looked after more than 150 children, as well
as raising three children of her own. She was
awarded a degree in education and psychology
as a mature student, and writes under a
pseudonym. To find out more about Cathy
and her story visit **www.cathyglass.co.uk**.

A Terrible Secret

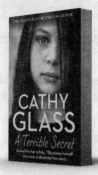

Tilly is so frightened of her stepfather, Dave, that she asks to go into foster care

The more Cathy learns about Dave's behaviour, the more worried she becomes …

Too Scared to Tell

Oskar has been arriving at school hungry, unkempt and bruised. His mother has gone abroad and left him in the care of 'friends'

As the weeks pass, Cathy's concerns deepen. Oskar is clearly frightened of someone – but who? And why?

Innocent

Siblings Molly and Kit arrive at Cathy's frightened, injured and ill

The parents say they are not to blame. Could the social services have got it wrong?

Finding Stevie

Fourteen-year-old Stevie is exploring his gender identity

Like many young people, he spends time online, but Cathy is shocked when she learns his terrible secret.

Where Has Mummy Gone?

When Melody is taken into care, she fears her mother won't cope alone

It is only when Melody's mother vanishes that what has really been going on at home comes to light.

A Long Way from Home

Abandoned in an orphanage, Anna's future looks bleak until she is adopted

Anna's new parents love her, so why does she end up in foster care?

Cruel to be Kind

Max is shockingly overweight and struggles to make friends

Cathy faces a challenge to help this unhappy boy.

Nobody's Son

Born in prison and brought up in care, Alex has only ever known rejection

He is longing for a family of his own, but again the system fails him.

Can I Let You Go?

Faye is 24, pregnant and has learning difficulties as a result of her mother's alcoholism

Can Cathy help Faye learn enough to parent her child?

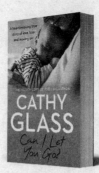

The Silent Cry

A mother battling depression. A family in denial

Cathy is desperate to help before something terrible happens.

Girl Alone

An angry, traumatized young girl on a path to self-destruction

Can Cathy discover the truth behind Joss's dangerous behaviour before it's too late?

Saving Danny

Danny's parents can no longer cope with his challenging behaviour

Calling on all her expertise, Cathy discovers a frightened little boy who just wants to be loved.

The Child Bride

A girl blamed and abused for dishonouring her community

Cathy discovers the devastating truth.

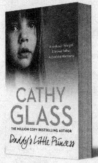

Daddy's Little Princess

A sweet-natured girl with a complicated past

Cathy picks up the pieces after events take a dramatic turn.

Will You Love Me?

A broken child desperate for a loving home

The true story of Cathy's adopted daughter Lucy.

Please Don't Take My Baby

Seventeen-year-old Jade is pregnant, homeless and alone

Cathy has room in her heart for two.

Another Forgotten Child

Eight-year-old Aimee was on the child-protection register at birth

Cathy is determined to give her the happy home she deserves.

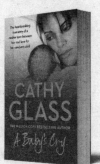

A Baby's Cry

A newborn, only hours old, taken into care

Cathy protects tiny Harrison from the potentially fatal secrets that surround his existence.

The Night the Angels Came

A little boy on the brink of bereavement

Cathy and her family make sure Michael is never alone.

Mummy Told Me Not to Tell

A troubled boy sworn to secrecy

After his dark past has been revealed, Cathy helps Reece to rebuild his life.

I Miss Mummy

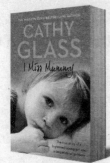

Four-year-old Alice doesn't understand why she's in care

Cathy fights for her to have the happy home she deserves.

The Saddest Girl in the World

A haunted child who refuses to speak

Do Donna's scars run too deep for Cathy to help?

Cut

Dawn is desperate to be loved

Abused and abandoned, this vulnerable child pushes Cathy and her family to their limits.

Hidden

The boy with no past

Can Cathy help Tayo to feel like he belongs again?

Damaged

A forgotten child

Cathy is Jodie's last hope. For the first time, this abused young girl has found someone she can trust.

Run, Mummy, Run

The gripping story of a woman caught in a horrific cycle of abuse, and the desperate measures she must take to escape.

My Dad's a Policeman

The dramatic short story about a young boy's desperate bid to keep his family together.

The Girl in the Mirror

Trying to piece together her past, Mandy uncovers a dreadful family secret that has been blanked from her memory for years.

About Writing and How to Publish

A clear, concise practical guide on writing and the best ways to get published.

Happy Mealtimes for Kids

A guide to healthy eating with simple recipes that children love.

Happy Adults

A practical guide to achieving lasting happiness, contentment and success. The essential manual for getting the best out of life.

Happy Kids

A clear and concise guide to raising confident, well-behaved and happy children.

CATHY GLASS WRITING AS
LISA STONE

www.lisastonebooks.co.uk

The new crime thrillers that will chill you to the bone . . .

TAKEN

Have you seen Leila?

THE DOCTOR

How much do you know about
the couple next door?

STALKER

Security cameras are there to keep us safe. Aren't they?

THE DARKNESS WITHIN

You know your son better than anyone. Don't you?

Be amazed
Be moved
Be inspired

Follow Cathy:

/cathy.glass.180

@CathyGlassUK

www.cathyglass.co.uk

Cathy loves to hear from readers and reads
and replies to posts, but she asks that no plot
spoilers are posted, please. We're sure
you appreciate why.

MOVING
Memoirs

Stories of hope, courage and
the power of love . . .

Sign up to the Moving Memoirs email and you'll
be the first to hear about new books, discounts,
and get sneak previews from your
favourite authors!

Sign up at

www.moving-memoirs.com